A TIME FOR PEACE

DUANE A. SMITH

A Time for Peace
FORT LEWIS, COLORADO, 1878–1891

UNIVERSITY PRESS OF COLORADO

© 2006 by the University Press of Colorado

Published by the University Press of Colorado
5589 Arapahoe Avenue, Suite 206C
Boulder, Colorado 80303

 The University Press of Colorado is a proud member of
the Association of American University Presses.

The University Press of Colorado is a cooperative publishing enterprise supported, in part, by
Adams State College, Colorado State University, Fort Lewis College, Mesa State College,
Metropolitan State College of Denver, University of Colorado, University of Northern
Colorado, and Western State College of Colorado.

∞ The paper used in this publication meets the minimum requirements of the American
National Standard for Information Sciences—Permanence of Paper for Printed Library
Materials. ANSI Z39.48-1992

Library of Congress Cataloging-in-Publication Data

Smith, Duane A.
  A time for peace : Fort Lewis, Colorado, 1878–1891 / Duane A. Smith.
     p. cm.
  Includes bibliographical references and index.
  ISBN-13: 978-0-87081-832-5 (hardcover : alk. paper)
  ISBN-10: 0-87081-832-5 (hardcover : alk. paper) 1. Fort Lewis (Colo.)—History. 2. Frontier
and pioneer life—San Juan River Region (Colo.-Utah) 3. Frontier and pioneer life—Four
Corners Region. 4. Frontier and pioneer life—Colorado—Pagosa Springs Region. 5. United
States. Army—Military life—History—19th century. 6. Indians of North America—San Juan
River Region (Colo.-Utah)—History—19th century. 7. San Juan River Region (Colo.-Utah)—
History—19th century. 8. Four Corners Region—History—19th century. 9. Pagosa Springs
Region (Colo.)—History—19th century. 10. Durango (Colo.)—History—19th century. I.
Title.
  F784.F566S45 2006
  979.2'59—dc22

                                                                                        2006010985

Design by Daniel Pratt

15 14 13 12 11 10 09 08 07 06   10 9 8 7 6 5 4 3 2 1

To the memories of

Silas Dexter Wesson,
Seth R. Woodruff Jr.
and
Stanley W. Smith

CONTENTS

PREFACE

In the book of Ecclesiastes, it is written: "For everything there is a season and a time for every matter under heaven . . . [concluding with] a time for war, and a time for peace." For the military garrison at Fort Lewis, Colorado, it was a time for peace.

In 1878 they came to a land that no longer could be defined as a frontier. Mining, with its rush and urbanization, had taken care of that. Now farms, ranches, settlements, mines, and cabins dotted the landscape. Roads crisscrossed the terrain and the railroad was coming. Tourists were even arriving to see the wonders of the mountains, visit the ruins of the ancients, and bathe in the medicinal waters of a score of hot springs.

The troops came not in war, although the fear of war motivated their arrival. They came to maintain and keep the peace. Their goals were simple:

to separate settlers from native tribes, to keep Navajos and Utes from pestering each other, to maintain peace among the settlers, and to ensure the continued peaceful settlement of what became known as the Four Corners region, where Utah, New Mexico, Arizona, and Colorado met.

It did not prove simple to attain their goals, but they did so without losing one man in combat. Like their comrades everywhere in the West, they, the army, and Uncle Sam were both praised and damned. Although they were in the region only from 1878 to 1891, their impact resounded beyond those few years.

The fort aided in settlement; provided jobs; created profits for local businesses, farmers, and ranchers; helped stabilize the region; and assisted in promoting the wonders of southwestern Colorado and the other states of the Four Corners region, thereby building a foundation on which later generations would build. The fort's buildings became an Indian boarding school, a rural high school, and finally a junior college before abandonment in 1956.

Today we have largely forgotten the military years of Fort Lewis and its garrison. Nothing remains of the first post, and the second Fort Lewis reflects more of what happened after the last trooper rode off than it does of their time there. Yet, Fort Lewis played a significant role in the military history of Colorado and the West.

The story that follows is that of the men, women, and children who lived there and their isolated post in a newly opened part of Colorado. They are all there: the young boy who grew up at this post, the officer who was nearly ready for retirement, and the wife who followed her young officer husband not to a glorious military life but to a life of isolation, low pay, and temporary housing. The immigrant who used the army as a school of Americanization, the man who was hiding his past, the soldier who came west then deserted for more alluring prospects, and the ambitious junior officer also have their moments on the stage.

Life at a small western post offered little glory or glamour. Guard duty, patrols, boredom, fatigue, poor food, isolation, discipline, and routine were relieved by good times at the sutler's, baseball games, dances, trips into Durango, cards, and social gatherings. The narrative also focuses on the post's role in the settlement of the Four Corners region and traces the relationship of the garrison and its troops with nearby communities, settlers, and native peoples. The Fort Lewis saga is that of the less glamorous, but typical, western post. Although not as famous as some of its contemporaries, the post and its people were part of the great westward movement that had started long before in Jamestown, Virginia, in 1607, or, perhaps, in 1492.

"Grieve not for what is past" an old-folk saying laments. When visiting the site of Fort Lewis, however, that past haunts you like a fresh-faced young girl you knew long ago. The echoes of yesteryear haunted me until I researched and wrote, but no book is written in isolation.

Any author, at least this one, owes a debt of gratitude to various individuals and organizations who assisted along the way. I owe a special thanks to Scott McGinnis, Ben Campbell, Jay Graybeal, and Sheila Biles for their assistance with this project.

The staffs of the Colorado Historical Society, Montana Historical Society, Museum of New Mexico, Arizona Historical Society, National Archives, U.S. Army Military History Institute, and the Southwest Center at Fort Lewis College were particularly helpful. Todd Ellison especially provided invaluable assistance in a variety of ways while I worked with the Fort Lewis papers.

"Three cheers and a tiger" to the enthusiastic, professional, and extremely helpful trio from the University Press of Colorado—Laura Furney, Daniel Pratt, and Darrin Pratt. Beth Green did some needed editing and my wife, Gay, provided her usual TLC and literary support.

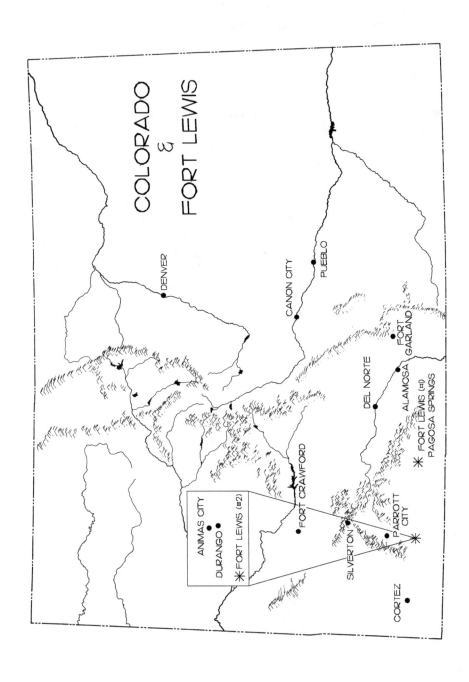

COLORADO
&
FORT LEWIS

DENVER

CANON CITY

PUEBLO

FORT
GARLAND

DEL NORTE

ALAMOSA

FORT LEWIS (#1)
PAGOSA SPRINGS

FORT CRAWFORD

SILVERTON

PARROTT
CITY

CORTEZ

ANIMAS CITY
DURANGO
FORT LEWIS (#2)

Punished Woman's Fork
and Pagosa Springs

A GREAT INDIAN OUTBREAK

Rapine and Murder in Kansas

    Intense excitement at Dodge City and in the Surrounding Country—Several Men Murdered, Cattle Camps Plundered, and Houses Burned by the Cheyennes—Engagements in which the Indians were victorious—the Border in an Uproar.

New York Times, September 20, 1878

Homesick, starving, desperate, disease-wracked, and tired of watching too many of their people die, Dull Knife and Little Wolf led their Northern Cheyenne people, about a third of the tribe, out of their desolate reservation in Indian Territory. They struggled back toward their traditional and much beloved homeland, far northward in Montana and Wyoming Territories. Quickly alerted, troops and scouts from Fort Reno took up the chase. But the Cheyenne managed to elude their pursuers and pushed on in what amounted to an off-and-on running skirmish, while worried settlers in Kansas and Nebraska feared the worst. Despite the peaceful intentions of their leaders, some Cheyenne warriors raided homesteads, adding more panic among town and farming folk. Rumor and fear fueled press reports, making matters worse.

1

Residents of neighboring Colorado also were alarmed. The *Rocky Mountain News* on September 20, 1878, headlined "RAIDING REDSKINS" and lamented the murdering of ranchmen and the burning of houses. But the worry was short-lived. The new state, caught up in a hot political campaign, soon returned its attention to politics.

Dodge City, Kansas, residents, on the other hand, were wracked with worry as rumors of Indian violence spread. The weekly *Dodge City Times* published extra after extra full of "almost hourly" reports of murders and depredations. These newspaper reports transformed a few struggling, poorly armed Cheyenne crossing the prairie into a warmongering, 1,000-man army traveling northward to join "Uncle Sitting Bull." The headline in the *Dodge City Times* on September 21 did not help matters: "THE RED DEVILS THE WILD AND HUNGRY CHEYENNE COMMIT MURDER AND ARSON, DODGE CITY UNDER ARMS."[1]

Yet the editor had mixed feelings about these events, blaming them, with typical western bombast, on "the starving and imbecile policy of the Indian Agents and the Government." The paper almost sympathized with the "destitute" Cheyenne who had not "taken the war path" but "simply wanted to get back upon their old reservation in the north."

Meanwhile, the government's weary troops reached the Cimarron station on the Arkansas River Wednesday, September 25. To their great relief, infantry and cavalry coming from Fort Dodge, commanded by Lt. Col. William Henry Lewis, joined them. The veteran Lewis now assumed the expedition's command, pushing on after Dull Knife.

Forty-eight-year-old Alabama native Lewis was raised in New York and graduated from West Point in 1849. (He was fifteenth in a class of forty-three.) Early in his career he had served in Texas before working for a year as assistant instructor of infantry tactics at West Point. In 1856 Lewis transferred to Florida during the Seminole hostilities before joining the Utah Expedition to calm the Mormon "war" in 1857. Stationed in the Department of New Mexico throughout the Civil War, Lewis twice was cited for gallantry and meritorious service (brevetted a major) during the 1862 New Mexico campaign to halt the Confederate invasion of the Southwest. "Intrepid" Lewis had helped capture the Confederate supply train and also was cited for bravery for capturing and spiking a gun during the March battle of Apache Cañon.

Elizabeth Burt, a frontier army wife, left the following portrait of Lewis, who commanded a battalion that included her husband's troops on their way from Fort Sedgwick, Colorado, to Fort Bridger, Wyoming, after the war:

His reputation was that of a fine officer and an experienced plainsman who was capable of guarding us from harm. We admired him and felt safe under his watchful eye, knowing he had his scouts on the alert and his officers always ready for duty. Socially he was agreeable, and often joined us in a game of whist, bezique or cribbage after dinner.

Colonel Lewis, she concluded, "we respected and admired."[2]

Lewis also had been involved in Montana's Indian scare in 1867. The excited Montana press called it a "war to the knife," expecting, it seemed, one side to be annihilated. At the time, Montana's distraught territorial governor requested the authority to raise volunteers and attack the hostiles. Gen. William Tecumseh Sherman, not so sure about the actual situation, ordered a discreet officer—Maj. William Lewis—to go to Virginia City to assess the real necessity of calling out volunteers. Major Lewis reached Virginia City on May 19. Although he had been given the power to raise volunteers, Lewis decided no danger existed, much to the displeasure of some Montanans. After a month, he returned to Salt Lake City.[3]

Lewis also was stationed on frontier duty in Camp Douglas, Dakota Territory, and commanded Fort Fred Steele, Wyoming Territory. A fellow officer described him "as an officer of great frontier experience" and possessing "a varied knowledge of the best methods of the administration and management of frontier posts." Lewis, who had entered West Point at age fifteen, matured into a man of "physically large stature, of pleasing address, and of a genial and happy nature." He had, according to Gen. Samuel Holabird, with a bit of Victorian sentimentality, "given his brother officers a chivalric example of noble conduct."[4]

By 1874, Lewis was commanding Camp Supply, Indian Territory, with two companies of the Nineteenth Infantry. During the 1874–1875 southern plains campaigns, he had the unenviable task of trying to supply troops in the field while guarding against attacks. At the time of the Cheyenne outbreak in 1878, Lewis was commanding Fort Dodge. Anxious to understand why this had happened, he interviewed scout and interpreter Amos Chapman, who told him that the tribe did not have sufficient food and had been driven to eat horsemeat and even diseased animals.

Upset with this, he wrote a letter to his departmental commander, Gen. John Pope, to be forwarded to the general of the army, William Tecumseh Sherman, in which he described the Cheyenne as a people driven to the brink of despair. The communiqué eventually appeared in newspapers, adding to the public outcry from others who believed an injustice had been done. Lewis was not the only officer to sympathize with the plight of the Cheyenne, but as one of the first, his views received press attention.

Despite his sympathy for their plight, Lewis led his troops northward after the fleeing Cheyennes. With their women and children tired and struggling, Cheyenne braves dropped back to blunt the approach of the troops. At Punished Woman's Fork on the Smoky Hill River they set a trap.[5]

They traveled through a deep ravine, hoping that Lewis and his troops would follow. The Cheyennes waited on the surrounding ridges to open fire on their pursuers. At about five o'clock in the afternoon, the Fourth Cavalry approached, struggling to take five wagons across a difficult stretch of the trail. Everything was going according to the Cheyenne plan until an overeager warrior fired just before the trap was closed.

A sharp fight ensued. Pressed from two sides, the troops fought back. Mounted Lewis steadily rallied his men, directing their fire, before receiving a hit in the thigh that severed his femoral artery. The trap failed, but it slowed Lewis's pursuit and the Cheyenne were able to escape under the cover of darkness. The battle left Lewis and three troopers wounded, and the Cheyenne lost one killed, along with some ponies and stock. With an escort, the badly wounded Lewis, already weakened by a two-week dysentery siege, and two others headed toward Fort Wallace, Kansas, by ambulance. The next day Lewis died en route.[6]

Lewis, who "was looked upon as one of the best officers in the service," must have been respected and liked. A memorial plaque was placed in his honor in the chapel at Fort Leavenworth and his fellow officers would soon honor him in another way as well. The Cheyennes simply felt that Lewis had been a brave officer. His fellow officers concurred, stressing that he "had been highly esteemed for his bravery."[7]

The *Dodge City Times* paid tribute to Lewis on October 5, 1878. "Col. Lewis was a man highly esteemed by both citizen and soldier, and news of his death was received with a profound sorrow." The "always active and aggressive" Lewis would be missed "at this critical time" because of his "thorough knowledge of the frontier." "The deceased left no family" and was buried at Fort Leavenworth with full military honors.

The official Department of Missouri announcement of Lewis's death described him as the man who had "devoted the best years of his life to the service of his country." It concluded, "[C]alm and deliberate in judgment, courteous and refined in bearing, active, firm and upright in the discharge of every duty, Lieutenant Colonel Lewis had won the respect and esteem of all who knew him." A eulogy praised his "gallantly setting an example to the men of his command, by exposing his person on horse back to the direct fire of the Indians."[8]

Two weeks later, far to the southwest, the Fifteenth Infantry marched peacefully up the San Juan River toward Pagosa Springs, Colorado, to establish a cantonment. Long known for their healing powers, the hot springs there had been a gathering place for generations of Utes. In the early 1870s settlers moved into the area, attracted by the fertile land, water, and abundant timber, and these two groups now lived as uneasy neighbors. Many settlers feared the Utes, who in turn did not appreciate Whites' trespassing on their land and monopolizing the healing springs.

This area also contained one of the main trails to the Animas Valley and the swiftly opening San Juan mining region. The troops were sent to guard this transportation route along the San Juan River and keep peace between the settlers and the Utes.

The army had considered establishing a post in this region for more than a decade. A reconnaissance in January and February 1864 to select a possible site for this post was unsuccessful because the deep snow and inclement weather prevented a thorough investigation. Hindered further by "very broken and frightfully rough country without a road," the officer in command concluded that it "almost prevented the possibility of doing it accurately."[9]

Three years later another report recommended establishing a fort on the Rio de Las Animas instead of the San Juan. A post at the former would "not only have a moral effect upon the Indians" but would control their "roam[ing] over the country during the summer." The 1867 report additionally offered the opinion that such a post "would open undoubtedly the best agricultural and mining land" in the region. On the other hand, a post on the San Juan, "in the vicinity of the boiling springs [Pagosa], would not afford any protection to the settler on the river west of this stream. In the wintertime, troops would hardly be able to move out of the fort." The "best commanding site is decidedly on the Las Animas." The report concluded that "all requirements necessary for the establishment & maintenance of a post are close at hand in superabundance, and a four company post according to the herewith submitted plan would cost the government very little."[10] The report's findings were correct; the timing proved premature. White settlement had not yet taken root in this region, which remained part of the Ute reservation.

It would not be long, however, before a military presence would be needed. The San Juan Mountains had attracted prospectors for more than a century, since the days when the Spanish ventured out of New Mexico. The Pike's

Peak rush of 1859 had caught the nation's attention and brought miners about 100 miles, as the crow flies, of these rugged mountains. In the following year prospectors traveled up the San Juan and Animas Rivers, creating a mini-rush in 1861.

To the relief of the Utes, the region's isolation, difficult terrain, hostile Indians, and, primarily, lack of gold temporarily drove away the miners. Long known as a mining mother lode, the San Juans again were besieged by prospectors in 1869–1870. Initially they came only during the friendlier summer months, when they could more easily cross the passes, climb the lofty mountains, and scurry about the deep canyons of this difficult mountain range, the highest mining region in the United States.

Prospecting soon gave way to underground mining, which the miners could not conveniently or economically conduct seasonally. Thus by the mid-1870s, Whites had established a permanent settlement on land guaranteed to its longtime residents, the Utes. Uncomfortable with their Ute neighbors, the trespassing Whites wanted the Utes to leave. Unlike the generally slow advance of the farming frontier, the mining front moved quickly, and by 1873, pressure and demands forced the Utes to sign the Brunot Agreement, ceding the mountains and their valleys to the U.S. government. But this solution proved temporary and the Utes continued to wander freely throughout this region.

At the same time, farmers and ranchers, attracted by the market created by the growing mining communities, drifted into the Animas Valley and even eastward toward the San Juan River. Settlement also took hold south in the northern part of New Mexico Territory where the Animas River joined the San Juan. Economically, the residents of the northern part of New Mexico Territory had more ties to their Colorado neighbors than to the rest of their territory because they were separated by desert and native tribes from the main settlements along the Rio Grande. The establishment of these farming communities was essential if the mining communities were to thrive. With little, if any, growing season in the mountains, the miners could not provide enough food for themselves, nor could they rely on winter-closed trails to furnish supplies from the more settled eastern parts of Colorado. The river valleys to the south, however, offered lower elevations, rich land, a decent growing season, and water for growing the necessary agricultural products, and was accessible to the miners who, in theory at least, had gold and silver to purchase this produce. The transportation routes, although mountainous, were shorter and the products fresher than when hauled from Cañon City or other points east.

As the settlers and miners ventured into the area, they created villages and camps. Urbanization was a major component of mining. High up in the mountains, Silverton and neighboring Howardsville, Eureka, and Animas Forks served the needs of the prospectors and miners. In the valley, Animas City, Colorado, and the communities that became Aztec and Farmington, New Mexico, answered the needs of their farming neighbors.

The White settlements thrived but the settlers continued to worry about the presence of the Utes in Colorado and the Navajos to the south. With various Ute bands living both north and south of the San Juan Mountains in close proximity to so many mining and farming communities, rumors, worry, and exaggerated reports of danger were rife. It had happened since the first English settlers had arrived at Jamestown and Plymouth 250 years earlier and had followed settlers as they journeyed westward. The cry went out for the government to send troops and establish a military presence.

John Moss, who had been prospecting and mining in the La Plata Mountains since the early 1870s, sent a resolution in 1876 to Washington, asking Congress to establish a military post in La Plata County. He also wanted a military road to connect the county to Fort Garland, the nearest Colorado post. As his first issue of the *La Plata Miner* came off the printing press, editor John Curry called for the need of a military post in the Animas Valley. The residents of Silverton, along with Curry and his readers, were convinced that danger was lurking on all sides. So, finally, the government sent troops up the San Juan River in October 1878.

Despite the concerns and recommendations of the 1867 report, the army chose the Pagosa Springs site that year. The order went out to "without delay select the most suitable ground and proceed to erect buildings for your cantonment."[11]

This as yet unnamed cantonment had become part of the network of military posts stretching across the West in the 1870s. Not surprisingly, these military posts were often established as a result of a knee-jerk response to pioneer demands without deliberate planning. In the years after the Civil War, more than 100 such posts were scattered across this vast region. Most were small—one- or two-company stations—as the terribly undermanned postwar army tried to protect the ever-changing and rapidly advancing (and occasionally ebbing) hodgepodge of settlement.

The forts provided nearby towns and settlers a comforting reassurance, although not always the immediate security everyone wanted. The officers and men of the cavalry and infantry often found themselves trapped in a nearly impossible situation, caught between the tribes who wanted their land protected from settlers and the settlers who wanted protection from the Indians.[12] Without question, however, the forts provided local markets that locals never overlooked and always appreciated. Uncle Sam, the tacit partner of western settlement, had deep pockets to resolve numerous needs but even these funds were limited. As senators, representatives, governors, and voters in the West demanded protection, Congress cut the size of the military force and its appropriations as a part of largely popular (at least to easterners), peacetime cost reduction measures.

It was in this situation, on a crisp, cold October day, with morning frost accenting yellow aspens and snow dusting the mountaintops, that the army found itself, as it traveled along the San Juan River in southwestern Colorado, amid a few ranchers and farmers and near a small hamlet. The troopers arrived at their new headquarters, a beautiful river valley location nestled among the mountains, which provided a spectacular site and hot springs, a luxury that few western posts could claim. The army had come to southwestern Colorado.

ONE

Pagosa Springs

It is not likely to be a place of military importance.

Maj. Alfred Lacy Hough,
Twenty-Second Infantry, October 16, 1878

The San Juan River cantonment, a military term for temporary quarters (a *fort* was a permanent station), was initially designated Pagosa Springs. On October 26, 1878, it was renamed Camp Lewis in memory of Lt. Col. William Lewis, following the recommendation of his fellow officers. In January 1879 it became Fort Lewis; land around the post became a military reservation in February 1879.

Located on the west bank of the San Juan River about 400 yards north of the main mineral springs, Fort Lewis was commanded by veteran Capt. Wilson Hartz, who had selected the site. He had moved the site from the location originally planned because he was worried that it was too near the mineral springs and had northern exposure. "By crossing the river at a good ford," Hartz found a splendid bench, about twenty feet above the river, with

9

"a fine southern exposure," overlooking the springs and the San Juan River. The new location, isolated though it was, allayed Hartz's concerns.

The troops initially stationed at Fort Lewis consisted of the Fifteenth Infantry (I Company) and the Ninth Cavalry (D Troop). The garrison totaled ninety-two enlisted men and six officers according to the November 1878 Post Returns. The Ninth was the larger of the two with fifty men.

Troops quickly began constructing the frame buildings, log stables, corrals, and shops. The government purchased lumber and shingles on the open market, which helped the local economy. Work was ordered to be "pushed ahead as rapidly as possible so that the work may be completed before winter." But winter comes early to this part of the San Juans, so the men were fighting a losing race.[1]

A good description of the post appeared in a January 1879 report from 2nd Lt. Charles McCauley. He approved of the site selected because it was convenient to water, commanded a good view, and was sheltered by a line of low hills from the "cold winds descending from the high mountains." At the time of his report, the site had ten buildings for enlisted men, five officers' quarters, two company kitchens, four storehouses, one guardhouse, a hospital, and other assorted buildings built or under construction. Hartz had determined the order of construction—first soldiers' quarters, then stables and corral, and then officers' quarters—to ensure the comfort of his men and animals. The men had finished construction by late winter.[2]

Built around a parade ground, the fort was shaped like three sides of a rectangle with the west end open. Each of the ten troop quarters housed ten men and was warmed by an open stone fireplace. Each set of officers' quarters, the guardhouse, and the hospital were divided into two rooms.

With his brief description of the layout, McCauley included information about the site's history and mused over what it might become. "The springs must have always been to the aboriginal inhabitants a place of great resort, attracted by its wonderful healing properties, since Indian trails from all directions converge thereto, all deeply worn." The Utes, the lieutenant believed, "venerate the springs," and the pipe of peace "is said to have here had an unusual supremacy." The Indians wanted the "great father in Washington to retain possession of the place so all persons whites or Indians could visit it when sick."

Of the future, McCauley foresaw great promise. "At no distant day it is destined to be a great resort and to play no mean part in the sanatory [sanatoria] economy of Colorado." Its position on the shortest route from the east to the lower San Juan country would also prove important.

McCauley's report also revealed a problem with this site. Settlers had claimed the springs through "perjury, misrepresentation, or fraud," and various squatters claimed the area as "agricultural land, omitting the springs on their plat" for record and file. A few devious locals made a doubly ingenious attempt to stake the springs as a placer claim after deciding that a mill site claim might be invalidated. According to McCauley, "[A]t a convenient point to the spring, the ground was duly 'salted,' in the most approved manner, by firing gold-dust from a shot-gun into the earth, after which in the presence of a witness, a pan of the earth was washed and 'color' found by the merest accident." These actions had alienated the Indians who watched as the Whites took over their treasured springs. Before troops arrived, the Utes had threatened settlers and even burned cabins.

To offset the fraudulent claims, President Rutherford B. Hayes reserved Pagosa Springs as a town site in May 1877 by executive proclamation. A six-mile-square military reservation was surveyed around the post, measured from the center of the main spring. By the time the army arrived, a small village had been started, occupying one square mile and leaving the military reservation the remaining thirty-five square miles. The Utes could only watch with anguish; their hot springs now belonged to others.

At first the Fifteenth and the Ninth camped on opposite sides of the river. This practice was not unusual in the military because the horses of the cavalry needed space and easy access to water. It also could have been based on who got the first quarters completed. In this case, it might also have been the result of the racism prevalent in nineteenth-century America. The Ninth Cavalry was part of the buffalo soldiers and consisted of former slaves and freed Blacks who had stayed in the postwar army. They faced discrimination both inside and outside the service. Racial incidents from slurs to fights marred the army's integration efforts in the West. The troops at Fort Lewis never displayed any open racial tension, but there is little question that it existed. All the troops, however, would be quartered together at the completed Pagosa post.

Heavy snow isolated the new post in early December. Even without the snow, however, isolation was a harsh reality at Fort Lewis. Mail arrived only once a week. The nearest Colorado military post, Fort Garland, was in another military district and could be reached only by traveling over the mountains and across most of the cold, desolate San Luis Valley. Passing through Del Norte, then Alamosa, couriers journeyed 140 miles by wagon road from the post. Alamosa had the nearest telegraph station and railroad connection, the Denver & Rio Grande. Before winter had stopped their efforts, the army had been working on a road that would cut that distance to ninety miles. District headquarters were located in Santa Fe, which was easier to reach than some of the other posts in New Mexico because it was only about 150 miles away over fairly easy terrain.[3]

Fort Lewis's isolation caused a multitude of worries and problems. Finding forage for the horses and mules quickly emerged as a major one. The nearby ranches could not furnish enough hay, particularly with the troops' late arrival; thus, an officer was forced to travel sixty miles west to Animas City as early as December to make "arrangement for the immediate delivery of hay." Squatting next to the Animas River, that "city" (westerners loved to baptize their small villages with such a status) had been settled five years earlier to help supply San Juan miners. One of the most isolated communities in the state, Animas City nonetheless offered an available market. With plenty of water and with a longer growing season, more accessible agricultural land, and more developed farms and ranches than Pagosa Springs, it offered the nearest and easiest-to-reach settlement.

As winter closed in, it became obvious to the commanding officer that they could not maintain all the horses and other public animals at the post. As a result, 2nd Lt. John Guilfoyle, commanding Troop D of the Ninth, rode to Animas City to arrange for necessary stabling and corral accommodations and an allowance of hay for those animals not needed at the post. The party awarded the contract for hay, however, "failed to meet his obligations" and the recent heavy snows prevented others from obtaining an adequate supply. The horses and mules were forced to go on half allowance.[4]

Not until mid-April could an adequate hay supply be readily obtained at a comparatively modest price from Colorado and New Mexico sources. That improvement, combined with increased local grazing, meant that the horses of the Ninth finally returned to the fort. With new recruits "greatly in need of drill," Hartz felt the time had come to bring back the horses, particularly if the troops were going to be ordered into the field in the coming summer. As Captain Hartz complained, they had the usual "new country to contend with," with its corresponding want of transportation and its terrible roads.

Fortunately, the troops, unlike the animals, did not suffer from lack of provisions. Supplies for the troops had come from Fort Garland, the last two wagons arriving in early January 1879. They contained much-needed stores, which, along with those on hand, provided a five-month supply.[5]

Mail service was another story. In March 1879, new post commander Capt. Francis Dodge, Ninth Cavalry, went so far as to write to Postmaster

General David Key in Washington about the inefficiency of mail service between Pagosa Springs and the East. Mail to the fort traveled a round-about route from New Mexico via Animas City but the service was slow at best.

Although a weekly mail route had been established between Fort Lewis and Del Norte, "carried on foot over the summit," Dodge had no faith in it. "I have yet to learn that a single letter has been brought into this garrison by [the mail service]. I cannot tell where the fault lies, but there is evidently a screw loose somewhere." Mail was slow, stored at length, and sent in round-about ways. Dodge recommended that the contractor carry the mail on buck-boards or travel using some light vehicle instead of riding on horseback. Expressing his frustration with the situation, he averred, "We might then hope to get what belongs to us, and there is also a possibility that we might get it on time, something as yet almost unknown."[6]

Mail service continued to be an issue the commandants worked to improve. Hartz pushed for daily, or at least triweekly, service, but he never achieved this goal because of Fort Lewis's remote location. He also wanted the post trader to be appointed postmaster and the office, currently a little over one mile from the fort, moved to Fort Lewis. In his estimation the present site proved "very inconvenient for transactions of public business." Locals would not have been pleased to read his next comment: "If necessary that office may be discontinued as but few persons are accommodated by the present location."

In spring, warmer weather and improved roads finally produced better mail service. But the post continued to suffer from staff and supply shortages. The hospital ran short of supplies and the post's surgeon had a hard time finding a hospital matron. To resolve another shortage, soldiers were forced to serve extra duty as hospital stewards. Yet another problem arose when the post surgeon wanted to bring his wife to Pagosa Springs, only to have the commanding officer turn him down because no available quarters for families existed "without inconveniencing other officers."[7]

Adding to the difficulties, on one occasion two badly needed twelve-pound mountain howitzers arrived without any wheels, rendering them useless for field service.

Another, less serious, problem arose—dogs. The post was overrun by proliferating canines, and this situation finally led to Special Order 59 in August. "Each company at this post hereafter will be allowed three dogs & no more. Any excess of this allowance must be disposed of by the end of the present month or they will be shot."[8] Undoubtedly this order was unpopular.

As with other military posts, the troops endured the boredom of the relentless routine of army life. The day started with 5:35 reveille (in winter, 6:30) and a second call ten minutes later. The rest of the day was organized around the following schedule:

7:00: breakfast	3:30: stables
7:30: fatigue	4:20: guard details
10:00: recruit drill	sunset: retreat, followed by supper
12:00: dinner	9:00: taps
1:00: fatigue	[Sunday—company inspection]
2:00: recruit drill	

At least one infantry officer thought the time allowed for stable call was entirely inadequate. His men could not turn out the mules; clean out the stables; and deliver fresh grain, hay, and straw in the time set aside. He gave orders to his troops "that hereafter stable cleaning shall come first." The time problem probably developed because infantrymen were not used to stable duty.

Fatigue detail was never popular, but it was essential for maintaining a post. Stable detail, police work, kitchen detail, working as orderlies, cleaning latrines, garbage detail, and gardening, not to mention the more arduous work of ice cutting and logging, stirred up discontent among the enlisted men. They resented being used as "cheap labor" when they had enlisted as soldiers.

To somewhat alleviate the routine, troopers could be assigned to extra duty and earn a small amount of extra pay. Extra duty might include work as a teacher or as a teacher's assistant in one of the army's post schools. These schools were maintained to teach the "three R's" to men lacking such skills. Other examples of extra duty were performed by soldiers serving as cooks and "strikers" (servants) for the officers, hospital stewards, or handymen.

Particularly when building a new post, men with experience as carpenters or stonemasons or who possessed other necessary skills received extra-duty pay, which in the 1870s was thirty-five cents a day. Soldiers designated as laborers were paid twenty-five cents. Noncommissioned officers were not eligible for extra-duty pay so it was possible for a private to earn more than a corporal or a sergeant. In addition to the extra wages, performing extra duty often excused the men from some of the drills and guard duty.

For the officers, service on the council of administration, which handled matters such as dealing with traders, and the numerous board of survey sessions took up much time. The latter handled a wide range of army matters, such as determining who was responsible for lost revolvers, lost ordnances, and property taken by deserters; establishing the quality and price for lots of trousers; and even examining twelve cans of "corn beef found to be bad."[9]

Officers also spent hours on garrison courts-martial and, for more serious offenses, general courts-martial. The former handled cases such as absence without leave, "conduct to the prejudice of good order and military discipline," drunkenness, and some issues involving violation of an article of war. The Articles of War, which had been revised and passed by Congress in 1874, along with other general and special orders and decisions of the War Department, governed the military. Customs of the service, an unwritten part of military law recognized as having the force of law, supplemented these written rules. The garrison court comprised three officers and was frequently called. Considering that generally only six officers were stationed at Pagosa Springs, garrison court duty almost amounted to regular duty.

Fortunately, many offenses were minor and "good order" could cover a multitude of sins. Private Fred Hill found out the value of good order when he pled guilty to all charges levied against him, except having uttered "this god damn way of one man doing all the damn work by god is a hell of a note." For this he forfeited three dollars in pay, and Hill previously had been reduced to a private. The typical penalty was forfeiture of some pay, spending extra time in the guardhouse, or, for something more grave, a reduction in rank.[10]

Prisoners guilty of serious crimes were taken by escort to Fort Marcy in Santa Fe or Fort Garland to await trial. Such was the case for two privates of Company D, Ninth Cavalry, who were sent to Santa Fe in August 1879. The order did not specify their offenses.

The Ninth had low desertion and alcoholism rates, but frequent incidents of insubordination and negligence offset this positive record. The offenses of theft and absent without leave also regularly occurred.

These cases did not involve just enlisted men. One officer was placed under arrest for drunkenness while on duty. And there was the incestuous marriage of 1st Sgt. William Braun to his niece. This one left the officers in a quandary and received no further mention.

Because the trial was more to determine punishment than guilt or innocence, conviction was the norm; however, the accused was not automatically found guilty. Private Patrick O'Neill was acquitted of charges, and Pvt. Charles Anderson had the charges remitted because it represented his "first offense and [he has a] good character." The defendant's prior record, as in Anderson's case, was as important as the facts of the case. An excellent soldier could get away with more than a sorry one could. Still, Fort Lewis had no shortage of disciplinary problems. In February 1880 Capt. George Thorkley reported to the Department of Missouri that because of the "large number in confinement," the post guardhouse had reached its capacity. To resolve the situation, three prisoners had been "temporarily restored" to duty while awaiting trial.[11]

Such problems were not unusual for the army in the frontier. Isolation, boredom, dashed expectations, outside allurements, and a host of individual issues took a steady toll on the men. Across the West, an astounding number deserted and Fort Lewis proved no exception. Indeed, because of its proximity to mining camps and districts, even more temptations existed.

In the years between 1867 and 1891, the army's desertion rate averaged 14.8 percent per year, for a total of 88,475 deserters during this time frame. Considering that the army averaged only 25,000 enlisted men during most of this period, that number was shocking. Nearly one third of the regulars deserted in 1871 and that number again in 1872. More than nearby attractive mining districts was responsible for this high desertion rate. The army's haphazard recruiting system brought unfit, undesirable men into service. And the poor food and quarters, garrison monotony, and low pay did not encourage men to fulfill their enlistment.[12]

The dearth of social and relaxation outlets available at the post did little to distract the men from the harsh realities of military life. In 1878 and 1879 the entertainment at Fort Lewis consisted of the post trader, who offered a small variety of goods for sale, and the post library, which offered a few books and twenty-four newspapers and periodicals, such as the *Harpers Weekly, New York Herald,* and *Atlantic Monthly.* How frequently the library was patronized remains unknown.

But the men at Fort Lewis were more fortunate the most. For officers and enlisted men alike, a relaxing time at the hot springs broke up the long, monotonous days. They must have enjoyed the pleasant diversion the hot springs offered. Several officers, in fact, built their own private baths at the springs in 1879, undoubtedly not open to enlisted men. It seems likely that the troops played baseball, or at least tossed the ball around, because records indicate that the game was popular when the post moved a year later. Shooting contests, fishing, and hunting occupied leisure moments in this area where game and streams provided abundant opportunity. Card playing and probably gambling, despite the army's disproval, also helped the men pass many hours.

Occasionally the fort or community hosted social events, one of which led to a fight with definite racial overtones. When troopers from the Ninth

Cavalry crashed and broke up a July Fourth ball in the village of Pagosa Springs, four troopers were promptly arrested and ended up in the guardhouse. The post commander who investigated the matter learned that the party had been a private affair with an admission charge and "only guests having invitations" expected to attend. Apparently that excluded the Ninth. In October, with the "citizen who caused the charges to be preferred" having fled the country "to avoid debt," and the four imprisoned troopers having "conducted themselves properly and given no trouble," Lt. William Davis successfully petitioned the district commander for permission to release the men and dismiss the charges.[13]

Another fight that appeared to be racially motivated occurred when a Mexican mail carrier attacked two Ninth couriers at the Piedra Station west of the post. The report did not specify a reason, but Blacks and Mexicans had a history of not getting along in the Southwest. Racism knew no cultural or geographic boundaries even in newly settled southwestern Colorado. When the Ninth came to southwestern Colorado, therefore, it was likely to expose underlying racial tensions in this region, which now had the largest concentration of Blacks in the nineteenth century and most of the twentieth as well.[14]

When the troops were idle and bored, conflict was bound to ensue. One way to relieve the tension was to send the troops into the field and keep them occupied with something beyond routine garrison duty. Before winter closed in, D Troop of the Ninth was charged with the responsibility of escorting the crew surveying the boundary between Utah and Colorado. Other individuals carried mail and army correspondence between Fort Lewis and posts in New Mexico and provided escorts for wagon trains, paymasters, and special officers, including Gens. Phil Sheridan and John Pope. Other men worked on the road between Alamosa and Pagosa Springs or helped with a survey of the military reservation.

The troops also worked to maintain peaceful relations between the Indians and the Whites. In 1879 the post received reports about troubles—or potential troubles—with the Utes and Navajos. Patrols might have been sent out to investigate matters, but no major campaigns happened during that spring and summer. The troops continued to keep the peace at the springs, where the appearance of Utes generally evoked strong feelings and fear among the settlers.

Fort Lewis and its garrison were an important part of the community. The troops interacted with civilians throughout the region for social and economic reasons. This interaction was an economic boon to the hamlet of

Pagosa Springs and even more so to the larger and better located Animas City. The 1880 census recorded 223 residents in the former and 286 in the latter, making them the two largest communities in southwestern Colorado, apart from Silverton. The entire La Plata County had 1,110 settlers, and the western end of Conejos County (Archuleta County had not yet been created), where Fort Lewis was located, probably did not have more than 400 people.

The military purchased hay, beef, charcoal, corn, lumber, and vegetables, among other things, from locals. Post commanders also rented stables and corrals for their animals, always bargaining for the lowest price. The fort was the best local market available but not one that could be taken advantage of; the army took great care in its purchases and saw that its contracts were fulfilled to the letter.

Local businessmen Thomas D. Burns, who had a hay contract with the army, and Thomas Graden, who owned an independent lumbering outfit, found out that the government was taking an active interest in the business affairs of the community. When cold, snowy winter weather and poor roads prevented Burns from meeting his deadlines, Lt. George Cornish went to Animas City to check on the hay and the feasibility of transporting it to Fort Lewis. He concluded that the effort to bring it to the post was hopeless, as long as freighters refused to haul at the contracted rate because of the snow and bad roads. "The road from Animas City to here is in bad condition, being built along hill sides, in many places and in some sloping to one side at an angle of about 15 degrees, rendering it dangerous for top heavy load."

Graden attracted the army's attention by illegally harvesting trees on the military reservation. The commanding officer had the honor of informing Graden that he was not to cut any more timber on the military reservation. "Failure to comply with this order will necessitate the removal of your saw mill from the reservation." Sometimes, however, civilians learned that the army took without asking. Local resident Matias Dominques informed the commander that troops camping on his land had used his fence poles for firewood and he requested a payment of $50.[15]

In 1880 the federal census taker finally reached isolated Fort Lewis. It was now a one-company post; the original returns provide a glimpse of the men stationed there. Only two young officers, 1st Lts. Cyrus De Lany and George Cornish, remained, along with surgeon John Cochran. Alabama-born and a West Pointer, Cornish was one of the few southerners ever stationed at Fort Lewis.

The enlisted men, all but two in their twenties, were 71 percent American-born. Almost everybody came from New England or the Midwest. Considering the army's postwar profile, it is interesting that only one man listed Ireland as his home. The company contained thirty-three men, which was below regulation strength but typical for those stationed at Fort Lewis.

Three enlisted men's families lived on the post, with a total of six children. One family had their seventeen-year-old niece staying with them, who probably enjoyed being the belle of Fort Lewis. No officers' families were present. A scout also served with the company. Unfortunately, the census taker did not bother listing previous occupations; following tradition he simply put down "soldier" for everyone.[16]

Despite its isolation and small size, Fort Lewis attracted some notable military heroes. Local Civil War veterans and northerners alike cheered the late May and early June 1879 New Mexico and Colorado tour of Lt. Gen. Philip Sheridan, the famous northern cavalry leader and well-known western commander of the Division of the Missouri. A preeminent figure in the army and the West, Sheridan journeyed west that spring to tour some of the Department of Missouri posts. Escorted by troopers of the Ninth Cavalry, he bounced over Stony Pass into Silverton, greeted by excited residents and buildings bedecked with flags. He then traveled on to Pagosa Springs and other posts.

Another Civil War general who had briefly served as commander of the Army of Virginia, Brig. Gen. John Pope, commander of the Department of the Missouri since 1870, followed in August 1880. His visit resolved several pressing matters and was part of a longer inspection of his department, a section of the larger Division of the Missouri. Although Sheridan and Pope had become noted Indian fighters, Pope had a progressive and humanitarian attitude toward the Indians. His and similar views, regrettably, failed to influence a large audience.[17]

The American public in general was far from any national consensus on what was rather quaintly termed the "Indian Question" or on what their place should be in a society dominated by Whites. At the time Fort Lewis was established, peace and Indian rights advocates were squaring off against westerners who did not want the tribes anywhere near them.

The troops who were charged with the thankless and dangerous job of trying to keep the peace and allow settlement to continue encroaching on Indian land tended to share westerners' views about the Indians. Sheridan showed much less sympathy than Pope toward the people he called savages and who he believed needed to be curtailed and punished for every crime.

Like many others, he thought that the best solution was to place them on reservations where they could learn farming while being absorbed into main-stream American life. (Later in his career, Sheridan revealed a more under-standing view of the tribes' plight: "We took away their country and their means of support, broke up their mode of living, their habits of life," and against this "they made war.") General of the Army William Sherman agreed that the Indians needed to be punished and placed on reservations. He be-lieved that their way of life was doomed, but told them that if they would keep the peace, "we will be kind to you." This so-called pacification policy was at odds with the growing humanitarian movement.[18]

The officers at Fort Lewis were well aware of the controversy surround-ing the Indian policy. They also knew about the tensions that existed be-tween the army and the Indian Bureau. As they strove to keep the Utes and their neighbors on a peaceful path, they tried to strike a delicate balance between the two sides. But soon they would be swept up in events outside their control.

Meanwhile, events beyond the reach of the Fort Lewis garrison changed its history forever. Despite the continued unease of the residents of Animas City and the nearby cattlemen, who were still "very anxious on the subject of the Utes," the settlers and Indians continued to coexist fairly peacefully in southwestern Colorado. Then came trouble. Fort Lewis became the head-quarters for some 500 troopers from the Ninth Cavalry and the Fifteenth, Nineteenth, and Twenty-Second Infantries, who were there as part of a mili-tary campaign, when the so-called Ute War broke out in northwestern Colo-rado in 1879. This war would mark the end of the post along the San Juan River.

Fort Lewis at Pagosa Springs had not been situated correctly to protect the largest number of people and settlements. The Animas Valley, from its headwaters high up in the San Juan Mountains to its entry into New Mexico Territory through the Southern Ute Reservation, was home to 2,197 miners, farmers, ranchers, and city folk. The post was located too far away from most of these people to be of any immediate help in case of trouble. Furthermore, the winters effectively isolated Fort Lewis for weeks or months at a time. And nearby settlers could not provide enough foodstuffs and other necessary goods, forcing the army to haul supplies over long distances, which was an expensive venture. Support posts were miles and mountains away. It all boiled down to isolation, something that could not be overcome.

Maj. Alfred Hough and his companies of the Twenty-Second Infantry camped at Fort Lewis in October 1879 on their way to Animas City and the river valley to protect the settlers. During his stay, when writing his wife Mary, he unintentionally provided the perfect epitaph for Fort Lewis at Pagosa Springs: "It is not likely to be a place of much military importance."[19]

TWO

THE UTE WAR

Oh the drums would roll, upon my soul,
This is the style we'd go,
Forty Miles a day, on beans and hay,
In the regular army O.

"THE REGULAR ARMY, O"

Several long days to the north of Fort Lewis, the White River Utes, infuri-
ated at their agent Nathan Meeker and his policies, plotted a revolt. The Ute
War did not explode overnight. It had been smoldering for a decade. War
had become almost inevitable, since the prospectors and miners had returned to the San Juan Mountains, searching, always searching, for the gold
and silver hidden in this mother lode country, that fabled land where all the
mineral veins originated. It bothered them little that they trespassed on land
guaranteed to the Ute people.

In some ways, this war had been coming for centuries, long before the
first prospectors ventured into these high, rocky, and ragged mountains. Since
the first seventeenth-century Europeans journeyed across the Atlantic and
settled in North America, an ongoing skirmish had ebbed and flowed between

two peoples whose cultures, religions, economies, concepts of landowner-ship, governments, and attitudes toward war differed markedly. As the Span-ish settled in the Southwest and the English marched westward, the conflict flared in hundreds of locales. The French briefly took part before they were knocked off the continent by other eighteenth-century world conflicts.

The Utes, in their mountain and river valley domain, had traded and warred with the Spanish for more than two centuries before the 1859 Pike's Peak gold rush. The creation of Colorado Territory two years later claimed land that had been the home of many Utes for years. The Utes were unaware of these changes and would not have been able to affect the outcome even if they had known or even realized what this could potentially mean to them. At the time, the federal government "generously" gave the Utes the land beyond the snowy range, as the Continental Divide was known in those days, because settlement and mining were then primarily east of the divide. That this land had already been their home for ages did not seem to matter.

In the years that followed, Coloradans and the Indians to the west watched each other with a wary eye. Treaties were made and temporarily postponed a confrontation, but the rush into the San Juans in the 1870s again brought the matter to a head. The Brunot Agreement opened the district to more settlers, but the Utes still lived in the surrounding lands to the north and south, too close for comfort for many settlers. Yet, the area continued to attract more Whites because of the numerous opportunities it offered. Mining became year-round by the mid-1870s and little camps took root in canyons and mountain valleys. To the south, along the Animas River, ranchers and farmers gathered where water, a longer growing season, and a large fertile valley allowed them to cultivate their land and tap the mining trade. Animas City became the economic center of this region.

Fort Lewis at Pagosa Springs had been established to protect these var-ied and widely scattered interests, but it was too far away and too isolated to do the job. At best, it might have protected part of the trail into the region, a few settlers, and the area around the hot springs. It might have been some-what reassuring to know that the military had a presence in the region, but the post could not offer the security that newcomers felt they needed and deserved.

As settlement rolled westward and settlers moved in, the push to re-move Indians from the land generally followed. The speed with which the Utes were pushed out was the only difference between what happened in the mining West and what had happened time and again beginning with Jamestown, Virginia, in 1607 and Plymouth, Massachusetts, in 1620. Mining, fast moving and often transitory, had come to the San Juans to stay. The changes that this rush made to the region brought matters rapidly to a crisis, as they had during the California gold rush and all those that followed. From the perspective of the newcomers, the Utes threatened transportation lines to the north, east, and south; hindered development; scared investors; raised the cost of living; and claimed some of the best farming land in Colorado. And who knew what mineral resources lay trapped within their reservation?

From the Ute perspective, these interlopers scared away the game, overran their land, disrupted their traditional way of life, and cared little for the tribe or for upholding any agreements or treaties made by the government. The two sides did not understand each other and in many cases did not really care to. Each side had its own interpretation of the Brunot Agreement and these two interpretations had little common ground. The balance between the Whites and the Indians on Colorado's Western Slope, the land beyond the "snowy range," teetered precariously, an explosion waiting to happen.

As soon as printing presses had been carried over the steep mountain passes to the region, local newspapers were filled with headlines like "The Utes Must Go." That cry, echoed by other newspapers throughout Colorado, doomed the Utes. And this sentiment was not focused solely on the Utes of the San Juans. Coloradans also craved the fertile land of the Ute reservation to the north of the San Juans and sought to tap the riches of the famed Gunnison Country, slightly northeast of the San Juans. It was to this situation that idealistic New England newspaperman, dreamer, and colonizer Nathan Meeker came. In 1870 he had traveled west to create a model world resembling the transcendentalist efforts at Brook Farm and elsewhere in the pre–Civil War years. With the help of Horace Greeley, Meeker had founded the Union Colony and its town of Greeley.

The success of Meeker's Union Colony and Greeley could not be denied, but Meeker's welcome there had worn thin. Many colonists did not agree with his views, nor did they think highly of "Father" Meeker. Meeker's views clashed with those of the more materialistic settlers who were not looking for a utopia, so he looked elsewhere to find his dream. It was at this time that the frustrated Meeker turned his attention to civilizing the Utes. Appointed Indian agent to the White River Agency in northwestern Colorado in 1878, he immediately began implementing his ideas, which meshed well with those of the Indian Bureau. He pushed the Utes to sell their surplus horses, turn to farming, settle down, stop gambling, and send their children to school. Yet within a year Meeker's plans had produced only mistrust, tension, threats, and downright hatred among his wards. Ute men did not like to do women's work, such as planting and harvesting crops. Hunting deer and buffalo was more to their liking. It was a classic clash of cultures, as misunderstanding and idealism crashed into reality.

Meeker continued pushing his agenda despite Ute protests. By September 1879, as the garrison at Fort Lewis prepared for the upcoming winter season, Meeker recognized that a storm was brewing and called for troops.

On September 21, 1879, troops left Fort Steele, Wyoming, in response to Meeker's call. But it was too late. On September 29, the Utes ambushed the oncoming cavalry column at Milk Creek, killing thirteen men, including Maj. Thomas Thornburgh, and wounding forty-three. The beleaguered, pinned-down troops sent for help. On October 1, relief forces swiftly left Fort D. A. Russell near Cheyenne and were joined by a company of the Ninth Cavalry from nearby Middle Park. Other troops stationed at posts farther away prepared to come west as army officers ordered an overwhelming force to quickly stamp out this resistance.

Many Americans envisioned another Custer's last stand, so recent in their memories. Screamed the *Rocky Mountain News* on October 8, 1879:

The Milk Creek Massacre

The White River Utes on the Warpath. Major [Thomas] Thornburgh's command ambushed

The gallant commander killed while leading the charge.

A Bloody War Predicted

The relief troops appeared, prepared to attack, but no bloody battle ensued. Instead, the Utes raised the surrender flag. Ouray, their most noted leader, skillfully managed the complex task of convincing his fellow Utes that further fighting would not only be futile, but would lead to disaster for the tribe. With that crisis averted, troops moved on to the White River Agency headquarters. But it was too late to save Meeker. He and eleven employees lay dead at the agency and their wives and children had been taken prisoner. The long-expected Ute War had begun.[1]

Until the captives could be located and rescued, no pursuit or revenge was possible. Once again Ouray proved invaluable as he secured the captives' release. Although the captives initially said that they had not been mistreated, eventually they told about the outrages they had suffered in captivity. Coloradans and others now loudly called for the army to mount a punitive expedition and make the Utes pay the price for their "treachery," as the Whites called it.

When word of these events reached the mining camps and Animas City, fear took hold and imaginations ran wild. Only four miles south of Animas City lay the Southern Ute reservation. Although these Utes had nothing to do with Meeker's demise, the threat existed that they might join their brothers to the north and attack. And protection was days away up the San Juan River.

The settlers had wanted a post in the Animas Valley long before Meeker had forced the uprising along the White River. Indeed, Fort Lewis had been established in part to satisfy this need. After the Milk Creek disaster the need was magnified as Coloradans rallied to demand the removal of the Utes. The unprotected residents of Animas City, Silverton, and other nearby communities saw danger everywhere. Rampaging Utes could ride in from the north or south and then the men would be killed, the women would "suffer a fate worse than death," and their children would be taken prisoner.

Full-scale panic gripped the upper Animas, when a would-be Paul Revere barged into a Howardsville saloon about eleven in the evening, breathlessly shouting, "The Indians have massacred everybody in Animas City and are moving on to Silverton." Located only a couple of miles north of Silverton, they feared the worst. After a drink, their well-fortified informant hurried off to spread the alarm. Word spread like wildfire; men, women, and children looked for hiding places. The chaos abated only after a few citizens from Howardsville arrived in a sleepy Silverton and found most of the residents still sleeping peacefully in the early morning hours.[2]

But there was no turning back now. Short of men and arms, Animas City hoped Fort Lewis could supply the latter. On October 10, the post adjutant informed the U.S. deputy marshal at Animas City, James Heffernan, that the post had no ordnance to spare. Somewhat encouragingly, he went on to say that more troops were expected to arrive in a few days and would be deployed to protect settlements in the area, including the Animas Valley.

Keeping a close watch on the state of affairs at Animas City, the army planned to move all available forces to the valley. Troops from Forts Wingate and Garland and beyond were moving in. From the military's perspective, "[T]heir apprehensions had been allayed as far as practicable," but the army also understood that "the presence of troops in their immediate vicinity will alone fully satisfy them." On Saturday, October 11, Animas City was informed that troops from Fort Wingate "should be in southern Ute country on the weekend."[3]

Meanwhile, troops gathered at Fort Lewis as part of the overall plan to put down the uprising and protect settlements throughout the Western Slope.

Recent visitor General Pope directed the movements against the Utes. But the troops marching out of Fort Lewis would play only a peripheral role in the final campaign and a rather frustrating one from a military standpoint. Once again the army was caught between the Indian Bureau, humanitarians, and western settlers and politicians.

The Fort Lewis troops got no closer to the White River Utes than the Animas Valley, mountains and miles away from their reservation, and would serve to calm fears more than anything else. It was this move to the Animas Valley, however, that would have significant implications for the history of the post.

Among the infantry rushing to Fort Lewis to reinforce the troops were the four companies of the Twenty-Second, commanded by Maj. Alfred Hough. In subsequent months, his letters would provide a fascinating view of the 1879 crisis, military life, a moment in Fort Lewis's history, and southwestern Colorado.

Major Hough and his companies came from Fort Gibson, Indian Territory, by rail to Alamosa, then over the mountains on a cold march to Fort Lewis. Hough observed upon awaking one morning, "[T]he night was cold, ice formed a fourth of an inch thick which showed a rugged change from Gibson with the mercury at 90 when we started." During the march, which he described as having begun with "a series of blunders," a company took the wrong road and wandered almost all night before reaching Hough's camp.

Shortly after starting, Capt. Charles Parker's troop of the Ninth Cavalry reported to Hough. "These were the first colored troops our men had ever seen but there was no demonstration at the meeting besides some looks of wonder and surprise, and from that time on there was never any difficulty between our men and them." Parker, a Civil War veteran from Illinois, had reenlisted in 1874 to join the Ninth.

Reaching Fort Lewis, they went into camp near the post. Hough left behind a description of the area and a prediction about its future.

> The springs are truly wonderful. A boiling sulphur spring of irregular form some 60 or 70 feet in circumference is situated at the apex of a slight elevation from the surrounding plain. . . . The San Juan is a fine mountain stream and very cold, though sufficient water runs from the spring into it to modify its temperature. . . .
>
> Nature though was being despoiled of its beauty by a new town of board shanties, which were being built near the springs, between them and the timbered hills which bound the valley of the San Juan. Bathhouses were already erected, and at no distant time, after the railroad reaches this place, it will no doubt be a resort of invalids.

He concluded that Fort Lewis was not likely to be a place of "much military importance."[4]

As "war chief" (a Ute designation), Hough attended an afternoon council with the leaders of the three bands of the Southern Utes—the Weeminuche, Mouache, and Capote. "The Indians expressed great sorrow for the misconduct of the Northern Utes and declared they had no sympathy with them, that they were peaceful Indians and wanted to know why troops were brought into their territory." Hough told them that the troops were there to meet the Northern Utes if they came south. Warned that they must not harbor any of them, the Indians agreed they "would not." Hough had his doubts, however, and felt the army had come at the right time. "No doubt our coming into the country prevented the young men from going north to aid the White River Utes."

Speeches took up a large part of that afternoon, and Hough's respect and admiration for the Utes grew, despite not understanding the Ute language. "There was eloquence in their manner of delivery and I wished I could have understood them." Ignacio, "the chief of the Winnemuches [*sic*] and the most powerful man among the Southern Utes, was not present." He had gone to meet the column marching from Fort Wingate. At its conclusion, Hough felt the council was "impressive and interesting." Afterward he confided to his wife, Mary, "[T]hey were very humble and all *looks* well but still we are vigilant."

Joined by Capt. John Bean and his company of the Fifteenth, Hough, riding a mule (his horse was still at Fort Gibson), led his column toward Animas City. The country impressed him. It was along the Los Pinos River that they "found a cultivated valley, the first since leaving the Conejos; and passed on to the Florida, another pretty valley and cultivated." On October 22, the troops finally reached Animas City after an easy march from Fort Lewis.

Despite the trials of his 180-mile trip from Alamosa, Hough waxed enthusiastic about what he had seen. "In all my experience I never campaigned through a country so beautiful, mountains, forest, valleys, clear rushing water, everything to make nature lovely, and here in the Animas valley we found quite a large settlement and a thriving town."

He thoughtfully wrote his wife not to worry: "The streams are full of trout of which we have plenty. We are well supplied and suffer from nothing." They drove cattle with them and ranchers supplied them with butter and vegetables. Hough observed that the ranchers took advantage of the miners' dependence on them and sold "their products to the miners in the mountains west of here at a high price."

As they moved into the valley, the troops found citizens eager to profit from the troops' arrival and little evidence of the worry that had brought them here. "The Indian scare if there had been one was over, and all anxiety of the inhabitants seemed to be centered on trying to make as much money out of our coming among them as possible." In fact, the day after the column arrived, Hough received news that all military operations would cease while the government conducted an investigation and worked on a peace treaty. "We therefore went into a permanent camp and made ourselves as comfortable as possible." Hough and most likely the other officers were frustrated with this decision. Tension between many in the army toward the Indian Bureau and the federal government's policy toward the Indians continued to simmer.

In his usual style of run-on sentences separated by commas, Hough later wrote in his personal story of the expedition how deep his feelings still were.

> Thus have these Indians by boldly resisting the government brought it to negotiate; if they had been a weak tribe our magnanimous government would have crushed them at once. Indians who will fight are always better treated than those who submit, and Indians know from experience that if they can successfully commit a depredation, killing a number of people and robbing some stock, do enough to compel the government to proceed against them, they are safe as to a settlement of the trouble by a concession to them. In other words it does not pay them to be peaceful.

At the time, he told Mary, "I don't care how much of a peace they may patch up now, every man, woman and child in Colorado are in favor of removing the Utes and they will force it and bring on a war sooner or later." The Southern Utes may be "peaceable," but when threatened with removal, "they will fight for their homes." Of the federal policy, Hough wasted no words. "Our whole Indian policy is a mere system of make-shifts and must result in much bloodshed in the end. I have not much comfort in looking at it."[5]

Settling down on the east bank of the Animas River across from Animas City, Hough described Animas City in a letter to his wife: "There are not more than 20 houses in this city but it has true Yankee enterprise—church, a school & newspaper." Despite being an economic center for the surrounding mining communities and one of the largest cities in the region, Animas City did not entirely impress the major, for he told Mary it was "somewhat decayed at that." The Presbyterian minister visited the camp to invite them to attend his church; alas, the next Sunday the mail came in at church time, and Hough had to remain in camp.

Hough went on to describe the excitement of the projected arrival of the Denver & Rio Grande Railroad, which people hoped would be completed by the end of summer. The railroad promised to bring greater opportunity for prosperity and ease of transportation, heretofore unexperienced in this part of Colorado. Unfortunately for Animas City, that promised day of prosperity that seemed inevitable in the fall of 1879 would not come to pass. But this information was not known to the locals, who would have been pleased with Hough's summary of their town. "Prospects are good for their expectations being realized, as there are rich but undeveloped silver mines in the mountains near, and the Animas valley is a good place for a town. The climate is compensatingly mild and pleasant with short winters."

Four troops of the Ninth Cavalry, one company of the Nineteenth Infantry, and two companies of the Fifteenth Infantry had joined Hough and his four companies camping across from Animas City, for a total of about 600 troopers. This detail was originally under the command of Edward Hatch, colonel of the regiment. Able and personable, the Maine-born Hatch had been one of the organizers of the Ninth Cavalry.[6] Col. George Buell, Fifteenth Infantry, assumed command after Hatch received an appointment to the peace commission. Hough, who admired the able and personable Hatch, had reservations about the change. "I do not believe it will be as pleasant for us as it has been. For while Hatch is the most amiable of men, Buell is the reverse." General Hatch "had endeared himself to us by his soldierly bearing and uniform kindness to us." Interestingly, Hatch had planned to move the troops over to the La Plata River until the war sputtered out and peace efforts started. But with the change in command, that move would wait another day.

Happy with his campsite, Hough described it for his wife: "My camp of five companies looks pretty and very picturesque with the men washing their clothing and cleaning up generally after their long march." Sounding almost like a chamber of commerce spokesman, he praised the climate. "The days are mild and pleasant, no fire needed and the night comfortably cold for good sleeping." It must have been quite pleasant, particularly in comparison to the heat of Fort Gibson.[7]

Although pleased with the campsite, Hough was frustrated with the situation: "Lying in camp so long is very tiresome and monotonous." And he concluded, "[T]his campaign has fizzled terribly." Without any military plans to occupy his thoughts, he wondered when he might get home and thought about visiting the ancient Toltec ruins on the Mancos River only 30 miles away. Interestingly, he had not been interested in the Mexican villages his troops had passed through on the way to Fort Lewis.

Among the troops camped with Hough was 1st Sgt. George Courtright's Company D of the Twenty-Second Infantry. One of the problems that Courtright encountered at camp was the mysterious, ongoing disappearances of pan holders, knives, tablespoons, and the like. "A careful investigation determined the stealing was not by soldiers, so I posted a scout to be especially careful in the early hours of the morning." Finally, they caught in action "several big, saucy blue jays, picking up the small, bright objects" and flying to nearby nests. The mystery was solved, and the story probably entertained the troops.[8]

When the commission to look into the Meeker mess was established, Hough did not believe that it would be the best solution.

> If the troops had been allowed to go on in all sides we could have done a great deal, if not settled the matter this fall. As it is, before the commission can proceed to the points necessary [to] get all the information, report to the government and get from it a decision or get action, the season will here nearly [be] gone and nothing can be done before spring.

Hough judged that "there is no possible use of our staying here any longer and I would not be surprised at any movement or receiving orders to go back to Fort Lewis. And there await events."

Hough was not impressed with some of the locals, or most Coloradans for that matter. The newspapers, he thought, tried to inflame the public and were supported by people who had one goal in mind: "To have an expensive war and bring in money and eventually to drive out the Utes. These frontier people are really unscrupulous." The army, Hough continued, has been "made such catspaws of, mere tools of ambitious men, who care only [to] further their own interests and cotton to the public for publicity." By mid-November, he was worried about being stuck at Camp Animas, as he called it, all winter and not getting out "until the Utes are conquered and the proscribed ones captured next season."

Despite his complaints, Hough did get along with his neighbors and conveyed a more positive attitude as he wrote about a party given at Animas City.

> The officers gave a hop in the city last night [November 12] in return for the hospitalities received. They danced in the schoolhouse and had supper at the "Shaws" hotel where the young ladies received. . . . It was a grand success and they outnumbered the natives. They are lounging around today looking sloppy.

Silverton's *La Plata Miner* imagined it a "grand ball," not a hop. Hough had stayed home, however, with three other officers, and they had a short party and played whist in his tent before turning in for the night.[9]

A few months later, he recalled those lazy, chilly days camped along the Animas.

> On pleasant nights the camp resounded with songs, and the "colored troops" were mighty with instrumental music. Many of the officers and men hunted and fished with great success, trout and venison were common food for us, the time afforded some society. On the whole the memory of Camp Animas is pleasant.

Hough remembered some excitement occurring when cowboys from nearby ranches came into town "and [were] 'running it'—in their language—which consist[s] of doing just as they please, riding into stores and through houses, etc., and firing pistols." When the city marshal killed one of the celebrants, his companions sought to avenge him. The marshal and mayor fled to Buell, who sent them to Hough's camp. "After the whiskey was out of the boys they left town peaceably, previously burying their late comrade, from whose funeral they returned in full gallop shooting and firing pistols. We were however in an anxious state of mind all the time."[10]

According to the *Miner*, much of the excitement in Animas City was the result of the troops' presence: "[Animas City] seems to be a lively place these days." Horse races, dances, concerts, and the like "are the order of the day there. Uncle Sam's blue coated laddies are the cause of all this commotion in our neighbor village."

But the village had something to worry about, despite the good times and presence of the troops. It soon became clear that the Denver & Rio Grande Railroad intended to start its own settlement two miles downstream, because Animas City had refused to accede to the railroad's demands. This new town would "knock the stuffing out of the present town," predicted the *Miner*. The editor recognized that the coming of the railroad would be a good thing for the San Juan mining district, but he also accurately predicted that urban jealousy and a fight over the railroad could be brutal. In 1880 these predictions would prove accurate.

Seemingly unfazed by this threat, the locals were focused on the Ute question. They sent a petition to Washington, requesting the removal of their southern neighbors. On this issue Silverton and Animas City agreed that "the Utes Must Go."[11]

The army remained vigilant even though southwestern Colorado faced no immediate danger. Courtright's company was sent out on a scouting expedition in the La Plata River country. After marching twelve miles in cold weather and deep snow through Wild Cat Canyon, they set up camp. The cook and his helpers "cleared away the snow enough so that he could operate his famous Dutch ovens." Moving on, they went into a second camp, passing along the way the future permanent site of Fort Lewis. There was so much game in the vicinity that "hunting was fine—in fact, we soon tired of game and were glad to go back to the old reliable bacon and beef."[12]

Meanwhile, as Hough and his troops lingered along the Animas ("two months in tents in winter expresses a deal of discomfort, of this we had our share"), the war in the north was resolved. After Ouray's and former Ute agent Charles Adams's efforts had led to the release of the captive women, the commission tried to take testimony, but the Utes would not talk and would not accept as valid the females' testimony against their male captors. With only the former captives' side of the story, the commissioners found themselves in a quandary. If trials were to be held, the Utes demanded they be held in Washington, because, as Ouray correctly argued, a fair and impartial verdict could not be reached in Colorado. Many Coloradans wanted the guilty parties punished, and almost all wanted the Utes removed—and quickly. But where should they go? That issue proved contentious and hard to solve, as the surrounding states and territories did not want them either.

It soon became obvious that the Utes' days in Colorado were numbered. Coloradans were ardently determined to be rid of them and to open the Western Slope to White settlement. Early in 1880, an ill Ouray led a delegation to Washington. Predictably, another "treaty" was signed, forcing all the Utes out of the state except those south of Animas City in southwestern Colorado. It would not be until September 1881 that the last of them dejectedly departed for Utah, and the aftermath of the war officially concluded. Coloradans had gotten their wish. By this time, Hough and his companies had departed Camp Animas, with one company returning to Fort Lewis at Pagosa Springs.

Hough had assumed command of the companies when Colonel Buell moved his headquarters from the camp along the Animas River. He wrote Buell on December 13, "I have not seen the men as comfortable and happy since we have been here." Most of the letter, however, discussed the problems of getting feed for their animals at a reasonable price. Hough even suggested that they send men to Fort Lewis for grain, "as these people are determined to squeeze us."

The lonely Hough confided to his "Dearly Beloved Wife" that on a sunny, cold Christmas day, the "glories of God" pale here with everyone "thinking of their homes far away. How many of us are now thinking of their loved ones at home? Or the happy children glorying in their new treasures? How many of us are wondering if it is a happy Christmas at home?"

Like soldiers everywhere, Hough wrote about his loneliness, asked about matters at home, wondered about the missing paymaster, and expressed his frustration with the campaign and his desire for a change. He talked about their leaving, speculated about going back to Pagosa or maybe even being transferred to Texas, but heavy snows had come to the mountains and winter had taken hold.

Then came the news Hough had been awaiting for months. "On the 1st day of January 1880 I received orders for my battalion to proceed to Texas via Fort Gibson. This was good news." Directed to march to Fort Garland, if practical, Hough decided to move south to Santa Fe to avoid the snow and "where orders would be found for further movements."

"On the morning of the 4th we started for the San Juan valley, and our part of the threatened Ute war was ended." He could not resist one more blast. "The whole proceedings had been disgusting, and was another instance of the want of a plan in our dealing with the Indians." Hough's attitudes toward civilians and the government policy were complicated. As western scholar Robert Athearn wrote, however, "[W]hile Major Hough was disgusted with the 'make-shift' policy of the government, as he called it, regarding the Indians, he had the professional soldier's dislike for the civilian population, which served as an irritant in the Indian solution."[13]

As the troops marched out of the Animas Valley, plans were already being made to establish a new Fort Lewis. Gen. William Tecumseh Sherman and Secretary of War Alexander Ramsey had "fully discussed the situation and affairs" in the Ute country. They proposed to give up Pagosa Springs and move the camp "well out to southwest Colorado" on the Animas or San Juan River.

Sherman, writing his friend Phil Sheridan, another recent southwestern Colorado visitor, explained what he thought would be best. "I prefer the point near where the Mancos enters the San Juan because if located too near Animas City it will soon be interfered with by emigrants." The $40,000 left over from appropriations would be used to build a post somewhere to the southwest of Animas City.[14]

That concluded Fort Lewis's first, and only, major military campaign, and it had been bloodless. The post had served only as a staging point for the

advance to Animas City and had assisted in the placement of troops between the Southern Utes and their northern cousins. Only a corporal's guard
had been left at Pagosa after Hough and the others marched westward to
their camp on the Animas.

The only question that remained was which site would be the best for
the new post. As spring became summer, that question would be decided. On
May 14, 1880, Col. George Buell and command started on a march that
would eventually take them nearly 350 miles in an attempt to find a good
location for the post.

THREE

A Remote New Post

Our hearts so stout have got us fame,
For soon 'tis known from whence we came;
Where 'er we go they dread the name
Of Garryowen in glory.

"Garry Owen"

Colonel Buell and his companies of the Fifteenth Infantry finished their long march on May 14, having found several good locations for the new post. Along the way they traveled the spring-bedecked valleys of the Dolores, Mancos, La Plata, Animas, and San Juan Rivers, the latter all the way to the Hog Back (a geological formation west of present-day Farmington, New Mexico). Buell favored two sites on the Mancos River (he spelled it "Mancas"). The sites had water, timber, farmers nearby, and what he judged to be "much warmer" locations. A third spot on the "La Platta" had almost equal advantages of fuel and building timber, but in the summer the river was almost dry, and the location had the disadvantage of "being a cold, bleak spot, with very deep snow in winter." A site on the Southern Ute reservation was ruled out as too cold and snowy and too far east.

The Indiana veteran Buell recommended "that the post to be built shall be not less than a ten company post—six of Infantry and four of Cavalry" or mounted troops. During the summer, outlying camps, or sub-camps, could be established without extra expense. He assured his superiors that doing so would "have a good moral effect on both the southern Utes and Navajos and the citizens could be protected."[1]

Having made the decision to establish a permanent post in southwestern Colorado, the army set about to occupy a site with the least practicable delay. Civil War veteran of the western theater Lt. Col. Robert Crofton, Thirteenth Infantry, had been cited for gallantry at the battles of Shiloh, Chickamauga, and Missionary Ridge. Now serving in the West, he was ordered to take four companies out of Santa Fe and travel to Pagosa Springs and then to the Mancos location with an eye toward "comfortably quartering your command at an early day and with consistent economy." He was instructed to avoid placing the post and the cantonment on a mesa as the cost would largely be increased thereby and the exposure to cold weather much greater.

After reaching Pagosa Springs, he left one company there to dismantle that post before continuing westward. By August 15, they had reached the Rio Florida and were well on their way to the Mancos River when their goal changed. By a verbal order from district headquarters, their destination was changed to a point on the La Plata River, obviously not what Buell had recommended.

Why this sudden change? Someone in Washington had decided that the La Plata "possesses manifold advantages" over the previously chosen Rio Mancos. It had, as the headquarters of the army informed the Secretary of War, closer proximity to timber, the most important consideration, and it contained "well watered splendid" hay and grazing country. Furthermore, a proposed move of the Ute reservation seemed to be in the works, although nothing ever came of the idea. The new location "is apparently a good one from which to operate" troops in order to control the Ute and Navajo Indians and protect miners and settlers "in that section of the country."[2]

Although his site recommendation had been ignored, they took Buell's advice on another matter. He had strongly urged that land be withdrawn immediately for a military reservation and that the army should "make the best terms possible with the parties who may have [been] found" within its boundaries. Already homesteaders had taken out two or three claims on this land, but a September 20 report confidently noted that none of the ground was under cultivation and "no person is living in the 2 or 3 dugouts built on these claims."[3] Although a seemingly insignificant matter amid all the hustle and bustle at the time, it would later come back to haunt Fort Lewis.

Located 0.68 mile south of the mail road between Animas City and Parrot City, the cantonment was established on the site originally proposed by Buell for the new post. Its buildings would be useful for garrison purposes when the permanent post was built one mile farther south on the La Plata River. This site would be abandoned as soon as the latter was ready for occupancy. Officially it became a substation of the post in December and was closed the following month.

On September 20, 1880, 1st Lt. Thomas Bailey of the Corps of Engineers was ordered to survey the La Plata site for the permanent post. The troops had arrived on August 15 at the new site and a sawmill and shingle mill were en route to the cantonment. The next month (September) the Department of the Missouri ordered six "good" carpenters, one of whom was also competent to act as a master mechanic who could repair machines, and two bricklayers sent to Crofton. To aid them, soldiers were detailed for extra duty as carpenters, cooks, and laborers to help unload lumber.[4]

Letters and reports detailing the progress went out regularly. Doors and sashes came from Fort Union and nails from Fort Leavenworth; funds from Washington went to local individuals for a variety of needs. Naturally, there were problems, both major and minor. An order for nails that should have gone to Leavenworth was sent instead to Santa Fe. Even if the order had been sent to the correct location, it would not have been filled because the nail sizes ordered were not clear. And government regulations caused other difficulties. Screwdrivers could cost sixteen cents, no more, and vouchers had to be presented for payment.

A special request for a planing machine, wood lathe, and two circular saws did not go out until September 4, and it was September 13 before the sawmill was operating. Then a severe storm struck, shutting down construction until October 16. Bad weather, combined with the late arrival of needed equipment, put construction way behind. Most supplies had to be brought in from New Mexico or Colorado cities on the other side of the divide, so weather would be an ongoing problem.

To assist with construction, soldiers were detailed for special duties, but some were more proficient than others. One soldier had to be replaced on wood-chopping duty by a more proficient axe man. An April 1881 report from the busy sawmill showed that it had manufactured 12,000 feet of lumber and 81,000 shingles since the last report and 1,000 feet of lumber had been dressed with the planing machine.

Building this new post would be expensive. Each barrack was estimated to cost $4,603 and an officer's quarters, $3,679. Initially plans called for four sets of the former and eight of the latter. By the time construction was finished nearly a year later, roughly $37,000 had been spent on building the post.[5] All had not gone that smoothly during construction. Crofton was having trouble with some of his officers. Second Lieutenant Charles Hall, an 1872 West Point graduate, accused his commanding officer of threatening that "he could have me arrested and court martialed for making a false statement." There the matter stopped. Crofton, who had earned his rank in the Civil War, may not have thought too highly of "green" West Pointers.

In December 1880 and January 1881, another junior officer, 2nd Lt. John Peshine, had filed complaints about Crofton with both the district and department commanders and had requested a department inspector be sent to "the post at as early a date as is consistent with the interests of the service." Peshine, who had started his military career as a naval midshipman during the war before transferring to the Fourteenth Colored and finally to the Thirteenth Infantry, stated "that there is much dissatisfaction both among commissioned officers and enlisted men of this command."

Crofton promptly relieved Peshine of command of his company, although by July he was back and the fight went public. In a long report to district headquarters, Peshine spelled out his complaints about how Crofton had managed the construction process. The first building constructed had been the storehouse and the second building was the commanding officer's quarters, which was occupied on November 16. On that date four companies of infantry, ten officers, four ladies and two children, and the laundresses and their children still resided in tents, tents "being unframed, generally without doors, and in several cases improperly heated."

As of December 27, three and a half months after the sawmill went into operation, no attempts had been made to house Companies E and B. While the commander was having wainscoting placed in a reception room of a house, the troops lived in "gopher hell huts," with the men compelled to sit up all night over their fires for warmth. Crofton also made "reproachful or provoking speeches or gestures to me in person [or to others]. . . . I was 'simply a dammed second lieutenant'" and "'no soldier.'"

He also accused Crofton of ordering extra furniture—bookcases, dressing tables, bedsteads—and having these items built for his personal use while officers and men continued to suffer in tents. The lieutenant further contended that chicken houses, hitching posts, and the like had been ordered constructed while the infantry remained in exposed tents. Back in July,

Crofton had been commanded to properly house his troops to "avoid any contingency of wintering prior to completion of the post." In Peshine's opinion the "post commander had not exercised" his military authority "with kindness & justice." Furthermore, in a "violent fit of temper," Crofton made "reproachful" speeches "or gestures to me in person."

Jealousy or insecurity might have motivated Crofton to accuse the Thirteenth Infantry of being a "volunteer mob." His rationale for doing so was that those officers of the regiment "who had served during the war in the volunteers" had to be "repeatedly" corrected. Interestingly, with the exception of Lieutenant Hall, all officers who supported Peshine had been in the volunteers.

Crofton also threatened to have Peshine arrested and court-martialed, but the lieutenant rebutted, "I beg that the District Commander will not consider my grievances as of a light or frivolous character." By summer, Crofton, based on the eyewitness account of 2nd Lt. James Goe, had accused Peshine of examining his private records without permission. Peshine blasted back that "no such examination took place" and that the charges were a "deliberate and premeditated defamation on the part of my accuser."

Peshine fired another round, accusing Crofton of injuring "my professional reputation" and jeopardizing "my social status in the profession." Hall, supported by Capts. Henry Pratt and Benjamin Rogers, jumped into the fray, supporting Peshine against the "spying" charges, and claimed that Peshine had been "given permission" to examine the records.

For an isolated, small garrison, this scandal must have been a savory topic of conversation. It clearly did not help the morale at the post. Matters calmed down briefly when spring came, then heated up again in midsummer. The stress associated with winter confinement, the site's isolation, and the inadequate housing probably played a role. Thus, calm temporarily returned with the start-up of spring patrols and the completion of housing for all the troops.

That calm ended in August when each man charged the other with conduct unbecoming "an officer and gentlemen." Upset with what he considered an unfair quarters assignment, Peshine fired another blast. Crofton had given a junior officer "ample quarters to the prejudice, discomfort and injury of a senior." Should the department commander decide to order a court for trial, Capt. Arthur MacArthur Jr., a friend of Peshine for years, was selected to be his counsel. Because of "his long personal intimacy" with Peshine and "his reputation as a lawyer at the bar and his special experience in the army as counsel under the articles of war," MacArthur would certainly have proven an excellent choice. Undoubtedly, he was the accused lieutenant's personal choice.[6]

The accusations did not cease until Crofton was eventually transferred in October 1881 to Fort Wingate, New Mexico, where the Thirteenth Regiment was stationed. Fortunately, the dispute never reached the point of a departmental hearing but the confrontation must have caused a great deal of tension. What seems to have been simply a personality conflict that exploded into something much larger never reached a conclusive result. Neither officer covered himself with much glory in this spat. But the well-known commanding officer appears to have survived Peshine's accusations unscathed.

Throughout the bickering, work went on. Dr. Bernard Byrne, a contract army surgeon at Fort Lewis, described his living conditions that first winter. "There was a rush to have the barracks and officers' quarters finished before the heavy snows set in. This kept a large force at work from sunup until dark." Of his quarters, he reminisced:

> The quarters assigned to me were two rooms of narrow boards, nailed up vertically, unplaned inside and out, with a tent dining room and kitchen attached. Of course, no one complained at having no plastering. We were glad enough to get undercover before the cold weather over took us. But the rough boards did not make an attractive interior, so during my leisure hours I began to decorate the walls and soon became quite absorbed in the work.

Planning for the arrival of his wife-to-be, he painted and secured a few pieces of furniture through the quartermaster.[7]

An independent inspection of the post's buildings in December both confirmed and undermined some of Peshine's charges. Two barracks were finished and two sets of officers' quarters were sufficiently complete for occupancy. Three other barracks, however, had not been completed and only three out of five sets of the laundresses' quarters were even under construction.

It appears that Peshine thus had some basis for his charges. The contrast between Crofton's construction plan and that of the original post at Pagosa Springs was startling. Recall how the commander there had ordered the troops' barracks to be built first, so that the largest number of troops could be housed as soon as possible. On the other hand, Crofton's initial construction phase was focused on ensuring the comfort of the officers and himself and did not display regard for the whole of his command.

Although it was undoubtedly a continued source of tension among the troops, civilians did not notice. Caroline Romney, editor of the *Durango Record,* visited the post in February and described it in the February 19, 1881, edition as "quite a little village with seventeen or eighteen different houses" arranged, for the most part, around the parade ground. With five companies, or a battalion, stationed there, the barracks "are to be enlarged shortly with the addition of a wing." For the rest of the post's life, some form of construction always seemed to be going on or was in the planning stages.

While the construction continued and the argument between Crofton and Peshine wound up and down, the Secretary of War officially designated the new post Fort Lewis on January 21, 1881, and renamed the still occupied earlier post Pagosa Springs. A small detachment of men remained at what was now designated a temporary post.

For the next two years, a few soldiers would reside at the Pagosa Springs post mostly to guard the government property still there, which was primarily buildings. All the public stores and "such buildings as should be transferred" had been removed. The army would officially abandon the post in November 1882. Material from buildings that could be dismantled would go to Fort Lewis, and although there would be some discussion about garrisoning a few soldiers at Pagosa Springs, nothing ever came of it. Locals would be loath to see this revenue windfall leave, but they would not be able to prevent it. Finally, in July 1884, no longer needed for any military purpose, the military reservation at Pagosa Springs would be turned over to the Secretary of Interior.[8]

To assist in forwarding supplies to Fort Lewis, the quartermaster's department sent John F. Leonard as its agent to Durango. He arrived in August 1881 and soon was busily engaged in receiving goods and sending them on by wagons. Leonard served for at least another two years and was described by the post quartermaster "as the most faithful and trustworthy man I have ever seen in the position."

Fort Lewis officially became part of the Department of the Missouri, which was divided into four military districts. The army designed each district to control a particular group of tribes. Fort Lewis was in the District of New Mexico, which was headquartered in Santa Fe. Under this district's jurisdiction fell the Utes, Navajos, Apaches, and a scattering of smaller tribes.

By April 1881, the troops at Fort Lewis were beginning to settle in. They planted post gardens and dug a system of irrigation ditches and a large reservoir with pipes leading to all buildings and eight fireplugs. A fence enclosed "some twenty acres," including the gardens and hospital. An inspection in May found the post generally in acceptable order. "General sanitary conditions are good," the guard "is well instructed" and their duty "well performed," barracks and kitchen "are inspected daily," and "no officer is known to be of intemperate habits or to have unfit associations." Framed shops for the blacksmith, carpenter, and wheelwright "are adequate," but insufficient and imperfect tools hindered their work.

Well enough, but the fort was not built yet. As late as August 15, 1881, with construction still not finished, another inspector concluded, "I suggest that temporarily military drills and exercises, in part at least, be suspended, and the men used in the best manner to complete the work in providing shelter as early as practicable."

The same thing happened at other western posts. For example, Fort Hays, Kansas, originally built for temporary duty, was in constant need of repairs. Construction and maintenance were continual at both posts and even at larger ones, such as Fort Leavenworth.

Despite its unfinished condition, Fort Lewis already was serving an important purpose. Gen. John Pope succinctly outlined the post's role.

> The post is one of the most important of the posts along that frontier, and should be thoroughly finished and kept garrisoned to its full capacity. It is placed practically between the Navajoes and Utes, where their limits are conterminous along the San Juan River, and where it can best overlook the country as against both tribes.
>
> It is also well situated for commanding to a considerable extent all that region of the country west and northwest of it . . . where some of the best mining in Colorado [is] found, and which is being rapidly filled with people. The communication, too, with Southern Utah and the lower valley of the Grand River is direct and easy, and for effective protection in any part of that country the garrison of Lewis will be easily available.

In his February 1882 report to Secretary of War Robert Lincoln, General of the Army William Tecumseh Sherman concurred: "Fort Lewis is a remote new post, deemed absolutely necessary for the protection of southern and western Colorado." Lincoln agreed.

Remote it certainly was. Other posts lay in all directions, but far distant. Fort Wingate, New Mexico, by the shortest route was 160 miles away "over difficult country almost destitute of water." Fort Union, New Mexico, by road and rail, lay 433 miles to the southeast. To reach the cantonment on the Uncompaghre, which was only 100 miles away as the crow flies, involved a trip of 593 miles via Pueblo and Montrose and a detour around the exceedingly difficult mountainous country north of Silverton. District headquarters in Santa Fe by trail and train remained a couple of days away. Fort Garland, the nearest post by road, would be abandoned in 1883.[9]

The post's isolation was exacerbated by human error. As commanding officer, Lt. Col. Peter Swaine observed to the Adjutant General of the Army, when a Washington clerk used the abbreviation CAL, letters were sent to California, not Colorado, and then were returned to Washington before finally being sent to their correct destination. Apparently, poor penmanship can be blamed for this error.[10]

Construction at Fort Lewis never quite seemed to be complete or at the level that the army wanted; thus, Fort Lewis's building program became an ongoing project that spanned into the next decade. Poor construction, new needs, fires, and bad site selection added to the ongoing work. One of the officers was shocked to have his quarters' chimney fall; subsequently all chimneys were checked. New cavalry quarters, a barrack, and stables were needed in 1884 as more troops arrived. The post quartermaster reported that in 1886–1887 a guardhouse, commissary store, magazine, coalhouse, and his office had been built for a total cost of $11,526.54. A sergeant's home that had been built of green, rough, undressed lumber was in bad condition and had to be replaced. The cavalry barracks needed to be rebuilt on higher ground because of drainage problems. An October 1885 fire burned the blacksmith, paint, carpenter, and wheelwright shops and the laundry buildings. Two other fires were reported that same week, causing suspicion of arson, but the culprits were never found.

In spite of the fires, the post contained a good water system, which had cost $6,000 and comprised a pump, boiler, pipes, hydrants, buildings, and other needed equipment. It also had a fire engine, although the district initially forgot to send along the wheels. The troops stationed at Fort Lewis could count on cool, clean water, a luxury not always available at western forts.

In his annual inspection report 2nd Lt. George Williams described the dilapidated condition of Fort Lewis. It was "absolutely necessary to place the post in a proper state of repair." Sidewalks and fences sagged in a state of decay, needing constant repair. "Every wind storm detaches shingles from some roofs[;] a recent one blew down the coal shed." If the buildings "are kept in a fair state of repair, damage would be lessened." Fort Lewis seemed to be continually, in his estimation, on the threshold of "rack and ruin."[11]

A November 1889 report that mentioned building new barracks provides insight into at least part of the problem: "The building could be merely a temporary structure." Such thinking often led to poor construction. Two years later the commander complained that the superintendent sent by the department had not properly constructed his projects: "It is worthy to note that all the buildings constructed under his supervision have fallen." Because the construction superintendent received one of the best salaries on the post, $150 a month, they expected more from him.[12] Cost-cutting by a penny-wise and pound-foolish Congress added to the problems as the army struggled to secure funds. The Army Appropriation Act passed Congress each year only after bitter debate.

This ongoing construction, however, provided a windfall to local contractors. At any given time, civilians and soldiers—who earned less on extra-duty pay than their civilian coworkers received—could be found repairing and building.

Officially established in February 1882, the military reservation around the post covered more than 50,000 acres. The land surrounding the post was for the use of the military and included timber, agricultural and grass land, water rights, and coal deposits. The purpose of a military reservation was to keep civilian activities away from the post, but at Fort Lewis, as with other military districts, this boundary was often disputed.

Fort Lewis in particular faced some problems stemming from homesteaders' claims that had been made prior to establishing the Fort Lewis military district. Although not in residence when the military claimed the land, the homesteader eventually proved up on his land and gained ownership. And others with claims were planning to do the same thing. Additionally, Colorado's superintendent of schools worried about the school land that was now within the district but had been set aside by the government prior to the military's claim. Fortunately, General Order #5, which created the reservation, addressed that conflict by exempting all school sections.

Despite its isolation and many troubles, Fort Lewis fascinated Colorado newspaper readers with a variety of news stories about the army. "At 8,500 feet [actually 7,800 ft.], Fort Lewis is said to be the highest military post in the world." It "is already one of the most important posts of the frontier." "Over 500 soldiers are stationed at Fort Lewis," and "more are coming," and the band from Santa Fe "will enliven the place." The visit of the paymaster caused "many a soldier to take French leave" and the remaining cavalry "went out in all directions" looking for "the fleeing guards of the nation." An instructive feature of the fort "is the school master," who happened to be a regular enlisted man receiving extra pay. "It is amusing to see how the soldiers rush into the school room at the opening of the term and seem so very eager to learn. But at the close of a week or two they begin to drop out, leaving only a few persistent men at the end of a session."

Reporters visiting the post gave their readers a peek into military life, usually a positive one. In September 27, 1884, the Durango *Idea* offered a detailed view of the post's layout with its buildings enclosing a large square used as a parade and drill ground. Among the buildings listed were seven company barracks, seven officers' quarters, one hospital, a headquarters building, sutler store, pool hall, and bakery, with the "buildings occupied by the officers being opposite the quarters of the privates and non-commissioned officers."

In the "commodious officer quarters," nothing was spared to add comfort and attraction, similar to those of affluent citizens' homes. Entertainment was provided to break the "monotony of the dull routine" of the soldier's life. The post's excellent band gave a concert every Wednesday night and plays every evening from five to six on the parade ground. The reporter encouraged visitors to come to the full-dress Sunday inspection and parade day as the excellently drilled troops "go through various maneuvers with remarkable grace and precision."

The article concluded with an admonition that reflected one of the problems the peacetime army faced. "There is quite a sentiment existing in this country against the soldier element, which is both unwise and unjust." Should a war ever threaten the country, "the little regular army is the nucleus around which defenders of America must rally."[13]

A love-hate relationship existed between the military and the federal government on one hand and westerners on the other. Westerners wanted the military's and federal government's support, yet not their accompanying rules, regulations, and supervision. Westerners liked having troops around for protection, sources of income, and assistance in developing the West, but they did not want to be deprived of their assumed rights and privileges. They did not want troops to be used to protect Indian reservations, enforce laws, protect natural resources, uphold various treaties and agreements, or settle land disputes.

Easterners, meanwhile, questioned whether the country needed so many troops and so much money to protect westerners who, in their opinion, often stirred up trouble and then cried for protection. Economy in government was considered the key to good government, and the government's western policy did not seem economical or practical. Eastern taxpayers wanted a lean, unobtrusive government. The army found itself caught between these two sides. An aroused public looked over their shoulder with a jaundiced eye.

In Fort Lewis, these conflicts were temporarily set aside as civilians and enlisted men alike celebrated the arrival of several war heroes at the post. Former general John Logan, who had become a U.S. senator and chairman of the Committee on Military Affairs, toured the post in July 1883. An even more famous visitor arrived, Lt. Gen. William Tecumseh Sherman, in September while on his final inspection tour before retirement. Sergeant Courtright remembered his visit: Sherman "made a thorough inspection of all services and branches and was especially pleased with our pack mule train drill we had put on at the corral down near the river." Dressed in a long, black Prince Albert coat, "ordinary civilian togs," Sherman seemed indifferent but handed "out quizzical quips here and there, the old war horse never missed a thing."

The old hero managed a short stay in Durango and had hoped to travel across the mountains from Silverton on his way to Salt Lake City. That idea he forthrightly canceled after crawling up the precipice of Red Mountain Divide, and he concluded "not to try that hazardous experiment." Returning to Durango by train, he left for Pueblo soon after.[14]

As time passed, Fort Lewis was becoming an accepted, even prized, part of southwestern Colorado and the neighboring territories. An excellent description of the post appeared in the August 28, 1888, inspection report of Capt. Adam Kramer. His report provides an engrossing look at 1880s garrison life and of the army's concerns about "spit and polish." Six companies of the Sixth Infantry and two troops of the Sixth Cavalry made up the garrison. Following a review and inspection, Kramer wrote a long report about conditions. For any mistakes or violations he found, he carefully listed the regulation in question.

> In the passage in review a few officers failed to salute at six yards. Music did not play while reviewing officer was going around the battalion. Several of the companies failed to execute the halt and carry with precision. In other respects the review was creditably executed. The arms were minutely inspected and found generally in clean and serviceable condition, some neglect in the screw heads. Brasses and buttons good. The clothing conformed to regulations, except that need of tailors to make better fit is apparent with all the men except D. Co. [infantry].

The cavalry horses "were restive and evidenced need of drill, it is claimed that, opportunity has been lacking for this. It will not be hereafter however—daily drills are now ordered for Infantry and Cavalry."

Kramer stated that "discipline of the whole command is very good." Generally, the post seemed in good condition, with a few problems noted.

> The barracks were found with respect to cleanliness, ventilation and sanitary conditions in very good order; flooring is not good and paint required.

Messes and food supply very satisfactory. Meat and bread are excellent. Slops in some instances were thrown on the ground near the kitchens,
proper remedy was ordered. The sinks are a bad feature, badly constructed, needing disinfectants.

The guard house and prison rooms well adapted for their uses and
clean. The hospital in excellent order and commendable neatness.

Only a few minor cases of sickness were reported in the hospital, which
pleased the captain. But religious services were another issue: "There is no
chaplain at the post and religious services are only held when some visiting
minister happens at the post."

Among the items discussed were the bathing facilities: "For Officers
none. In barracks, small and uncomfortable tubs & each bather needs to
carry to & away all water used." The post had no drainage system except
"that offensive matter is carried away—ordinary washing water has been
thrown on ground near barracks." The post's water supply rated "good and
abundant" and the gardens "excellent and under good cultivation." The fire
department suffered from a defective hose, but requisitions had been forwarded to resolve that problem.

Kramer was concerned about the post school because "with only one
teacher allowed [it] cannot accomplish good results." He also felt the "general police of the post affords room for improvement and this is now constantly kept in view and prosecuted." Because the army had a protocol for
filing reports, which included using proper forms for all reports, Kramer included an explanation of why he had not used the proper form in this case:
"[the proper blanks for reports] were not at the post, . . . so the form of
'general report' is respectfully submitted."[15]

One of the great problems the postwar army faced was securing and keeping
men. Retirements, disability, and desertion caused a steady drain on forces
throughout the West and Fort Lewis was no exception. Companies were
often undermanned, making their forts vulnerable and compromising their
ability to take the field. Colonel Swaine, when reporting the post strength at
344 in February 1888, stated that he needed 100 recruits to bring the companies up to strength.

Sometimes, however, new recruits caused more trouble than they were
worth. As they arrived at a post, they had to be assigned to quarters, taught
drills, and fit into the company or troop structure. In June 1881, ten recruits
of the Ninth arrived at Fort Lewis, but their horses had been lost along the
way. Before their mounts arrived, much time was spent sending telegraphs

over the Denver & Rio Grande in the effort to find them. Because the track had not yet reached Durango, this communication was difficult and time-consuming. Fortunately, their horses finally arrived.

In January 1882, the post was threatened by smallpox after a group of forty recruits, including one infected with smallpox, left the recruiting depot at Columbus, Ohio, bound for Fort Lewis. It wasn't until a week later that the post surgeon received a communiqué notifying him that it was possible that some of the men had been exposed to smallpox on the way to Fort Lewis. Fortunately, no outbreak occurred. And with physical examinations somewhat haphazard, a share of the recruits were found to be physically or mentally incapable of serving in the armed forces. A few recruits who arrived at Fort Lewis were in need of immediate medical attention, inciting the exasperated Capt. Mott Hooten, Twenty-Second Infantry, to finally exclaim, "[A] reduction instead of an increase in the force would have been in the interests of the service."

Yet, recruits were necessary to maintain company and garrison strength and adequately keep the post functioning. In the years that followed, recruits regularly appeared and, at least in May 1885, with "each man having a full complement of ordnances."

Before the recruits even arrived at the fort, the army had invested time and expense to get them there. The post commander was required to have transportation available for the soldiers when they arrived at Durango, which sometimes was a problem when trains arrived late or in the evening, necessitating an overnight stay in town. Because travel was expensive, some men used recruitment as a means of obtaining a free ticket to the West and, once there, soon deserted for the mining regions or other prospects.

Starting in 1882, Fort Lewis had a designated recruiting officer. This officer was responsible for recruiting for posts throughout the region and the Missouri and Pacific Divisions. He had a difficult time, because army life and pay did not appeal to many late nineteenth-century Americans. And life at western posts generally was difficult.[16] The recruits sent to Fort Lewis, however, were fortunate. The site of the post at which they arrived and were stationed was a healthy one, unlike others scattered throughout the West. The elevation provided an invigorating climate of summers with warm days and cool nights, brisk autumns, cold and stormy winters, and short but energizing springs. The most extreme weather the garrison faced was the winter storms coming directly out of the north from the high La Plata Mountains. The dry climate, however, kept the discomfort to a minimum. And the surrounding scenery provided a beautiful, if challenging, setting with its deserts, high mountains, plateaus, forests, river valleys, and plains.

A host of available natural resources also eased their stay beside the La Plata River. Plenty of fresh water rippled right past the post for man and beast and the growing season allowed for company gardens and fresh vegetables. Nearby timber and coal made winter more pleasant and fishing and hunting provided recreation and food. Good grazing land existed for the post's mules and horses.

The men certainly thrived at the post, but this apparent garden of Eden did not always fare as well. As nineteenth-century hymn writer Reginald Heber intoned, "though every prospect pleases, and only man is vile."

It was not that these troopers, and other Americans of this generation, failed to appreciate their environment; they were just not as keenly aware of their impact on it. Farmers, miners, town dwellers, and soldiers opened, settled, and developed the West. The land they sought and the people who lived and worked there merged to become part of America's Manifest Destiny, the building of a greater nation no matter what or who stood in the way. That they might spoil their own nest did occur to them, even if they did not always pay heed.

Commenting on the environmental impact of the post, Dr. Bernard Byrne later described the construction process:

> [T]rees [were] cut for lumber for the dwellings, clearing the ground for sidewalks, and leveling the earth for roads, soldiers were digging irrigating ditches, a task which they deeply resented, and men were getting out firewood. Millions of feet of lumber were used and hundreds of handsome trees were destroyed in the building of Fort Lewis.[17]

Although he expressed more environmental concern than might be expected for the time, he still thought of the entire project as progress. Anytime men and animals are crowded together, it is bound to affect their environment and present potential health problems. Timber was cut, game killed, water diverted, and land farmed and physically changed, resulting in pollution and litter. It all followed in the wake of nineteenth-century Americans. All this happened while generating but little concern. Of more immediate concern was the health of the post and its garrison.

The various inspections were conducted daily, weekly, and, in the case of general post inspections, whenever an army inspector traveled to the post. On May 31, 1881, assistant surgeon Justus Morris Brown commented that after conducting his daily inspection of company messes, sinks (latrines), and the post overall, he had "the honor to report" Fort Lewis "in a good sanitary condition."

It would not always be that way. Over the years reports pointed to the hospital sinks being unclean and the condition of the water closets unsatisfactory. Privies had not been well disinfected, unsuitable conditions existed at the guardhouse, and slops were found at the rear of company quarters.

As might be expected, conditions would worsen during the winter months, but after winter eased, a spring cleanup usually improved the unhealthy garrison situation. In response to a negative inspection report, Colonel Swaine wrote the Department of Missouri that one such cleanup was under way in March 1888. Snowstorm after snowstorm had marched through in depressing regularity all winter and each storm only exacerbated the situation. Swaine promised that daily inspections would be resumed and all quarters would be checked as soon as possible. Once the ground was "sufficiently dry," it would be "policed as customary every spring." New pits would be dug for the privies and "upright seats" installed. "Disinfecting will be well attended to" and a urinal ordered for the guardhouse. He did not concur with the recommendation about using earth closets in the summer but agreed to "endeavor to cover the pits." (Troughs were provided for troop use in the summer!)

Fatigue duty involving digging pits, disinfecting and filling old ones with dirt, and cleaning sinks was not popular. Yet, working in the overcrowded guardhouse probably was less popular. The most common complaint at Fort Lewis concerned the conditions at the guardhouse, which usually was overflowing with prisoners. Repeated attention was called to its overcrowded and unsanitary state throughout the post's history. Attempts to get money to build a new one went nowhere with the cash-strapped army. The Secretary of War did authorize that "all worn but serviceable bed and pillow sacks may be issued to prisoners confined in guard houses."

Personal cleanliness also concerned officers and doctors. One officer recommended a post bathhouse instead of bathtubs in each barrack for sanitary reasons and the relative ease of disposing of used bathwater in a bathhouse. But throughout the post's history, individual barracks continued to have their own tubs, which was the typical practice at all posts. The result of the apparent efforts to keep Fort Lewis as clean and sanitary as possible appears to have been positive. Fort Lewis never suffered an outbreak of illness or an epidemic, nor did an unusually large number of men appear on sick call at any one time.[18]

Compared with many other posts and the army overall, Fort Lewis was indeed a healthy post. Crowding men together in barracks, often with wretched sanitation conditions, poor food, and poor medical services, left troops vulnerable. Finding good doctors willing to serve at isolated western posts was also hard. Nonetheless, the illness rate did drop for the army as a whole in the 1880s, and the next decade saw another drop, but by then the post had closed.[19]

One reason for Fort Lewis's good record was the relatively high quality of medical care at the post. Fort Lewis had a fine group of post surgeons and a more than adequate hospital. That had not always been the case. In Fort Lewis's early days, conditions had not been so suitable. Bernard Byrne, one of the two original doctors at the post, lost a patient because their hospital at that time was a field tent. A badly wounded civilian was brought to him on a bitterly cold night. "I put a constricting bandage around him, to lessen the pain, had him moved to our hospital tent, and sent for Dr. Fields. When we were ready to operate, the wind was so high that our only lamp would be blown out as fast it could be relit." Left in total darkness there was nothing the doctors could do but wait for daylight. The man died during the night.

Less then a year after the post's establishment, a frame building (with a capacity of twelve beds) replaced the tent. The new building proved "entirely inadequate to the wants of the sick," the post surgeon reported in 1884. Finally, two years later, it was replaced with a brick structure, which completely met current army regulations. It cost $10,044 to build and was one of the best in the Four Corners region. In 1889 Capt. Edwin Gardner, post surgeon, requested that the old frame hospital be removed to the rear of the new hospital, where it could be utilized for many purposes, from drill room to dead house.

Byrne later made an interesting observation about military doctors and civilians' expectations of them:

> In case of serious illness, in those early days when settlers lived miles apart, a man would rather travel a longer distance to secure an army surgeon than call in a physician living nearer, the inference being that one could not be in the army unless he was a good doctor. It was not always agreeable for the surgeon, however, as the family would expect him to restore the ill member to health even if he or she were in extremis.[20]

It is true that civilians used the post's medical staff and facilities, as did troops from other posts who happened to be in the area. Nearby Durango, however, also offered excellent physicians and a fine Sisters of Mercy hospital.

Hospital stewards (a specific appointment by the medical department), stretcher-bearers, and ambulance drivers came from the rank and file of the post and their work was considered extra-duty detail. Women were appointed hospital matrons. Along with the doctors, they were the post's medical staff.

Treatments and prescriptions at Fort Lewis have to be put in the context of nineteenth-century practice. The practice of "modern medicine" was still decades in the future. Strides had been made during and after the Civil War in hospital sanitation, medical practices, and nursing, but many Americans avoided hospitals or saw them as the last resort. The hospital was still considered by many a place to die. So popular patent medicines and home remedies satisfied many civilians and soldiers.

Pain had always been a problem for doctors, but now some relief was available. Military doctors during the Civil War had begun prescribing various forms of opium, the "queen of medicines," as painkillers, but by the 1880s medical professionals were beginning to ask questions about its being addictive. Chloroform became the anesthetic of choice because it was not flammable; only a generation before, doctors had done operations without anesthetic, a devastating experience. In physicians' bags, chests, or cabinets could also be found the "wonder drug" quinine, which along with opium, ether, and chloroform became the standard postwar medical anesthetic.

A crucial factor in improving medical services, cleanliness of hospital and medical staff was finally recognized as vital to a patient's recovery. Because of the new interest in public hygiene and health, in 1886 the army ordered a series of medical lectures to be given at each post. The Fort Lewis surgeon dutifully delivered them in April 1887.

Fort Lewis provided a cemetery just northeast of the post for those who died on duty, their families, and government employees. Each grave had to be "plainly marked" and be "suitably secure," and a fence had to be built around the cemetery to satisfy army regulations.[21]

While infantry and cavalry garrisoned Fort Lewis, men trained for the artillery and signal corps. The ordnance at the post consisted of two twelve-pound field guns, one mountain breech-loading hotchkiss gun, and two Gatling guns. Army headquarters in Washington, however, limited practice to twenty rounds annually. That limit hardly seemed sufficient, but it helped to cut costs and prevent wasting ammunition. Four men from each company were trained to handle the Gatling guns and a similar number were trained for the field pieces. This arsenal gave the post more "fire power" than any group it might encounter.

Some of the troops at Fort Lewis were part of the signal corps. The post was actively involved with the communication wonder of the 1880s, the heliograph, which joined with flags, torches, telegraphs, and disks as one of the army's main reliances to send messages over longer distances. The post's most active signal officer was 1st Lt. Theodore Mosher, who had entered the signal corps in the 1870s as a private. When first stationed at the post in 1885, Mosher discovered that the "signal property is in unserviceable condition." He tested one heliograph model for the army in 1887 and found it adaptable, but could not secure any because of fiscal restraints. Two working heliographs were finally shipped. With its reliance on mirrors for signaling, the heliograph worked particularly well in the sunny, dry Southwest with its abundant high points from which to flash signals. Under ordinary conditions the field heliograph could transmit messages (called heliograms) thirty to forty miles at a maximum rate of ten words per minute. If conditions were ideal, the message could be transmitted up to ninety miles.

Mosher trained the men to use heliographs and other military signaling. After debating the relative merits of Morse code versus continental or English code, the army decided to continue using Morse code for both the telegraph and heliograph because changing it to English code would have been difficult and confusing. It would also have made it a challenge to talk with civilian telegraph operators, who used Morse code.

To operate the heliograph, four people were needed—one to operate the device, another to receive messages, another to record messages, and yet another to keep the mirror adjusted as the sun moved. From the ridge behind the post, signals could be sent to Point Lookout (about twenty-three miles away) and then on to the Blue Mountains in Utah (another fifty miles distant). As Mosher brought the post up to standard, heliograph signals could be seen flashing back and forth, much to the amazement of locals. At least one old-timer specifically mentioned seeing flashes from Point Lookout as he rode past with his freight team.

Connecting Fort Lewis to Durango and the outside world, telegraph service was established in 1881. With seventeen miles of wire, poles, and other equipment in place, the post's military telegraph operator clicked into operation. Morse code was used "to insure secrecy of transmission."

When the telegraph failed, which happened occasionally, the district would advise the commanding officer to use couriers to carry dispatches. Some of the failures might have been the result of not always having a qualified operator at the post. At least once, a request was made for an operator among the recruits being sent.

The post by 1884 also had a telephone line, which was to be utilized only for military purposes. It ran to the railroad station and included two telephones, receivers, and batteries. In case of an emergency, the chief signal officer in Washington pointed out that this system could use the telegraph line.[22]

Fort Lewis also acquired a typewriter in April 1889. Although penmanship among officers and clerks had not been terrible over the years, the typed documents made writing and reading the innumerable required reports much easier and faster.

The typewriter must have been particularly helpful to the post adjutant, whose job it was to file and answer reports on a host of issues. Nothing was new about that; he had done the same at Pagosa and his contemporaries did likewise at every western post. Because the adjutant was responsible for all official correspondence, the variety of subjects that passed through his office was truly amazing. At Fort Lewis, the clock in the adjutant's office was deemed "entirely unreliable" and, because the "necessity for a standard time at the post is evident[, that] standard must be in the hands of the post adjutant." At another time, the guardhouse clock became "unserviceable." Another memo stated that the iron safes at the post "are not considered secure enough" to keep large amounts of money; therefore, "a good safe needs to be sent." Another statement to the district's chief quartermaster listed the number and condition of all iron bunks, barrack chairs, buffalo coats, and fur hats.

Myriad other issues passed through the adjutant's office. Who was accountable for the camp kettles and the printing press? Why did a woolen stocking shortage occur at Fort Lewis? (In response the district sent 225 pairs.) Bathtubs and urinals "are chargeable to what account"; but there was no question about pipes and sewers: "they are properly chargeable to army transport." It took three letters to get fences built around some officers' quarters, yet, two years later, only one report was necessary "to prevent wagons driving too close" to those fences.

To expedite the change from wood- to coal-burning stoves, a report was forwarded to the Department of Missouri, requesting the proper grates and explaining the reasons why the present stoves could not be changed. As I result of having so much correspondence, the adjutant sent a report noting that extra issues of the following stationery "are absolutely necessary—five quires of letter paper, seven quires of legal paper, 150 official envelopes, two gross of rubber bands and one lead pencil." The need for black wool hats for the company required several months and a number of inquiries between post and department to settle the matter. Other reports discussed items such as coal scuttles, bookcases, Pear's shaving soap, and "the want of lamp chimneys," which, according to Kramer, "leave[s] the companies almost in darkness." Even the quality and variety of cigars (not more than six) available for sale at the post had to be determined.

This amazing potpourri of issues, some directly affecting the safety of the men, occupied the staff and the post council. Unsafe matches captured Swaine's attention after a package caught fire on his shelf. Incoming recruits had to be searched for knives. Officers protested against shoes with screws that punctured the insole, and endorsed the adoption of Smith & Wesson revolvers as the Colts "are deemed deficient." A discussion about washing or drying clothes in company quarters led to these being prohibited. It took eight endorsements before they could destroy a company guidon, after which authorization arrived (but too late!) to cut the staff for broom handles.

Depending on the nature of the request, these reports and requisition orders went to Washington, the department, the district, the post commander, or the post council, and a careful record was made of each report. The post council was made up of officers and handled smaller post matters, such as repairing the adjutant's clock and building bookcases. As at all posts, the necessities of supporting and maintaining the troops required a lot of paperwork.[23]

Fort Lewis never emerged as a major western post, despite being described with local pride as "one of the most important posts of the frontier." Indeed, by the troops arrived, the region had grown from frontier to a land dotted with established communities of farmers, ranchers, lumbermen, miners, and town builders and linked to the rest of the country by the railroad in nearby Animas Valley. It wasn't long before growing numbers of tourists arrived. The routine of military life went on during the decade-plus of the post's existence along the La Plata River while more settlers swarmed into the area, hemming in the Utes. Contrary to the stereotype of life at a western post, life at Fort Lewis in these years was not marked by romantic or exciting events or personalities.

By the time Fort Lewis was established, Sheridan's strategy had become one of watchful waiting. The foe was weakened and definitely on the defensive. Posts now ringed the reservations, guarding against outbreaks by disgruntled tribal members. The Utes and Navajos were surrounded by forts in Arizona and New Mexico as well as Fort Lewis, which monitored their activities.[24]

The army had come to the West to keep the peace. Troops from Fort Lewis did take to the field in campaigns, scouts, and patrols, upholding the tradition of the western army, as will be seen in a later chapter. But first we will take a look at the men who garrisoned Fort Lewis during its existence along the La Plata River.

His Hour upon
the Stage

"Life's but a walking shadow, a poor player that struts and frets his hour upon the stage, and then is heard no more," observes Macbeth in Shakespeare's play. For Fort Lewis that brief moment lasted only from 1878 to 1891.

The two Fort Lewis posts were quite similar and had unexceptional but strikingly beautiful locations. Built according to typical military plans of the post–Civil War era, they probably reminded their residents of other garrisons at which they had served. The second Fort Lewis, located along the La Plata River, was already showing its age by the time the army turned the site over to the Interior Department for an Indian boarding school.

This second Fort Lewis has a better photographic record, captured on glass plates and preserved for future generations. These images of the fort and its men will not remind the viewer of Hollywood's romantic image of western forts and garrisons. They display a nineteenth-century post with little excitement, less glamour, and no glory.

Now the bugles are silent, the guards no longer march their duty in snow and sun, and reveille and taps last sounded here more than a century ago. Nothing remains of the original post at Pagosa Springs, and only little remains of Fort Lewis on the La Plata River. What endures are the photographs, drawings, and plans. For a moment then, drop back generations ago and savor a time that helped lay the foundation for today and tomorrow.

The site of the first Fort Lewis in 1878–1879 on the north bank of the San Juan River. Courtesy, Duane A. Smith

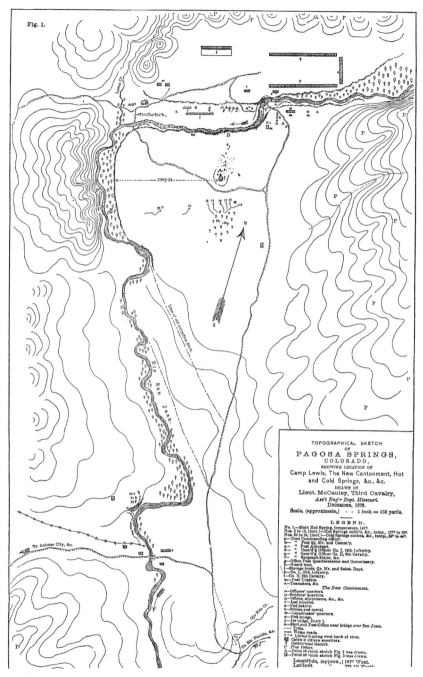

Fig. 1.

TOPOGRAPHICAL SKETCH
OF
PAGOSA SPRINGS,
COLORADO,
SHOWING LOCATION OF
Camp Lewis, The New Cantonment, Hot
and Cold Springs, &c., &c.
DRAWN BY
Lieut. McCauley, Third Cavalry,
Ass't Eng'r Dept. Missouri.
DECEMBER, 1878.
Scale, (approximate,) · · 1 inch = 150 yards.

LEGEND.
No. 1.—Main Hot Spring, temperature, 141°.
Nos. 2 to 19, (incl.)—Hot Springs outlets, &c., temp., 137° to 99°.
Nos. 20 to 24, (incl.)—Cold Springs outlets, &c., temp., 52° to 64°.
a—Post Commanding officer.
b—   "   Post Qr. Mr. and Comm'y.
c—   "   Post Adjutant.
d—   "   Com'd'g Officer Co. I, 16th Infantry.
e—   "   Com'd'g Officer Co. D, 9th Cavalry.
f—   "   Sergeant-Major, &c.
g—Office Post Quartermaster and Commissary.
h—Guard tents.
i—Storage tents, Qr. Mr. and Subst. Dept.
k—Co. I, 16th Infantry.
l—Co. D, 9th Cavalry.
m—Post Traders.
n—Teamsters, &c.
        The New Cantonment.
o—Officers' quarters.
p—Soldiers' quarters.
q—Offices, storerooms, &c., &c.
r—Post hospital.
s—Post bakery.
t—Stables and corral.
w—Laundresses' quarters.
x—Foot bridge.
y—Ice bridge, Dec'r 1.
z—Store and Post-Office near bridge over San Juan.
——Trails.
———Wagon roads.
• • • Limited fencing west bank of river.
▨ Cabin of citizen squatters.
◻ Cottonwood timber.
⟨ Pine timber.
A—Point at which sketch Fig. 2 was drawn.
B—Point at which sketch Fig. 3 was drawn.
Longitude, (approx.,) 107° West.
Latitude   "   37° 15' North.

Lt. Charles MacCauley sketched Camp Lewis in December 1878. Courtesy, Duane A. Smith

61

An artist's rendition of the isolated post at Pagosa Springs. Courtesy, Center of Southwest Studies

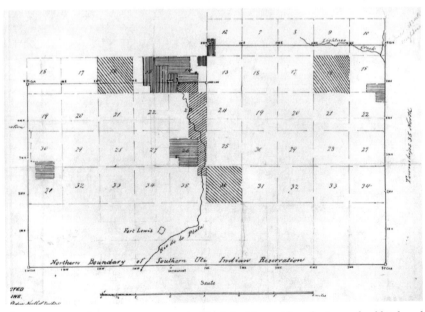

The Fort Lewis military reservation on the Rio de La Plata with coal mines, school land, and homestead entries indicated. Courtesy, Center of Southwest Studies

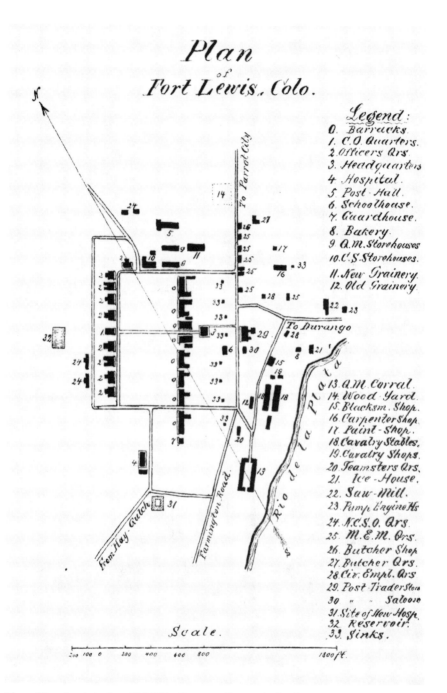

Plan
of
Fort Lewis, Colo.

Legend:
0. Barracks.
1. C.O. Quarters.
2. Officers Qrs.
3. Headquarters
4. Hospital.
5. Post-Hall.
6. Schoolhouse.
7. Guardhouse.
8. Bakery.
9 Q.M. Storehouses
10. C.S. Storehouses.
11. New Grainery.
12. Old Grainery.

13. Q.M. Corral.
14. Wood-Yard.
15. Blacksm. Shop.
16. Carpenter Shop.
17. Paint-Shop.
18. Cavalry Stables.
19. Cavalry Shops.
20. Teamsters Qrs.
21. Ice-House.
22. Saw-Mill.
23. Pump Engine Hs
24. N.C.S.O. Qrs.
25. M.E.M. Qrs.
26. Butcher Shop
27. Butcher Qrs.
28. Civ. Empl. Qrs.
29. Post Trader Store
30. " " Saloon
31. Site of New Hosp.
32. Reservoir.
33. Sinks.

To Parrot City
To Durango
Rio de la Plata
From Hay-Gulch
Farmington Road

Scale.

200 100 0   200   400   600   800   1800 ft.

Plan of Fort Lewis in the mid-1880s. Courtesy, Duane A. Smith

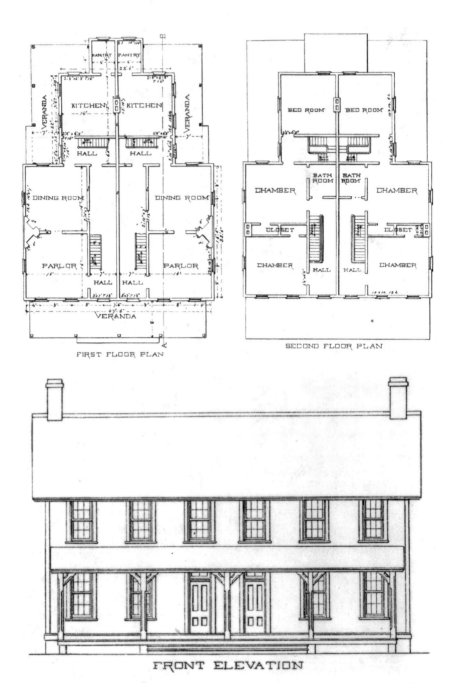

FIRST FLOOR PLAN

SECOND FLOOR PLAN

FRONT ELEVATION

Drawing and plans for officers' quarters. These are standard quartermaster-designed buildings for the era. Courtesy, National Archives

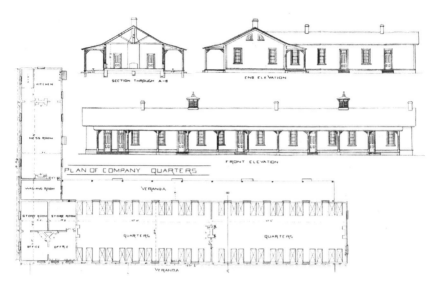

Company quarters provided room and board. Courtesy, National Archives

Fort Lewis, defender of the Four Corners region. The building with the cupola was the post headquarters. Courtesy, Center of Southwest Studies

Fort Lewis looking west in the mid- to late 1880s. Barracks are in the middle and the stables are in the foreground. Courtesy, Montana Historical Society

Fort Lewis looking east. Officers' quarters are in the foreground with the commanding officer's in the middle. Courtesy, Montana Historical Society

Post trader's store, the scene of both relaxation and troubles. Courtesy, Center of Southwest Studies

Unidentified Fort Lewis buildings; perhaps one was the schoolhouse. Courtesy, Center of Southwest Studies

One of the few photographs taken inside the garrison. Courtesy, Duane A. Smith

Utes and occasionally Navajos visited Fort Lewis, which is showing its age in this photo-graph. Courtesy, Duane A. Smith

Durango was the nearest community to Fort Lewis. Courtesy, Duane A. Smith

FOUR

THE TROOPERS

The soldiers were a superb lot of men physically. The out-door
life had developed them into perfect specimens of vigorous
manhood.

ELIZABETH CUSTER, *BOOTS AND SADDLES*

Who were the men of Fort Lewis? The best available information about the
garrison at its peak comes from the original returns of the 1885 Colorado
census. Typical of the army at the time, the officers all were native-born,
with only two exceptions: one came from Canada and another from Ireland.
The sixteen native-born officers came from New England and the Midwest,
with New York and Ohio contributing seven men. Only two officers had graduated from West Point (which is low because at other posts nearly half the
officers were West Point graduates), but the post's commanding officers generally were West Pointers. Those who did not graduate from West Point were
former Civil War volunteer officers (seven) or men promoted from the ranks.

Of the eighteen officers reported, six were single, one did not list his
status, three were married with their families not present at the post, and the

71

remainder had their families with them. Nine children roamed around officers' row. Three officers listed female cooks as part of their household, but
only one of this group had any children still at home. Sixty-six percent of
the officers were forty or older and only two were younger than thirty.

As expected, the enlisted men presented an entirely different picture.
Most of them ranged in age from their early twenties to early thirties, which
meant that few Civil War veterans served among them. The number of men
under twenty and older than forty was very small. It has been said that the
western army in the post–Civil War era was a popular way for immigrants to
receive a crash course in Americanization. That seemed true at Fort Lewis.
Nearly half of the 1885 garrison was foreign-born. The Irish predominated
among the foreign troopers, followed by Germans. The other immigrants,
almost without exception, were from other northern European countries,
reflecting the population of the United States at that time. Descriptions of
the postwar cavalry have called it "one of the busiest sections of the great
American melting pot." It definitely seems to have been that way with the
troops stationed at Fort Lewis.

New York and Pennsylvania, followed by Massachusetts and Illinois, contributed the largest number of American-born recruits. A smattering came
from southern states, but none had served in the Confederate army because
they were too young. Four troopers listed wives as post laundresses and only
one had a child with him.

The popular Fort Lewis band presented a slightly different portrait. Its
eighteen members included four Germans, three Englishmen, and one Swede,
but no Irishmen. They were also older, with more than half in their thirties
or forties, and only one was married.[1]

The preservice occupations of the garrison presented a cross section of
nineteenth-century America and represented a variety of skills that could be
used at the post. Most of the troopers had been common laborers before
joining the army, and farmers made up the next largest contingent. Of particular interest for maintaining the fort were painters, carpenters, and engineers. Blacksmiths, butchers, saddlers, hostlers, shoemakers, molders, bakers,
tailors, and upholsterers may have come in handy as well. The bookkeeper
and clerks would have been useful. The photographer and watchmaker probably would have been less useful, but the latter might have been able to help
the post with its ongoing clock problems. Only three men at Fort Lewis in
1885 listed soldiering as their only occupation.[2]

One notable change between the 1885 census and the 1880 federal census of the Pagosa Springs post is the large increase in Irish recruits. The

earlier officers had also been younger, but the number reported had been too small to form an accurate basis for comparison. Otherwise, the returns proved quite similar. Because most of the original census returns of 1890 were destroyed, it is not possible to compare personnel in 1885 with those present at the end of the post's life.

A comparison between the 1885 census results for Fort Lewis and the Seventh Cavalry enlisted men and officers who died with Custer at the Little Big Horn on June 25, 1876, displays a similar portrait of the post–Civil War army. Forty-two percent of the men were of foreign birth. The Irish led the contingent, followed by Germans and Englishmen, then a smattering from the rest of northern Europe and Canada. For the American-born, four states provided the most recruits—New York, Pennsylvania, Ohio, and Massachusetts. Only four men came from the ex-Confederate states. "Thus the Seventh Cavalry still retained a distinctly Yankee flavor more than a decade after Appomattox," as did Fort Lewis.

Like the troopers at Fort Lewis, the men who died at Little Big Horn were young. The minimum age for enlistment in the army was twenty-one, but as one scholar noted, it was unlikely "that recruitment officers of an army plagued by high desertion rates were apt to be overscrupulous in rejecting underage volunteers." About half the men were between twenty-five and thirty-one years of age, with the officers and sergeants having an average age of about thirty. The officers were decidedly younger than those at the fort; the eldest were Custer and Capt. Myles Keogh, at thirty-six years.[3]

Civilians were fascinated by many things at Fort Lewis, including the troopers. The regiment that stood out most in locals' eyes was the Ninth Cavalry (the buffalo soldiers), which earlier had had a company stationed at the old Fort Lewis. This unit had been formed after the Civil War when Congress had authorized six black regiments for the peacetime army, including two of cavalry. When the newly formed Ninth and Tenth Cavalries headed west in 1867, a new chapter in U.S. military history opened. They would campaign for more than twenty years on the Great Plains and in the Southwest, with the Ninth often stationed in neighboring New Mexico. Indeed, the four troops of the Ninth at Fort Lewis had been sent there from New Mexico in May 1881.

When they arrived, a detail was promptly sent to Pagosa Springs and the rest camped at the fort because no barracks were ready. In August, the district ordered two companies with the pack trains to travel to Fort Craig, New Mexico, in response to a greater need there, providing fascinated

Durangoans a glimpse of these troops. After numerous delays resulting from poor roads and train delays, Gen. John Pope finally wired Lt. Col. Robert Crofton on August 17: "I desire you give your personal attention to seeing they get off as soon as possible as they are much needed." Crofton worried about losing his cavalry, but Pope reassured him: "I will take care of matters in your part of the country when necessary."

In 1883 the Ninth returned to Fort Lewis with two companies, 112 men, six officers, three packers, and 60,000 pounds of freight. Again they camped near the fort and scouted along the San Juan River before leaving in the fall. A minor problem arose when two of the officers brought their wives with them without the district commander's approval. In September, the women were ordered to leave, and just over a month later, the troops departed as well.

Although the men of the Ninth never used the term "buffalo soldiers" to describe themselves, that name has become identified with these regiments. The term's origins have been lost to history, but sometime around 1870 the Comanche or Cheyenne called them buffalo soldiers. Perhaps their Indian rivals gave it to them because they thought their hair resembled buffalo hides. It might also have been a sign of respect because the buffalo was so important to the plains tribes. Or, as one soldier remarked when watching an officer cursing a group of them, "[T]hey stood it like black buffalo sons of bitches."

Despite these favorable associations, these African Americans faced discrimination in civilian and military life because of the deep-rooted racism so prevalent among Whites. Many Americans considered them second-class citizens and soldiers and few thought they were qualified to be commissioned officers. But the members of the Ninth here, and elsewhere, proved to be excellent soldiers.[4]

As some of the only Blacks in southwestern Colorado, they had trouble finding other Blacks with whom to socialize. The 1890 census listed only thirty-four Blacks in all of La Plata County and only ten Blacks (four adults and six children) lived in Durango in 1885. Typical for the time, they worked at menial jobs and had little influence in their community. They faced tacit discrimination in town, even as people were sympathetic to their situation. Expressing the pervasiveness of racism, Durango's *Southwest* reported on December 22, 1883, that "there are two or three pretty hard Ducks among the coons in Durango." On September 22, 1883, the *Weekly Herald,* however, commented about a trooper arrested at Fort Lewis for robbery and murder in Ohio: "Being merely a poor devil of a negro, with neither friends nor influence, it is presumed he will be severely dealt with."

The army never stationed the Ninth's companies at Fort Lewis long enough to make a significant impact on Durango or southwestern Colorado. They, however, may have instilled pride in the African Americans living in that region. But there is no evidence that any of the men returned to settle in the region following their enlistment.

As new enlistees arrived at the post, records show that they maintained the same population patterns as in the 1885 census. Post enlistment records for 1883 and 1888 both reveal that most recruits from foreign countries were Irish and that only a slight variation among native-born occurred, with New York and Pennsylvania providing the most recruits. Preservice occupations also appeared nearly the same, as blue-collar jobs again predominated, with the exception of one banker. And these recruits were young; the vast majority were in their twenties.[5]

Neither saints nor sinners, the enlisted men stationed at Fort Lewis were similar to their comrades at other posts. They followed a daily routine of drill, fatigue duty, and inspection; did sentinel duty at four guard posts, with the cavalry furnishing its own stable guard; and marched their beat regularly. As Maj. Tullius Tupper reported, guard duty came about "once each week" with "extra and daily duty men" performing no guard duties "while detailed as such."

Enlisted men endured thorough inspections, drilling, guard duty, fatigue duty, and all the various demands on their time. They were detailed to reload cartridges, perform stable duty, and serve as hospital stewards, guards, cooks for bachelor officers, schoolteachers, and "strikers" (enlisted men serving as volunteer paid servants) for the officers' families.

The worlds of enlisted men and officers were separate for the most part. Sometimes this gulf caused complaints, as a July 26, 1888, letter, signed "private," to Durango's *Idea* plainly pointed out. A dance that had been held at the post had been a "very restricted affair," exclusively for officers and their ladies. The only representatives of the "lower ten" (enlisted men) to be honored with an invitation were the musicians. According to the private, the dance "was not considered a success." The private was fighting a losing battle; this behavior was typical of officers at western posts.

The enlisted men also complained about a host of concerns and problems. They did not like the food (the very heavy and half-baked bread "is utterly unfit for men to eat") and considered the rations insufficient, or at least some complained they were. Lack of variety may have played a role in this complaint. The uniform diet consisted of staples—beef, salt pork, bread, coffee, and beans—which amounted to a bland diet. They also complained when the paymaster did not arrive on time. "Unjust" treatment by noncommissioned officers and "hard usage" by officers raised their ire even more. When they grumbled about aches and pains, they did not receive the sympathy they had wanted. Trumpeter John Hildebrandt protested that the horse he had ridden for six years "was taken from him and given to a recruit trumpeter who does not know how to ride." Complaining worked this time; he got his horse back.

For some of their complaints, they had no one but themselves to blame. When they ran out of money before the next payday, for example, they did not always behave responsibly. Private Richard Green claimed that his lack of funds kept him from getting back to the post at the end of his leave. Others used that excuse too, sometimes finding themselves listed as deserters. Troopers occasionally borrowed money from each other but did not always repay their loans on time, if at all. Capt. Benjamin Rogers disgustedly informed one creditor that he felt the debtor "intends to evade payment."[6]

One possible reason for the troopers' defaulting on loans came from the army's frequent transfer of troops. Companies were moved about, but also individuals could request transfers. Private Charles Lawrence requested a transfer for health reasons because Fort Lewis's climate and elevation aggravated his "chronic bronchial affliction contracted during the war." The post surgeon concurred that a warmer climate would help. Another trooper who was a musician at the post wanted to return to duty as a private soldier, but he found his request disapproved because "this man is a good drummer." A cavalryman "unable to ride and manage a horse" wanted to exchange appointments with an infantryman who "is a good horseman."

Transfer requests happened too often and took up too much of the officers' time. Medal of Honor recipient Capt. William Carter's responses to two transfer requests suggest that the number of transfer requests he processed was significant:

> I think about half the troop would be willing to pay the cost of getting to posts near large towns.

> It is an expense to transfer this man to the Sixth Inf. to go east and be replaced here by a recruit. This is the third application of the kind. Coupled with the monotony of this post, these men evidently do not relish the idea of remaining here with two troops to guard and care for an eight, or nine company post, this coming winter.

Major Tupper concurred. Every transfer granted "seems to breed a desire for transfer on the part of about half a dozen other men, who had previously appeared contented where they are." It did not help when the Union Pacific Railroad patriotically offered half rates over their line for military personnel. The Santa Fe actually transferred officers and families for free but did not mention enlisted or noncommissioned regulars.[7]

Further increasing the officers' workload were those parents, wives, and others who wanted their men out of the army. They used a variety of reasons and pressures to persuade the proper officers. The local minister of Bookland, Scotland, wrote on behalf of the parents of Edward Gray, who wanted their son to return home. The mother of another soldier claimed that he "is not mentally responsible and has never been competent to take care of himself." Was this merely the plea of a desperate mother, or did it perhaps expose a flaw in recruiting and medical examinations? A couple wanted their son discharged as he had enlisted as a minor, only to find out that "no such man" served at Fort Lewis. Longtime U.S. senator Daniel Voorhees from Indiana wrote on behalf of a concerned mother, as did Kansas senator Preston Plumb for a lonely wife. Capt. Hiram Ketchum responded to one such request, writing that he saw no military reason that Charles Brown, a "corporal in my company, a large, strong, able-bodied man," should be discharged. A letter from the French consulate in Chicago noted that an Emile Lods was obliged to return to France to "serve a term in the French army." Some wives requested that their husbands be discharged to support the family. Private John Bowlen asked for a discharge because he was needed to tend to his sick wife and dependent children.

Sometimes the officers received letters from friends and family members who simply wanted to check up on their loved ones. A Delia Callahan wanted to find out about her brother, as did a man from England. A mother from Ohio wrote to request information about her son, asking that "he be stirred up as she is very anxious to hear from him." Serving under an assumed name was not uncommon, but this practice created more complications when loved ones requested information about particular troopers. Sometimes the family member was aware of the name change, as with the request about a brother who "is serving under another name." But sometimes they did not, as with Annie Griffin, who asked about her apparently wayward husband: Was there any "trace" of a person named David Griffin? No, replied the post adjutant Edward Casey. If her husband was here, it "must have been under an assumed name."[8]

If Griffin had used the army to escape an unhappy marriage, he was not the only one. More soldiers, however, were interested in escaping from the army. Desertion was a huge problem in the decades after the Civil War. The Secretary of War reported that one third of troops deserted in the years 1867–1891. And the troops at Fort Lewis were no exception. Troop F of the Sixth Cavalry reported thirteen deserters from March 25 through June 24, 1887. From April into mid-May 1882, thirty soldiers stationed at Fort Lewis deserted their companies—nearly one per day!

The military lost men to the dreaded "three D's"—discharge, death and desertion, but the last was the greatest drain on military manpower in the late nineteenth century. Brig. Gen. Nelson Miles asserted in 1889 that "the principal evil besetting the army is desertion." Desertion in the 1880s averaged about 40 percent of recruits. Secretary of War Redfield Proctor estimated that three fourths of the desertions happened during the first year of enlistment, which meant that the army saw little or no return on its investment of clothing, feeding, training, and equipping these "temporary" recruits. The military, hoping to mitigate this problem, instituted reforms in the 1880s, including improvements in housing, diet, and clothing. These changes seemed to help a little, but desertion remained a significant problem throughout Fort Lewis's history both at Pagosa Springs and on the La Plata River.[9]

Indeed, little deterred the men from deserting; troopers deserted from the cavalry, infantry, and even the band. The army paid $30 for each captured deserter. For local law enforcement agents and others, it became somewhat of a game to arrest deserters for the reward. "Are there any rewards?" was a standard question. When a sergeant appeared in Alamosa to pick up a deserter, the city marshal "refused to give him up unless he received a reward." The city marshal wanted $50, $20 more than the usual amount.

Once captured, the wayward trooper faced arrest, confinement, and court-martial. Often the army seemed more interested in retrieving the horses and equipment taken than in the men themselves. For example, in 1881, the district commander offered $25 for each mule taken by Fort Lewis deserters.

And they often went in pairs or, at least on several occasions, in larger groups. The city marshals at Alamosa and Pueblo were advised that trains out of Durango on July 4, 1884, were carrying "six or eight deserters from this post." One conductor single-handedly arrested four deserters on their way to Silverton, which made for a total of five in the local jail. Some, like the musician who surrendered in Illinois, got far away, but others didn't try to run too far. One was apprehended just two miles away, working at a ranch under an assumed name. Another deserter, John Carringan, was captured after winning a boxing match in Silverton on July 4, 1886; the next morning, he went back to the post in irons. Apparently a slugger both in and out of the ring, he was accused of punching a company sergeant before deserting.

It was a drain on army resources to track them down. In May 1886, 2nd Lt. Amos Shattuck and his detachment spent a terrible time trying to head off a deserter at the railroad station of Carbon, south of Durango. On their way to Durango they asked about the road, tried to follow directions, got lost at night, went back to town, and finally found the route only to discover the station closed. Not willing to give up, they crossed the mesa and stopped the train. Shattuck inspected the coaches, baggage car, and even the water closet but detected no one he recognized. As the train chugged away, his sergeant, who had searched the first car, hurried over to report that one of the deserters was aboard. Returning to Durango, Shattuck sent telegrams to stations along the route, asking them to arrest the men. Having lost the deserters on the train, the detachment did not return to the post empty-handed. Durango police turned over nine soldiers whom they had arrested and placed in jail. This search had taken two days.

Some men were quite open about their intentions to desert. Late one evening Pvt. John Garvey threw his dress coat and a pair of trousers into the company kitchen, "saying you can have them. I will have no further use for them." The next morning, he was absent from roll call.

Amazingly, some deserters reenlisted under different names and got into trouble for deserting a second or even third time. A frustrated Captain Ketchem refused to take a soldier who had served time in military prison for desertion and now wanted to rejoin his company. "My experience is that when men once desert they are quite likely to commit the offence again." Recent West Point graduate 2nd Lt. Alonzo Grey disapproved a transfer because he considered the transfer applicant likely to desert: "I recently had a transfer of this kind of man [fair character] who deserted." Because the army kept a record of the percentage of desertions from an officer's command, Grey added, "I do not want to have my records incumbered by men who are discontented in other organizations." Of course, some soldiers did better the second time around. One soldier who earlier had been dishonorably discharged from the Marine Corps gained the backing of his new commanding officer, who found no fault with him in his company.

Officers attempted to find out why men deserted. Sometimes liquor was blamed. One deserter who enlisted under the name of famous boxer John L. Sullivan claimed that he was "under the influence of liquor" when he signed. Capt. Adam Powell interviewed five deserters who offered a variety of reasons that he considered "trivial excuses." One was "disappointed in what he thought the army to be" and another did not like the country. Drinking caused another to desert, despite the fact that the army had been the best home this man had had since "he was eight years old." Another desired to see his wife, and yet another wanted to get a job to make "more money out of the army." Considering Fort Lewis's location, the allure of mining in the San Juans must also have been a factor for many. Boredom, isolation, inferior quarters, military discipline, disputes with superiors, and the tedium of garrison life were some of the more common reasons given by those who deserted.

Poor recruiting methods only contributed to the problem. Civil War hero General Oliver O. Howard put it bluntly in the 1880s: "[I]f we take bad men we cannot always reform them. Bad men will desert." And the generally negative public attitude toward enlisted men may have played a role in troopers' decisions. General George Crook, veteran of the Indian campaigns, pointed out, "Their attitude toward the unfortunate private soldier [causes a man to lose] his pride and self-respect when he finds that he is despised by the people he meets."

Fort Lewis tried to recruit locally without much success. One of the officers, designated as the recruiting officer, faithfully filed his trimonthly report. "I have the honor to state that no enlistments or reenlistments were made at this station" was the typical statement. Near to a prospering mining district and many promising opportunities, Fort Lewis could not compete.

The deserters were a discredit to the army, but many other soldiers reliably served the country. Comments such as "excellent, good, fine, steady, faithful in duties, and reliable" appear beside the names of many men who were cited in reports or who retired or were discharged for disability. Several men retired from Fort Lewis after forty years of service, including one who applied for a Mexican War pension.

Another issue for the military concerned the service of married men. Voicing the opinions of many, 2nd Lt. Frank Webster suggested that a recently discharged married sergeant should be replaced by a single man, who "would be infinitely better for the service." After one of his soldiers married, "without my consent or knowledge," and then applied for a discharge on the grounds that he could not support his wife "properly," Capt. William Rafferty observed, "I mention all these matters most respectfully, that the authorities may know what an evil is growing up in the military service and that if possible they may apply some remedy."

Soldiers intending to marry supposedly did so with their commanding officer's permission. That rule seemed to have been more "honored" by its avoidance by the troopers than by following the book. Most married soldiers were staff or company noncommissioned officers. Few, if any, at Fort Lewis did not fit into this category.

With their family commitments, married soldiers generally created more problems than unmarried ones. In one case, Sgt. James Corwin built a "shanty mostly at his own expense" for his family, which included four children. Because he did not consider the housing adequate, his commanding officer asked for better quarters before dropping the request because Corwin "expresses himself satisfied with his present quarters." Every post had a "collection of overcrowded sheds and shanties" where married troopers lived with their families. As one scholar noted, "[T]heir only uniformity lay in the fact that they were all equally unfit for occupancy."

Married men had to ask permission to reenlist, and the army recommended that only those considered indispensable be "allowed in the rare instance to reenlist [and] then only upon the condition their wives be entitled to no privileges as laundresses." Arthur MacArthur Jr., assistant adjacent general in Washington, discharged one married Fort Lewis infantryman for fraud because he had enlisted as a single man.[10]

The soldier's modest salary hampered married men and sometimes did not meet the needs of even the bachelors. To compensate, soldiers could perform extra duty for extra pay and temporary relief of more boring details. Enlisted men received an extra twenty cents per day for "the care and preservation of ordnance stores." The army paid like amounts for teaching school, painting, working in the quartermasters' department, carpentering, and serving as teamsters. An April 1890 report summarized a month's extra pay, which ranged from $3.50 to $15.00 per individual, with most averaging around $10.50. The availability of extra-duty pay depended on "limited appropriations," so sometimes no funds remained by the end of the fiscal year in June.

Enlisted men could also apply for furloughs. Captain Adam Kramer heartily approved of Sgt. John Martin's furlough request. After having served in his troop for a decade, "he is an *excellent soldier, honest, reliable and trustworthy and faithful* in the performance of his duties." Soldiers could even travel overseas by making a special request.[11]

Some soldiers were ambitious, such as the one who asked to start a post barbershop. Others, like the tailor assigned to Peshine's company, who was described as an "indifferent workman," did not make the most of opportunities available to them. All soldiers, regardless of their special skills, had to be ready to fight. To the military, target practice was vital if the troops were to conduct successful campaigns against an enemy. This emphasis on marksmanship was true even at Fort Lewis where they had few reasons to shoot at people. These skills had not been stressed in the post–Civil War army until late in the 1870s. The result proved an abomination. One officer complained that out of the 124 shots his company took at a 200-yard target, 68 missed the target completely and only 2 hit the bull's-eye. Another speculated that if Custer's troopers had been better shots, the outcome of the battle at Little Big Horn might have been different. It was true that in these years militia units often outshot the army in shooting contests. Sheridan and others pushed for reform and the army finally instituted regular target practices.

Without more pressing matters to occupy them, the troops at Fort Lewis used these target practices as an excuse to bicker among themselves. The men of Company A of the Twenty-Second complained that Company H used their target. Company A also ran into a dispute with Company K, which eventually led to counting the number of bullet holes in the target under dispute. Finally, K's commander checked the records, counted the holes, and promised to see that "this offence does not occur again."

Unfortunately, accidents happened on the firing range, and the wounded were carted to the hospital. In May 1885, the surgeon felt obligated to call "attention to the number of accidents." In 1889, the range was entirely reconstructed to limit the possibility of injury. The range officer believed that "a better [shooting range] cannot be found on any post." This assessment may have been true but the range's quality did not necessarily correspond to the skills of the soldiers who practiced there. Sometimes the shooting reports documented none too cheery results, even to the extent that the post commanders were nearly apologizing for them. Poor or defective eyesight could not be blamed because fortunately that managed to get both officers and enlisted men excused from target practice. Despite these problems, Fort Lewis trained some marksmen who went on to represent the post in competition.[12]

The role of the post surgeon was vital in the lives of the men. He was responsible for the health and welfare of the garrison and the sanitary conditions of the post.

The doctor—or doctors because sometimes there were two—stationed at Fort Lewis wielded wide influence. He was responsible for validating disability applications and deciding how disabled a man was. Private Fred Linkman, for instance, received quarter disability for dislocating his left elbow when thrown by his horse. A mild case of rheumatism, "contracted in the line of duty," earned half disability, and three wounds over the years in addition to being "broken down by exposure in service" gave Private William Halloran a full disability discharge. Consumption, spinal problems, syphilis, chronic diarrhea, night blindness, and myopia also excused troops from service.

One case that the post surgeon investigated was the result of a game of tug-of-war "for a large wager." He certified the disability, but he specified that the injury had been sustained "not in the line of duty." In another case, a veteran who had suffered through the hell of the Confederate Andersonville prison claimed to have a heart problem, which was intensified by Fort Lewis's elevation. After an examination the surgeon reported that he could find no evidence of "any serious disease" and in his opinion the subject was not eligible for disability discharge. Some men were declared unfit for service because of illnesses they had before enlisting. Chronic rheumatism, epilepsy, and alcoholism earned a number of men disability discharges, but one Pvt. Sherman Payton was denied a discharge despite claiming rheumatism and mental problems. The surgeon's report stated, "[H]e has the appearance of an awkward and silly country lad, still his mental condition is not such as to warrant discharge. Neither does his rheumatism trouble him to that extent."

The surgeon could also recommend medical leaves, sometimes sending patients to visit the popular hot springs (nineteenth-century medical elixirs), such as nearby Pagosa Springs or Trimble Springs or even as far as Hot Sulphur Springs, Arkansas, where the government established an army and navy general hospital. Applications for medical transfer to another post appeared occasionally and seemed to have been generally approved. Surgeons also approved applications for admission to the soldiers' home and once sent a soldier to the government insane asylum in Washington, D.C.[13]

Post surgeons probably spent a fair amount of time with patients afflicted with sexually transmitted diseases. Indeed, it has often been said that post surgeons "had nothing to do but confine laundresses and treat clap." Because there were no cures for sexually transmitted diseases at the time, doctors could only treat the symptoms, not the disease.

In addition to illnesses and discharge requests, the post surgeon was responsible for enforcing health guidelines to control the post's environment. The site of Fort Lewis was better than most, with good water, an invigorating climate, plenty of sunshine, and all those qualities so beloved by Colorado boosters, but sanitation needed to be managed. Army regulations kept litter to a minimum, the outhouses and stables were cleaned regularly, and garbage was removed from the post. But other, more unusual health issues required attention from the surgeon. One such problem was caused by the pigs that freely roamed the post grounds. They were welcomed because they helped remove garbage and provided a food source, but they also deposited "chips" and raided gardens. The post surgeon was responsible for setting guidelines to manage the pigs and the many other public animals stabled at Fort Lewis and establishing practices to control infestations of flies and rodents.

In addition to managing the post's general healthcare, certifying illnesses that excused troopers from guard duty, evaluating fitness to resume duty, giving physicals, and running the hospital, the post surgeon had to check fraudulent illness and disability claims dreamed up by less than enthusiastic troopers, as in the case of Pvt. George Kraft. Kraft's captain, Javan Irwin, tracked the trooper's medical history from the time he joined the company on March 30, 1886. In May Kraft went on the sick report for gonorrhea. A month later he was excused from duty for three months because of rheumatism. After arguing that Kraft's gonorrhea was "curable," the surgeon heatedly told Kraft that he "considered him a fraud of the worst character, and returned him to duty on September 20." Irwin concluded several months later that Kraft "is apparently in robust good health" and quite capable of carrying out military duties.

Another soldier managed to fool his medical examiner, who later conceded that the soldier had "evidently feigned illness" and gotten away with it. After receiving his disability discharge, this trooper foolishly took a job driving the stage between Fort Lewis and Durango. But the surgeon, who declared him a "fraud and liar, not deserving any consideration or help much less a pension," ultimately had the last word; he recommended denial of any pension application made.

The army maintained records on the health of its soldiers. Each company was supposed to file a monthly report with the surgeon, and the surgeon in turn reported on the health of the post. Usually this reporting procedure was unremarkable, but once, Company D of the Sixth Infantry turned in its report on part of a paper bag. Insulted, the surgeon considered this "action either intentional or careless disregard" and asked the company commanders to take more care in the future.

Among the variety of illnesses reported by the various surgeons, syphilis, gonorrhea, and acute alcoholism ranked highest. Pneumonia, frostbite, typhoid fever, apoplexy, heart problems, gunshot wounds, diarrhea, exposure, and cancer were other ailments commonly reported. Other maladies, such as consumption (tuberculosis), kidney disease, a variety of physical injuries to eyes and legs, and poisoning, were understandable; yet some diagnoses defy analysis, such as "softening of the brain" and "abscess of the middle lobe of the brain."

Doctors also treated patents for blistered feet, wounds, gas, depression, and a host of other ailments. The physicians vaccinated men for smallpox ("at such convenient hours as will least interfere with other duties"), recorded deaths, treated suicidal soldiers, and even cared for civilians and, more rarely, Indians. Suicides, unfortunately, were not uncommon. At least five suicides by gunshot occurred at the post during the 1880s. Another soldier suffering from "suicidal melancholia" tried twice to kill himself before finally being sent to an asylum. The post issued no official reports about what may have caused these suicide attempts.

Medical supplies available in the nineteenth century included nitric, sulphuric, tartaric, and acetic acid; ammonia; tincture of aconite and cinchona; alum; oil of lemon; borate sodium; and cocaine hypochlorite. It has been said that soldiers of the Roman Empire received better medical attention than soldiers in the Civil War. Strides had been made during the Civil War and in the postwar years in hospital sanitation practices and nursing, but popular patent medicines and home remedies satisfied many civilians and soldiers alike.

As previously mentioned, sometimes it was difficult to get enough hospital attendants from the ranks. Ambulance drivers, hospital stewards, and stretcher-bearers also came from the troops. When the troops were in the field, armed medical personnel accompanied them if possible.

The doctors were not above the fray when it came to post politics. At least once, the post surgeon and an officer got into a heated discussion over transferring a particular soldier to the hospital corps because the officer thought he had great potential to become a noncommissioned officer. Private Calhoun Lee (Company C, Ninth Cavalry) called the surgeon a "dead beat on several occasions," which led to the surgeon complaining that Lee had cast "reflection upon the professional character of medical officers." Bernard Byrne found himself in an argument with a company officer over whether a soldier should be on sick call, and was charged by Capt. Benjamin Rogers with unduly interfering.[14] Living at this small, remote post probably intensified small matters into larger arguments in many areas besides medicine.

Although soldiers received mostly adequate treatment for their illnesses, the same cannot be said for their teeth. The post surgeon had a "handsome tooth-extracting case" among his supplies, but no dentist resided at the post. Several practiced in Durango, but they probably received few patients from the military. Typical for the time, most soldiers did not bother with their teeth until they were in severe pain. At that point, dental care consisted primarily of extracting decayed teeth, which was the most common dental practice.

Extraction was a job usually left to the hospital steward. Having teeth pulled out was painful, but not unusual during this era. Most Americans had never met a toothbrush and preventive dentistry remained generations away. Until the days of nitrous oxide (laughing gas), trips to the dentist were painful affairs as the dentist used a pump drill—and no painkillers—to clean out cavities. So with regard to dentistry, the soldiers were really no worse off than the average American.

Another responsibility of the post surgeon was making sure that sufficient supplies of good quality were ordered. Securing the best possible food and supplies for the company messes and officers' tables enhanced the health of the garrison, improved morale, and hopefully eliminated some of the complaints. To take care of the soldiers at the post, many supplies were needed. In October 1880, 1st Lt. Harry Cavenaugh ordered 12,000 pounds of potatoes, 2,500 pounds of onions, 20 cases of condensed milk, and 300 pounds of oatmeal.

The post adjutant was responsible for securing a fair price for the necessary supplies but quality was also an issue. In one case, the quartermaster complained that no evaporated vegetable soup "can be obtained at reasonable price." Later he would not accept Woodwand Gold Medal Family Flour because of its "inferior quality"; thus, 600 pounds of flour needed to be shipped as soon as possible from another company. On another occasion, he warned that unless the Belger Refining Company packed its golden syrup more securely, they need send no more to Fort Lewis. Occasionally, a surplus had to be managed to avoid wasting supplies. In 1887, for example, Fort Lewis found itself with a surplus of dried cod. The Department of Missouri ordered the post to "issue to the troops such portion of the excess as is deemed expedient before hot weather to prevent loss to the United States."

Complaints about food were legion, and probably the troops lacked enthusiasm for the sudden emergence of so much cod. Company G of the Thirteenth griped to Crofton that they were not getting enough bread and vegetables and further "are compelled to wash their dishes in the dining room." Beef allotments divided unequally among companies also aroused ire. Some received more of the better cuts than others, or so they believed. Veteran Capt. William Conway complained that his company needed a higher bread ration. Another officer recommended purchasing evaporated vegetables from the best market to "prevent deterioration" of the product and to improve the appeal of the food served. How appealing evaporated vegetables might be, he did not say.[15]

Fresh vegetables from company gardens and local farmers resolved some food problems. The post's elevation and unpredictable rainfall, however, limited what could be grown. The water supply problem was mitigated by irrigation water from the La Plata, which was available until mid- or, occasionally, late summer.

Whiskey often seemed to be the most important sustenance for some of the men. One of the major problems faced by officers and the surgeon was drunkenness, a problem of near-epidemic proportions in the postwar army. After only sixteen months' service, Pvt. Patrick Murphy, for example, had been tried by a garrison court-martial six times for drunkenness and sentenced to the guardhouse for eighty-four days. Murphy's captain recommended that he be discharged and forfeit his retained pay. Captain Roger brought charges against Pvt. Henry Provost after he saw him come into camp "rolling about his horse" and when dismounted "showed still more evidence of intoxication, being scarcely able to walk." Private Richard Haven was discharged for "fraudulent enlistment, being an incorrigible drunkard." In the 1880s and into the 1890s, many such discouraging reports crossed the post commander's desk.

Captain Gustavus Bascom had a horrible time with one man. After finding him under the "influence of liquor" and quarreling, he ordered the soldier walked up and down to "sober him up." The soldier refused. After ordering the guard to knock him down "if he did not start [walking] at once," the rebellious drunk finally muttered, "he could stand shooting but not the butt of a gun," and walked, only to stop. A sergeant finally tied him inside a tent to restrain him "until satisfied he was duly sober."

Although the post commander had many problems to deal with, drunkenness, described as the "curse of the frontier army," was by far the most common. Other offenses included at least one case of sodomy and an opium addiction. For a time, arson was suspected after a series of suspicious fires plagued the post. Theft of government supplies or private items from fellow soldiers occasionally cropped up, as in April 1890 when the storeroom and hay yard were broken into and the locks destroyed. Additionally, other "locks around the garrison were tampered with and rendered useless." Private Charles Shafter was accused of stealing government property when he sold "or otherwise "unlawfully" disposed of $32.98 worth of army articles. Another was accused of "taking a quantity of tobacco" from a fellow soldier. Soldiers also made discourteous comments and disobeyed orders. Private Joseph Lynch was "absent without leave." Striking a fellow private led to Pvt. John Dunne being found guilty of "conduct prejudice to good order and military discipline." Destroying nineteen panes of glass, "more or less," and one coal scuttle while in the guardhouse gained musician Alfred Hanson twenty days of hard labor.

Many of these men had to go before a garrison court-martial or, if facing more serious charges, a general court-martial. The officers spent much time handling these cases. The hours involved must have been truly staggering, and the reports reflect only the more serious offenses because noncommissioned officers generally dealt with the more trivial infractions. In just February 1881, thirty-four courts-martial took place at Fort Lewis. For using foul language, writing "an indecent expression on a sign," talking loudly in quarters, or making threats, soldiers forfeited pay or performed hard labor. Private Joseph Mozingo pleaded to prejudicial conduct and was fined five dollars. Sergeant William Exener was found innocent of saying "Damn you, I will throw you out too," but was judged guilty of three charges of prejudicial conduct and lost one month's pay. Absent without leave for a night, Pvt. Joseph Lynch had to perform fifteen days' hard labor and was fined ten dollars. Another, Pvt. James Israel, was fined five dollars for using a "vile and insulting name" and writing an indecent expression on a company sign. More serious cases earned the offender a reduction in rank, dishonorable discharge, or confinement in a military prison for several years.[16]

The post guardhouse, "a splendid well-built stone building," contained three apartments and eight cells. The cells, according to an anonymous private writing in the *Idea* on August 1, 1888, were the "dark hell division" and housed "unruly and violent prisoners." The main cell, "large and spacious," handled less obstreperous prisoners. Private James McGintry, who had been sentenced to the guardhouse, claimed that his health had "become shattered" since his confinement and requested parole so that he could sleep in his company quarters. Permission was granted because the guardhouse was overcrowded, not because he complained.

A few probably were responsible for most of the infractions at Fort Lewis. In 1890, a report mentioned that a particular sergeant at the post was "entirely incapable of performing intelligently or correctly his duties. I regard him at the latter end of an ill spent life." In another report regarding two soldiers in the guardhouse, Capt. Sumner Lincoln mentioned that one had boasted he "had been dishonorably discharged several times" and the other "is known to be a thief. These men are very bad characters and their influence in the company, particularly with young soldiers and recruits, is so demoralizing that I am very desirous of getting them out of the company."[17]

The tedium of military life at a remote post must have been difficult for the soldiers. Holidays such as Christmas, New Year's Day, Thanksgiving, and the Fourth of July, when "all duty except necessary guard, fatigue, and police is disposed with," must have been a welcome change of pace. The death of an important American or military person also was an occasion to break from routine, such as the day that assassinated president James Garfield was buried. On that day, the post suspended all duty and labor, the flag flew at half-mast, and a twenty-one-gun salute was fired in his honor.

Another notable event at the post was the arrival of the paymaster. Initially, he arrived bimonthly, if all went well, but it was not unusual for him to be two or three months late. As part of the army reforms of the late 1880s, a monthly schedule was established and adhered to as much as possible. Coming in by train to Durango, where the paymaster collected the payrolls and was joined by an escort, he then proceeded to prepare his accounts. When the paymaster was scheduled to arrive, troops were not sent "in the field unless necessary until after the arrival of the paymaster," so the men eagerly awaited their "very much needed money" at the post. Officers worried that the men might vanish to nearby communities to spend their money if they received their pay while in the field.

Not all community interactions involving the military resolved positively. The arrival of the mail was another event at the post. A particularly bureaucratic donnybrook late in Fort Lewis's history (June–July 1891) involved Durango's postmaster and Capt. Sumner Lincoln, the fort's commander, over poor mail delivery on Sundays. Lincoln called what he described as "gross and apparently inexcusable irregularities" in the Durango post office to the attention of the Postmaster General. Initially, these "inexcusable irregularities" involved returned mail originally sent from the post to the War Department, even though the letters were "properly and legibly directed." On another occasion, "an entire sack of mail from this post was missent" to Farmington, "causing a delay of three days." Durangoans had approached Lincoln, he explained, "while in town to make complaints, as to the inefficiency of this postmaster."

Although mail was delivered every other day of the week, in mid-June the postmaster refused to distribute mail on Sundays. Lincoln telegrammed Washington "to order him to deliver mail" to "our special carrier."

Although advised that they could not "lawfully" do so, Lincoln eventually got his wish and government officials ruled that postmasters on route 65301 (Durango–Fort Lewis–Dolores) could exchange mails on Sunday. They also stipulated, however, that the commanding officer would have to make his own arrangements with the local post office. After debate, the postmaster refused to deliver the mail to the carrier until 7:00 P.M. on Sunday, "although the office was open to the public in the morning when the request was handed to him." Lincoln complained that this delayed official mail ten hours.[18]

The modified Sunday delivery resolved one issue, but in August when it took seventeen days for a dispatch to reach Fort Lewis from Washington, a disgusted Lincoln did not know whether to blame the post office or the stage company contracted to carry mail to the garrison. With less than a month to go before the abandonment of the post, it did not matter. Problems with mail service were not unusual, particularly in smaller, more isolated western military posts. In this respect, Fort Lewis actually had less trouble than many of its contemporary posts.[19]

Copies and more copies of numerous reports, material lists, memorandums, and other correspondence passed across officers' desks. The paperwork covered topics ranging from uniform matters to living conditions. In order to build a fence around the Fort Lewis cemetery, the post quartermaster had to transmit triplicates for the necessary materials to the appropriate suppliers. One officer had to respond to a request from the fish commission about establishing an auxiliary station for propagating fish at the post. Another responded to the Department of Missouri's request for input regarding irrigation and reclamation of arid lands. From headquarters in Washington, D.C., came a demand to get reports straight and an order not to ship "gold and silver in mixed packages." Another officer looked into the matter of two missing field glasses and discovered that they had erroneously been returned. Another responded to a Department of Missouri missive decrying the use of excess stationery throughout the whole region, not just at Fort Lewis.[20]

Of more pressing concern to the troops was the need to care for the post's animals and maintain the stables. Mules and horses were vital to the post but they caused economic, sanitation, and health concerns. Particularly in the post's early years, it was difficult to find adequate forage for them. Once a supply was secured, it had to be paid for and the mixture of oats and corn used for feed was expensive. The post command carefully managed these costs, ordering that mules were "not to be fed oat mush except in special cases of hard service."

When new troops arrived, more public animals came with them. Two carloads arrived with the Ninth, totaling forty-six horses, and forty left with the Sixth Cavalry. Stables, with manure piling up, needed to be cleaned and maintained, and a gravel floor was preferred to one of dirt.

When not in the field, the troopers spent part of each day exercising horses and occasionally mules. Less enjoyable was the stable detail, particularly in the summer. Even the cleanest stables smelled terrible in hot weather and were filled with swarms of flies. Mice and rats also were a problem. But the maintenance of the stables was important for maintaining the post's health. Fortunately, the first fall freeze improved the situation immeasurably, as the flies and some of the smell abated.

Adequate facilities for the post's animals was an ongoing concern. Captain Adam Kramer petitioned the Department of Missouri for new stables. In 1889, when several horses came down with "pneumonia or severe colds," it was decided to rebuild the cavalry stables, which were located on low ground near the river, on higher, drier ground.

Now promoted to staff quartermaster, Sgt. George Courtright recalled the large corral. It served "pack trains, six- and eight-mule jerk-line teams, ambulances, escort and passenger wagons, saddle animals, etc. A man by the name of Scott was the corral master. He was one of the most efficient I ever knew."

The post's blacksmith was always in demand to shoe the animals, but Fort Lewis seems to have had a recurrent shortage of blacksmiths. With icy winter roads, particularly between the post and Durango, "the horses had to be rough shod to maintain traction."

Managing the number of animals at Fort Lewis was another problem. Horses were always in demand by the military. When the initial construction of the post took place, a shortage of draft horses caused some problems and frustrations. And the practice of each troop using horses of only one particular color complicated matters. When Troop B of the Sixth Cavalry realized that they had only thirty-eight, Capt. George Anderson requested enough black horses to increase that "number to at least 60." The Seventh Cavalry rode white horses, and other companies had black, gray, or sorrel. Acquiring specific colors of horses proved costly, time-consuming, and often impractical, but it remained a common practice for years past Fort Lewis's demise.

For a while, Fort Lewis had 106 mules, which was 23 more than allowed for a post of its size. The surplus mules had to be shipped to other posts. At another time, the garrison faced a shortage. And every transfer, acquisition, and death of an animal had to be accounted for, even if the loss occurred while in the field.[21]

Fort Lewis would never have been considered a prime assignment for the officers, but it also wasn't the worst post. For the men stationed there, Fort Lewis was much like their other assignments. The scenery might have been better and the climate more agreeable than at many western posts, but the isolation and higher elevation of the post negated these positive attributes.

FIVE

General Commotion
All over the Country

Full many a name our banners bore
Of former deeds of daring,
But they were of the days of yore,
In which we had no sharing;
But now *our* laurels freshly won
With old ones shall entwin'd be,
Still worthy of our sires each son,
Sweet Girl I left behind me.

"The Girl I Left Behind Me"

Throughout the nearly thirteen years of garrisoning Fort Lewis, both infantry and cavalry were stationed there. These troops included the Sixth and Ninth Cavalries and companies of the Sixth, Thirteenth, Fifteenth, Seventeenth, and Twenty-Second Infantries. The *Colorado Business Directories* during the 1880s listed populations at the post ranging between 175 and 1,000, but the actual garrison strength was never as high as 1,000. Garrison strength in 1887, for example, was 344 and a year later, 439.[1]

Rarely would a whole regiment be stationed at a single post. Cavalry regiments, for example, consisted of twelve troops, with each regiment divided into three squadrons of four troops. The troops were usually scattered around a military district and became the basic military unit at these western posts. The infantry regiment consisted of ten companies.

Before 1866, a cavalry troop was supposed to contain four officers, fifteen noncommissioned officers, and seventy-two privates. In reality, it seldom approached that number and sometimes could not muster half that. Following the Custer debacle at the Little Big Horn, Congress authorized the strength of cavalry companies to be raised to 100.

But a corresponding increase in the strength of the army did not happen because of the depression during the mid-1870s, congressional penny-pinching, and the public's desire to keep government costs low. Thus, to reach the goal for the cavalry, the number of men authorized per infantry company was dropped to a low of thirty-seven. Some infantry men suddenly found themselves temporary horse soldiers in mounted units.

A sampling of post returns during the 1880s found that infantry companies ranged from thirty-seven to forty-six soldiers, counting enlisted men and officers. Cavalry ran higher, numbering from forty-seven to sixty. Underfinanced and ignored by Congress and publicly criticized by those who lived in areas where no danger existed and who objected to the high cost of maintaining the western army, the army could not fill its quotas, particularly while relying on volunteers.[2]

The Four Corners region of Colorado and the territories of Arizona, New Mexico, and Utah presented a variety of potential troubles for the troops settling into the new Fort Lewis. Just to the south of the post lay the Southern Ute reservation and beyond that, across the San Juan River, were the Navajos. To the west were more Utes and Navajos and also the Piutes. Farther to the southeast but still within scouting range (actually closer to Pagosa Springs where the troops had recently been stationed) lived the Jicarilla Apache. North across the San Juans, in the valley of the Uncompahgre River, were more bands of Utes, which soon would be removed. Also in that area was a cantonment, Fort Crawford, which was Fort Lewis's sister post.

Preexisting conflicts between these tribes were exacerbated by the great numbers of White settlers flooding into the valleys and mountains. Racism and cultural differences produced tension and fear, imagined threats and strife. As each group struggled to secure its place in the region, long-standing conflicts were brought to the surface. Mix in a little racism between Anglos and Hispanics, along with jealousy between young Durango and isolated northern New Mexico, and the army found itself in a familiar mess.

Caught between taxpayers and tribes backed by treaties and agreements, the army could not satisfy both sides, and sometimes was able to satisfy neither. Throughout the West, the military tried to mediate between angry settlers and upset tribal members. These problems persisted even as the troops exchanged the San Juan river valley for that of the La Plata.

Further complicating matters was the tension between Colorado and New Mexico settlers along the Animas and San Juan Rivers. Cattle rustling and a smattering of outlaws—some of whom had been involved in New Mexico's notorious Lincoln County war, in which Billy the Kid gained national attention—stirred feelings and occasionally violence. As the new post opened, some 2,000 people were crowding into newly founded, yet still ungoverned and unpoliced, Durango. La Plata County's law officers were nearly overwhelmed.

The army was just getting settled when reports of trouble came. The locals accused the Navajos of causing troubles along the San Juan River and the Utes of taking horses near Bluff City, Utah. Whether these were Utes may be questioned; settlers did not always carefully check on who did what. The reports that Crofton received reveal the long-standing feuds that were at the root of these complaints. The one from the San Juan river valley called the Navajos "notorious petty thieves who use every opportunity to pilfer" and who "may seek revenge on lone persons, if acts of violence are committed against them." In his report, Henry Sage, Southern Ute agent, stated: "[The Utes] are indolent in habits, regarding labor as degrading to man only suited to the groveling nature of women. They subsist upon the bounty of the government." The Southern Utes, Sage maintained, remained at peace, showing "little disposition to engage in hostilities either white or Indian, but nearly all the males are supplied with fire arms of the best quality with a liberal supply of ammunition." Sage had no idea where and how the Utes had obtained the guns and ammunition. According to Sage, it was good that Whites had thus far made few attempts to sell them liquor.[3]

Crofton must have received this information with mixed feelings. This twenty-year veteran no doubt understood the underlying issues and realized the part that he might have to play. His neighbors in Durango, Animas City, and Parrott City expected his troops to be willing to uphold and defend their interests. For the Utes, the troops' presence was a constant reminder of what could happen to them if matters got out of hand. Fortunately for Fort Lewis's officers and men, 1880 ended without any actual field service, and the troops were able to complete construction and settle in at Fort Lewis.

But in January 1881, the cavalry was forced to intervene in a conflict unfolding in Farmington, New Mexico, between the settlers and the Indians. Settlers accused the Utes of trespassing and stealing stock and threatened, "If not removed immediately by proper authority, they will be removed by citizens." The Ute agent told Crofton that ranchers had their stock on reservation land and "in doing so consumed much grass now required by Indians to feed their stock."

As the conflict between the Utes and the settlers was heating up, the Navajos entered the fray. Settlers accused the Navajos of "committ[ing] depredations such as stealing our horses and cattle and other violence." On January 25, an armed party of Navajos rode into Farmington and tried to whip a White man; a Navajo was shot. Frantic Farmington folks warned Crofton that if the troops did not hurry, "it is certain there will be blood shed soon."

Fifty troopers dispatched from Fort Lewis temporarily calmed the situation and departed. Meanwhile, a scout down the San Juan River produced nothing but conflicting stories. But the conflict was far from settled. Some residents blamed the ranchers for the problems, and the ranchers blamed the Indians. Many were determined to drive the Navajos away from the rivers. Worried citizens petitioned Crofton to permanently station troops there. "We entreat you to afford relief and protection against this eminent danger." Captain Benjamin Rogers returned with a mounted company of the Thirteenth Infantry to try to ease the tension. They met with no success before departing.

Rogers returned in April and, to the dismay of many locals, recommended that the men who had shot the Navajo be arrested to prevent further trouble. Crofton requested Indian scouts to help, only to find the request turned down because "the district now has the full number accorded."[4]

In addition to trying to manage the situation with the Navajos, Crofton was forced to intervene between Durango and the Farmington cowboys. As one of the fort's beef contractors warned Crofton, his cattle were being stolen "by the hundreds" and the lives of his men and himself threatened. Durango parties "are making raid after raid on his herders" and "butchers had to go in bands for their own protection." This dispute had begun months ago, when rustlers, operating with two gangs along the border, started stealing cattle in New Mexico and Colorado. Local law enforcement had been unable to stop them. That episode had nearly split New Mexico earlier in 1878, and now it seemed the participants might be shifting to the northern part of the state. In the public's eyes, this development only made the situation worse.

These gangs were reportedly made up of men who had been involved in the Lincoln County war of 1878 and who were considered extremely dangerous. After Port Stockton—one of the two brothers who led the Colorado contingent—was killed by the gang from New Mexico in December 1880, the rivalry between the two groups became an all-out war, terrorizing the citizenry of both sides, as his brother, Ike, swore revenge.

Stormed a Farmington writer, "Stockton and his friends threaten to shoot everyone who opposes them" and the Colorado legal authorities "do not feel themselves called upon to restrain citizens entering our territory." To this writer, it seemed "obvious if there is not a speedy check put upon this turmoil, our country will soon be depopulated of its peace-loving, law-abiding citizens." A petition arrived from Farmington that shouted: "[T]o say the least, under the present reign of terror, our lives, our property, or anything we call our own, are not safe and if you can do anything to give our country relief, you will hasten a lasting favor upon all our law-abiding citizens." Another petition claimed: "[R]uffians have come in and broken up our schools. In conclusion, to say the least, our lives, our property, or anything we call our own, are not safe."

Crofton also received complaints from the Colorado side, including Colorado governor Frederick Pitkin, who had received a communiqué from Animas City's marshal that detailed the problems faced by the citizens of La Plata County. Stock owners and farmers had been driven from their homes: "[D]riven from thence by men who made Lincoln Co. N.M. a synonym of blood and massacre. These same murderers, for the past two years have made Farmington their headquarters." During this time, the governor bewailed, a "carnival of blood" resulted and "good farmers [have been] driven from their homes in the night with the wives and children trembling and frightened to death."

The editor of the *Durango Record,* Caroline Romney, fanned the flames in an April 16, 1881, article by blaming everything on Ike Stockton, his sidekick Dison Eskridge, their associates, and the Farmington folk. She went on to say that Durangoans "wanted to put an end to the Farmington troubles. As the situation now stands our people rule."

It all came to a head in the Battle of Durango, as Silverton's *La Plata Miner* jokingly called it. The Durango and Farmington gangs fought it out on April 11 on the mesa east of town. The invaders from New Mexico were forced to retreat south down the Animas. Although victorious in this skirmish, the Colorado side—including Durango, which had been established less than a year before—was left with a tarnished reputation, as Romney hastened to point out. Potential visitors, settlers, and investors failed to appreciate Durango's Wild West reputation. Even if she did call the first robbery "a sure sign of civilization," this went too far.[5]

The situation left Crofton in a quandary. Americans generally did not want the military to become involved in civilian affairs and were suspicious of standing armies. Based on the problems with the British colonial army, this preference was reinforced after the military was sent to Kansas in the 1850s, during an era known as "Bleeding Kansas," to prevent a civil war between the free-staters and pro-slavery forces. Later the army became involved in controlling the Mormons in Utah, managing various civilian issues in the southern states during the reconstruction period, and ending the 1870s war in Lincoln County, New Mexico. Additionally, the army had used federal policing powers throughout the West to arrest and place in confinement small groups of outlaws in situations similar to the one unfolding along the Animas. General Christopher Augur acknowledged the problems of military policing: "It is a very delicate and unpleasant duty, and one from which we would gladly be relieved by the establishment and enforcement of civil laws."

Protests over such military activity in civilian affairs, particularly in the south, led to the Posse Comitatus Act (1878), which strictly limited the power of the military and the president to authorize troops to assist civil authorities. Such force could be applied only when lawlessness proved "too powerful to be overcome by judicial procedures." During Fort Lewis's life, that happened twice—in Cochise County, Arizona, when Apache raiders crossed over the international boundary, and in Utah, where the Mormons were practicing polygamy.[6]

Given the political climate, Crofton wisely deferred from taking action at this time, adopting a wait-and-see approach. Fortunately, the Durango-Farmington conflict died without more violence. The Stockton gang broke up, Ike was mortally wounded while resisting arrest, the Farmington outlaws drifted off, and law enforcement finally gained the upper hand. The troops did not have to ride to the rescue.

But now that Crofton's troubles in the south were over, he was forced to turn his attention to the west. Settlers in the Dolores and Montezuma Valleys saw a war with the Utes as inevitable. A rancher wrote on May 2, 1881, that well-armed Southern Utes had threatened him, stolen three of his horses, torn down his fences, and "ruined my crops beyond redemption." He and twenty-five neighboring cattlemen were camped at the Big Bend of the Dolores River "where our numbers are enough to check the danger." But others were not so fortunate. Utes killed three ranchers near the Blue Mountains, and one of Durango's citizens was fired on within a mile or so of Durango.

Settlers blamed the Southern Utes for all of this trouble, but the Utes (and some Navajos), through their agent, blamed the Piutes. But were the

Southern Utes simply deflecting the blame? Explaining the discrepancy or perhaps revealing the government's inadequate understanding of the situation, Deputy U.S. Marshal James J. Haffernan noted that "when west of the Rio Mancos all southern Utes become Piutes."[7]

Settlers also blamed the army. One J. T. Williams complained, without worrying about exaggeration, "There is a military post within fifteen miles of Durango where there are fifteen fine companies of U.S. Troops drawing their rations regularly, with as little concern about the safety of American citizens as if we were a lot of coyotes." Williams foresaw another terrible scene like the one in Minnesota in 1862 during which the Sioux had killed more than 730 settlers. Why, he wondered, were "the lazy and bloodthirsty Utes" allowed to come and go as they please?

The settlers' complaints were forwarded by the governor to the commander of the Missouri District, who ordered Crofton to send fully armed cavalry and infantry into the field to assess whether the "depredations reported have been committed." To Crofton's relief, Capt. Henry Carroll and four veteran companies of the Ninth Cavalry were also on their way to strengthen his command, to be "used for no other purpose" than the Indian troubles. He also received permission to enlist five Indian scouts. Meanwhile, the Southern Ute agent advised him that the Utes "seemed to be in good humor and I don't think they will join any trouble."

Captain Rogers was a noted Indian fighter and had twenty years' experience in the Rocky Mountain states and territories. As he led the command into the field, he was slowed somewhat by searching for two deserters from his ranks. When he reached the Dolores, he reported that all "the ranches in this section have been deserted" and that he had not found out much information. Because they had seen no Utes, Rogers was convinced that there would be no problems here, but he feared that they would run into trouble farther west in the Blues.

At the end of May, Deputy U.S. Marshal Haffernan privately wrote Crofton that some cattlemen "are certainly doing mischief." The month of June was spent trying to run down rumors as Washington got involved. Apparently, the army was responsible for causing some mischief on the Ute reservation, as Samuel J. Kirkwood, Secretary of the Interior, asked the army to stop unauthorized parties engaged in "unlawful pursuits—selling liquor, gambling, dance house—at the new station [railroad] on the Ute reservation."

Around this time, there was a shooting in Durango. An investigation of the incident determined that it had been a Ute hunting accident and not an intentional act. But panic caused imaginations to run wild. Henry Page, now the Southern Ute agent, stressed that the Blue Mountains "are the favorite resort of renegade Indians" of all Ute bands, Piutes, Navajos, and Apaches and requested that a company go to the Blue Mountains to enforce the law. Page admitted, however, that few people were "able to distinguish White River, Uncompahgre, Unita [Utes] from Southern Utes."

In response to Page's request, Rogers advised Crofton to put a flying column in the field with "at least one hundred men, good *scouts*, a pack train, and thirty days' rations. Some blow should be struck." Troops in camps would be "useless in my opinion, as the Indians could pass around camps."

Meanwhile, the conflict showed no sign of going away as local ranchers sent reports that the Piutes "openly boast they can and will drive all cattlemen from the country." Suggesting that negotiation attempts might be futile, the Navajos explained that the Piutes "may have a few bad Indians from other bands with them."[8]

Stretched for men and resources, Crofton reluctantly sent his companies of the Ninth, under the command of Captain Carroll, on a long scout to the Blue and La Sal Mountains and the valley of the Grand River (now the Colorado River). Traveling with the Ninth, Dr. Bernard Byrne described the frustrations of this detached service: the Piute "knew every foot of the ground" and "led us a merry chase. We toiled up precipitous trails no wider than a man's foot. We dismounted and walked behind our horses as they jumped from rock to rock." And their campsites were sometimes awful: "There was no water and the ground was covered with cactus. Any place we selected to throw our blankets, the needles of the plants would come through, making a veritable bed of thorns." The doctor packed his mess supplies with 1st Lt. Thomas Davenport, Ninth Cavalry, who, unfortunately, "exercised no care in having the contents packed." Everything was ruined: sugar was mixed with salt, bread became soggy from a broken pickle jar. "There was not a mouthful that could be eaten." After two months in the field and having seen only one Indian, Carroll realized that "it was both silly and useless. His orders had been to capture the Indians and secure the horses and cattle they had stolen. We returned to Fort Lewis without Indians, horses, or cattle." When he returned on July 11, the captain reported that nothing important had occurred concerning any Indians. His troops and horses, however, were worn out: "Many men in my command are about barefooted and need clothing generally."[9]

Crofton's resources were further strained when a deputy U.S. surveyor requested a company of soldiers to guard his party. Crofton simply did not have the manpower. He received help, though, when two companies of the

Fourth Cavalry, coming out of the Uncompahgre post, took to the field in August. They rode as far west as the mouth of the Dolores River where it joined the Grand River. But he could not get Indians to serve as scouts. Fort Wingate's commander did not think any would enlist in an operation against the Utes. Former slave and Ninth Cavalry veteran John Taylor, now married to a Southern Ute, agreed to serve as an interpreter.

Will-o'-the-wisp rumors drove the troops hither and yon. A reported wounding of an Indian on the Mancos River led to an investigation by the Ninth. The investigation did not uncover any useful information because the locals denied having any knowledge of the matter. Then some of Crofton's companies of the Ninth were ordered to Fort Craig, New Mexico, to "look after raiding Apaches."

Caroline Romney witnessed the departure of the troops from Durango. Under the command of twenty-nine-year army veteran Maj. John Mix, two companies of the Ninth departed amid a "lively scene all forenoon around the depot." Some tardy officers were left on the platform as the train pulled out. Reacting promptly, they commandeered a switch engine and managed to catch the train a couple of miles outside Durango. Two other companies set up camp at the station to await transportation. Romney went to see these troops in the evening and described them as "a jolly and happy set of men. Both officers and men were dying for a fight, but the red-skins knew better than to give them a chance." The only reason they "didn't kill any Indians [was that] they didn't find any to kill."[10]

Expressing the widely held belief that the Indian Bureau favored the rights of its wards over those of the settlers, Romney stated that army officers, unlike Indian agents, "believe white people do have some rights as well as Indians." That the army "is sometime compelled to favor the red man rather than the white," she was convinced, "has done the brave men at Fort Lewis a grave injustice." Many officers must have applauded her editorial.

After visiting Fort Lewis, an inspector general touched on this same theme in a report to Gen. John Pope. He discussed the warring bands'

> return to the fostering care of the Interior Department at their respective reservations, where food, rest and protection will prepare them for the next opportunity to raid the settlement and exhibit their Christian proclivities & moral improvements developed and made manifest by the policy & teaching of the branch of the government & its agents having control of them.[11]

The army and the Department of Interior did not always agree about what to do with the Indians, and many westerners joined in the debate, generally favoring a solution that quickly removed the Indians. Their eastern cousins joined, too, often favoring the "noble red man," much to the chagrin of those who wanted the Indians on reservations, out of the way, and pacified.

Trying to maintain the fragile peace, Crofton had no time to debate the matter. The district commander ordered him to send a detachment of men to the lower San Juan River to "restore the confidence of the settlers." But restoring that confidence was made more difficult when a Navajo was caught "attempting to outrage" a white woman, who beat him off with a club. The uneasy settlers fretted and rumors continued to circulate. One rumor blamed all the trouble on a Mormon who was said to be inciting the Navajos and Utes to commit acts of violence. Camped on the Mancos, Rogers tried to run down rumors of a waylaid mail carrier, intercepted travelers, and stolen stock.

In the midst of all this, the few troops stationed at the original Fort Lewis had to chase a couple of stage robbers or, as 1st Lt. John Guthrie called them, desperadoes. Crofton was transferred around this time, relinquishing his command to the new post commander, Lt. Col. Peter Swaine. Despite never having led his troops into battle, Crofton had remained busy maintaining the peace as settlement continued unabated.

In many ways, the troops' experience at Fort Lewis was typical for a western military post. Dusty, dry, long days were spent marching or in the saddle to seek out an elusive enemy or investigate some rumored danger. Company I of the Ninth scouted 2,776 miles during 1881 over land in Colorado, New Mexico, and Arizona. All of this scouting meant that the troops spent a lot of time camping in isolated locales far from the post and civilization and faced weeks of worrisome boredom, sprinkled with upsetting rumors and fears.

After a temporary lull, rumors about Indian unrest started circulating in early February 1882 when a prospector was reported killed in the Navajo Mountains; he was later found alive and well. Reports of Navajos' stealing horses in the lower San Juan river valley drew troops again to the area to "give temporary protection and endeavor to restore confidence" to the settlers. The citizens of Farmington and its vicinity asked to "interpose the military arm on our behalf" to stop the "daily and hourly" encroachment of Navajo herds of horses, sheep and goats "upon our lands, grazing grounds." The settlers reported that the Navajos "fight any attempt made to move them and defiantly flourish revolvers."

Southern Ute leader Ignacio, who was responsible for maintaining the peace the year before, warned his agent about potential danger from the

Indian police killing a western Indian. He warned that White settlers might be in danger. Fort Lewis went on alert, but nothing came of Ignacio's fears. In July 1882, Capt. John Wesley Bean led his company to a station on the San Juan near the Navajo reservation where they remained for more than two months to keep the Indians from encroaching on settlers' lands. It appears that Bean faced no trouble from the Navajos, but he was reprimanded by the district commander after it was discovered that Bean's wife was living with him in camp. Bean was directed "to send her to the post or such point as he may elect." Such instructions "take effect with all other officers" as well.

The troops continued to respond to various requests for their support along the San Juan. Usually, their mere presence was all that was needed to settle matters. At the end of 1882, the citizens of Mancos asked for a cavalry force to be stationed at Navajo Springs and on the Dolores River to protect against the Piutes, Utes, and Navajos. In early 1883, the folks of Farmington again requested assistance for what they described as "those pesky Navajos next door." Winter weather prohibited immediate action but in February a station was established along the San Juan River and patrols were sent out as needed. They found a few Indians off the reservation, but nothing more serious. At one point, a local Indian trader was threatened, but the western veteran Capt. William Conway, company commander of the Twenty-Second stationed at Fort Lewis, responded quickly by sending a guard of four men to his store.[12]

In March the Indians in the vicinity of the Ute Mountains reportedly faced an epidemic of smallpox. And then it was reported that the Utes were "dying in large numbers near the post." The reports proved false, but the Ute Mountain smallpox rumor had heightened worries in the region. Fortunately, the situation along the San Juan and the rumors of smallpox were under control by May.

As trouble along the San Juan ended, a crisis flared near the Jicarilla Apache reservation. The agent felt he had matters under control, but a detachment of the Ninth Cavalry arrived from Fort Riley, Kansas, to help in moving some Apaches to a different reservation, the Mescalero Agency. Other companies of the Ninth had arrived at Fort Lewis late that spring to reinforce the garrison. The troopers camped near the post probably because there were not enough barracks and stables available. It is possible, however, that the Ninth faced tacit discrimination, as at Pagosa.

Soon after arriving at Fort Lewis, the Ninth went on patrol along the San Juan and over to the Blue Mountains as trouble again flared near the Blues when a rancher was killed. West Point graduate and veteran western officer 1st Lt. John Guilfoyle, who had been cited for gallantry in three 1881 New Mexico actions, commanded the detachment of the Ninth Cavalry sent to investigate the situation, which calmed before the troops arrived. The troops, however, were able to help by arresting the guilty party. Other problems between the settlers and Indians, such as the settlers' complaints about the Navajos' driving their animals onto their ranges, continued, but these problems did not lead to violence.

In December the Department of Missouri, finally recognizing that Fort Lewis was undermanned, authorized more cavalry to be stationed there. The result was a construction boom of needed quarters and stables in 1884.[13]

Busy with the construction projects at the post, the troopers probably were hoping to avoid protracted scouting trips, but that would not be the case. In January, a settler near Bloomfield, New Mexico, angrily reported that he had been shot at "by a drunken Indian. Indians would be peaceable if the whiskey business could be stopped." But the army and the agents did not have much success in controlling the sale of alcohol to the Indians. The post continued to receive reports that the Navajos and Utes were "troublesome."

By March, ranchers near Navajo Springs were told to leave the region, after one rancher was severely wounded and several herders were driven back to their ranches. Bluff's mail carrier felt so threatened that he refused to go on further trips without an escort, and the people of Mancos called for help. The post's adjutant major, Robert Hall, responded to this cry for help, saying that deep snow made it impractical to move infantry. He also questioned the need for army involvement because he suspected that Mancos cattlemen were trespassing on the Ute reservation and provoking the Indians: "We cannot protect [those] "trespassing on the Ute reservation." Worried that the conflict was worsening, locals gained no reassurance from a telegram from the New Mexico District's commanding officer, which said that he considered the Mancos people "able enough to protect themselves."

The situation deteriorated when Navajos robbed a store in McElmo Canyon, prompting Utes in the area to move to avoid trouble. The district commander ordered a detachment into the field to help in recovering stolen goods. Troops went out to Mitchell's ranch, near Navajo Springs and the store, and recovered some of the pilfered property, returning it to its former owners. Fort Lewis's officers generally had success handling small problems, like recovering stolen goods or investigating individual incidents, but they were at a loss as to how to address the problem as a whole. Clearly with the myriad reports of problems, some action was needed, but these requests for help were mixed with contrary reports, such as the one from a settler in late March, stating that there existed "no occasion for troops." These varied reports left Fort Lewis officers unsure about how to continue.[14]

But the problems seemed to be worsening. In March a messenger informed the post that Navajos had surrounded Mitchell's place and a fight was in progress. Troops arrived on March 21, passing Utes on the way who were leaving the country to avoid trouble, and found an armed group of settlers there. Mitchell claimed that the Indians had fired first in a fight that left two of them dead and two wounded. Proclaiming the situation serious, the army rushed more troops in from Forts Wingate and Lewis.

On the San Juan River front, the army received reports that the Navajos were "menacing" settlers. Again, Fort Lewis requested Navajo scouts from Fort Wingate and this time they received authorization to have some serve with the Sixth Cavalry. Fort Lewis's commanders advised the Fort Defiance Indian agent that the scouts "should be selected for good conduct and steadiness." The two "most reliable and best behaved will receive appointment as corporals." All were to report to Fort Lewis as soon as possible.

It was clear that more information was needed before it could be determined if the Utes or Navajos were indeed causing all of these problems. As some settlers blamed Utes while others blamed the Navajos, the troops in the field needed accurate information to ascertain the guilty group. Captain Hiram Ketchum, who was stationed with his infantry company at Mitchell's, finally brought some semblance of reality to a situation that had become highly inflated in the public mind. He confirmed that the disturbance reports had been greatly exaggerated, most of the stock had been recovered, and there was no need for a full company. Supported by other officers, he recommended that only one noncommissioned officer and six to ten enlisted men be left there for duty. His recommendation was accepted and most of the infantrymen, and all of the cavalry, withdrew.

The remaining detachment received orders "that Navajos and Utes off their reservation should have written authority from agents." Sergeant Christian Soffke and his men were to render "all possible assistance to the settlers" in case of a "hostile demonstration" and "make a stubborn fight" in the event of being attacked. His weekly reports to the fort should discuss "everything that transpires." Hopefully, settlers gained some reassurance from this lonely detachment.[15]

As spring turned to summer, a summer camp was once again established for a cavalry troop along the San Juan River and the field season opened. But high water promptly caused the camp to be moved.

In mid-June a report came in of two ranchers killed in the neighborhood of Navajo Mountain and troops marched out to investigate. After a second attack on July 3 and the loss of some horses and cattle, some local cowboys took out after the hostile Utes. They found them, killed one, and lost one of their posse.

Then trouble flared again at Mitchell's. The detachment there was about to leave, with two troops of cavalry now in the region, when it arrested five Utes suspected of being involved in the killing. On July 12, Ute chief Red Jacket appeared with armed warriors and demanded the release of the prisoners, whom he promised to deliver to the Ignacio Agency. Outnumbered and realizing the cavalry was too far away to help, Sergeant Soffke surrendered his prisoners. Red Jacket delivered the prisoners to the agency as promised but then appeared in Durango with "about forty well mounted, well armed, and highly painted" warriors. When one of his braves knocked down a city marshal who tried to arrest one of the band for carrying firearms, Durangoans assumed the worst would happen and demanded troops to "keep the Indians out of town." Their request was not granted, but Fort Lewis's commanding officer was ordered to protect life and property in Durango with troops if hostiles attacked the town. Mayor John Bell sent a telegram to the post, claiming the problem was that the Utes carried firearms and this practice needed to be stopped.

Durangoans could not understand why the army did not rush to their rescue immediately. Flustered civilians complained about army inefficiency and wasted tax money. Frustrated troops grew weary of trying to run down all the rumors, reassure settlers throughout the region, and find the various parties guilty of fueling the conflict. Spread too thin, the beleaguered troops in the field sent reports complaining about "shoddy narrow toed shoes" that crippled the men, the failure to send medical officers with the troops, lack of forage for horses and mules, and insufficient water supplies. And the Navajo scouts who had been approved already had still not arrived. When Fort Lewis commanders inquired about the missing scouts, it was the post's former commander and current commander of Fort Wingate, Lt. Col. Robert Crofton, who informed them that the scouts were enlisted and only awaited transportation. They finally arrived and some remained on duty until the next January.[16]

With rumors running rampant throughout the region, a telegram received in Ignacio claimed that nine citizens had fired at eleven Indians. After checking it out, a patrol reported that they could ascertain only that a party of citizens had fired upon Indians somewhere around Piute Springs. No casualties were sustained but it generated more panic and anger.

Further complicating matters was the relocation of Navajos and Utes around this time. A recently completed survey of the Navajo reservation found that two townships thought to be on the reservation actually were not and therefore were opened to settlement. An officer and an escort were sent to explain the matter to the Navajo and prevent any difficulties between them and the settlers now claiming the land.

In August, another escort went with the Navajo agent to Navajo Mountain to arrest suspects accused of murder. They reported that they had found a large number of Utes there. The Southern Ute agent replied that he knew nothing of his people being in that vicinity and they should be forced back to the reservation. The Ute agent thought that more troops would be needed to round them up but warned them to "act prudently as the area is full of renegade Utes and Navajos."

Reports of these problems appeared in newspapers across the country, leading to a request for additional information from former Colorado senator and now Secretary of the Interior Henry Teller. Teller then requested that Secretary of War Robert Lincoln send troops to "put back or kill Indians when off their reservations and recapture stolen stock." Such drastic measures did not have to be taken as the situation calmed down by late August. Anxious to keep the situation under control, Teller asked that the military provide assistance to Warren Patten, Southern Ute agent, to keep the Utes on their reservation.

What had initially seemed to be a simmering conflict settled down and Fort Lewis's troops fell back into what had become the usual routine. Small detachments of troops stayed in the field until mid-October, scouting and reassuring settlers that Uncle Sam was on the job. Durango, which had never been attacked or even threatened after the Red Jacket incident, relaxed. As the October 18, 1884, issue of *Idea* reported, the Sixth had been ordered to return to the post from the Blue Mountains and "no further trouble is expected from Indian raids." Thus, another rumor-filled year ended, just as it had started.[17]

The change of the readjusted boundaries of the Navajo reservation now came back to haunt the post. Some Navajos did not want to move. Trouble started in January 1885 and continued for months as troops again patrolled the river. By June, Utes, pleading hunger, ranged off the reservation to hunt. Ranchers worried that the Utes would steal their cattle: "They will and always do." The troopers at Mitchell's ranch reported that well-armed Utes were on their way to the Blue Mountains to hunt, but the residents "are not apprehensive of trouble with the Utes at present."

But others were worried about the problems that the Utes had already caused. The July 4, 1885, issue of Durango's *Idea* editorialized that a Ute outbreak would lead to serious consequences. It had already "caused general commotion all over the country which will not easily subside." In a previous article on June 27, 1885, the editor of the *Idea* reported, "The recent trouble has given us a black eye for the year and the injury that the advertisement abroad will give us is incalculable." He envisaged that these ongoing problems would hurt mining, tourism, and trade. Indeed, an article in a Georgetown, Colorado, publication indicated the validity of these concerns: "[R]eport of Indian troubles in southern Colorado has an injurious effect upon eastern people." It is why "many who intended to come to tour this summer are afraid of being scalped." Investors and visitors were not likely to appear where they believed "the redman is swarming."

Fearing trouble, post commander Lt. Col. Peter Swaine sent troops to the Mancos River. Demands for protection had brought them there, but tragically, they arrived too late. A house had been set on fire, killing the owner and wounding his wife; rumors swirled that other attacks had occurred, but they had not. An investigation revealed that this attack had come about because cowboys, after threatening to "shoot Utes on sight," had murdered six Utes, including two women and a child, in their tepees. And, despite clear evidence of wrongdoing, these cowboys escaped punishment. Veteran officer Maj. David Perry, Sixth Cavalry, who had been cited for gallantry in the Civil War and Indian wars, reported from the field that the "inoffensive Utes" had been massacred in a "most barbarous manner." Swaine, in his report to his district commander, denounced the outrage:

> All we can do will not prevent a disastrous and bloody war if this savage act of butchery is repeated, as it is feared it will, whenever a small isolated party of Indians again fall into the hands of the lawless element associated with the cowboys. They openly boast they will kill Indians on sight. These cowardly assassins care little for the fate of innocent settlers as they do the lives of inoffensive Indians.

Denver papers picked up the story about the Utes being killed and seemed to side with the Utes, calling their killers "horse thieves."

Exasperated residents of southwestern Colorado grew indignant. Reports from Denver, transmitted by the Ute agent, generated a "great deal of disgust in Durango," whose citizens felt misunderstood. Local opinion, which was decidedly anti-Indian, was fueled by sensationalist editorials and rumors. On June 27, 1885, Charles Jones, editor of Rico's *Dolores News*, concluded his editorial "Ought Squaws to be Killed": "Squaws in every Indian tribe are far more blood thirsty than bucks." They "torture" and "always take a willing hand [in a fight]. . . . The motto of the frontiersman is, and ought to be: 'shoot to kill spare nothing.'" Jones did not think much of "OUR NATIONAL PETS," his name for the Indians. The June 25, 1885, issue of Durango's *Idea* issued a more moderate call to arms: "The time for action is at hand. . . . [If the government does nothing,] every man [is] to defend his person and property, and to shoot every Indian that may be found in the country, no matter what his business."

Based on the reception that locals gave the Ute agent and his Indian police when they arrived to investigate the situation, this manner of dealing with the Indians was perfectly acceptable. The Ute agent reported that he was warned by locals that an armed party of men planned to fire "into my Indian police and if troops attempt to defend them they would also clean them up." In response, Swaine took the precautionary measure of advising district headquarters to have reinforcements ready should trouble arise; with a large "part of my command out, it would not be prudent to weaken the garrison" any further.

Durangoans panicked over this "war" and Swaine could not calm them despite his assurances that "we have enough troops" and "more in readiness." Swaine reported that Durangoans sent the "governor exciting reports" and clamored for state troops because they did not believe that regular troops could be depended on to afford protection.

Silvertonians joined in the chorus. The editor of the *Silverton Democrat* on July 4, 1885, suggested that a large force would have the "effect of restraining the Indians and prevent an outbreak." Perhaps tongue in cheek, the editor went on to say that the militia could enjoy a pleasant summer and become "acquainted with the beauties and advantages" of this area while keeping the peace. Colorado's militia, however, had not the best of reputations since the 1864 Sand Creek tragedy and massacre.

Swaine opposed using the state militia and wrote headquarters that Governor Ben Eaton should be informed that Swaine commanded a sufficient force for "present emergencies." The presence of Colorado militia "is neither advisable or necessary." Further, the government "will eventually be called up to pay expenses attending the calling out of state troops."

To calm fears, troops, infantry, and cavalry were stationed at Mancos, Big Bend on the Dolores River, and Mitchell Springs. Cavalry scouts were ordered throughout the region. Captain Mott Hooton was advised to have his troops "show themselves as much as possible to the settlers to assure them of your intention and ability to protect them." But rumors surfaced that the officers were saying "they were not sent there for the protection of the people, but for the protection of the Indians." Swaine insisted that this "idle rumor, of course, has no weight" and "might emanate from ignorant and panic stricken people," but it was one more thing for Swaine and his men to overcome. To add to Swaine's crowded concerns, in July he briefly served as the Ute agent.

Reports and editorials make it clear that the settlers in southwestern Colorado would be satisfied only when the Utes were removed from the region. A July 4, 1885, editorial in Durango's *Idea* insisted that it was a "suicidal policy to keep the Utes where they are." With the implied threat of violence, the locals warned that they would "teach the Indians a lesson to stay away" from their homes, herds, and lands because they needed to be removed from the "irritating proximity" to the settler. Tensions mounted as the settlers grew impatient with the army, Indian Bureau, and War Department:

> There is nothing to be accomplished by cursing the army stationed at Fort
> Lewis for the Ute troubles. If the army is not properly advised, curse the ear
> of the War Department, if it will do any good. The officers and men at
> Fort Lewis are eager enough to fight the Indians if they are given an
> opportunity, but the stupid head of the department would cashier the
> officer, and hang the soldiers if they were to kill an Indian without one
> year of red tape racket between here and Washington.

In the midst of this turmoil, Swaine was busy investigating stories of a woman "ravished" at her home on the San Juan River, spurring her husband to kill the guilty Indians. From throughout the region, rumors circulated about Ute plans to seek vengeance, including another false report of another threat to Mitchell's. Captain Ketchum and his troops tried to track down the origin of the rumors, but they could find "no reliable source." Fueled by these rumors, the settlers continued to provoke the Utes. Ketchum worried that the situation could quickly spiral out of control: "I believe eventually Utes will take lives of more white men to compensate" for the loss of their tribal members. To ensure the uneasy peace, troops remained in the field until winter and additional rations were issued to the Southern Utes to "prevent starvation and hostilities."[18]

The already unsettled residents were further provoked when the *Silverton Democrat* took the traitorous position of blaming the cowboys for the conflict with the Indians. Yet, the editor merely seemed to be grinding another axe because the article's purpose appears to have been to stir up a healthy dose of Anglophobia: "[M]ost sensational stories emanated from the agent of an English cattle company composed of men not American citizens."

More directly related to the Indian question, another article in the *Democrat* voiced the frustration of the American taxpayer. It seemed, the editor mused, that it "would be cheaper for the government to contract with some big hotel" to board the Indian wards at three to four dollars a day than to "maintain them on reservations." This system would have the advantage of keeping "rascally agents and traders" away from the Indians and doing away with the need for a "large force of inefficient soldiers" to guard them.

This tumultuous time proved as close as troops at Fort Lewis ever came to becoming involved in an uprising that might have led to war. Without question, the cowboys had caused the trouble this time and Swaine and the other officers rightly called them "despicable cowards." More serious trouble had been avoided thanks to Swaine's careful and professional handling of the situation.

In comparison, 1886 seemed calm indeed. Troops went out to the San Juan River in April to a camp established at the mouth of the La Plata River by the Sixth Cavalry. The controversy over ownership of Navajo land was quelled when the federal government decided to return to the Navajos the townships that had briefly been placed in public domain. To forestall further conflict, the government decided that the few settlers on these lands were not to "be disturbed until further orders."

Feeling more assured that the situation was under control, Captain Hooton, who was camping on the San Juan with his Twenty-Second Infantry company, recommended that for the moment only a small detachment of cavalry was needed to act as couriers, the river being so high that it "is simply impossible" to cross it with horses. So quiet appeared the situation that Hooton recommended that the company on duty be relieved every month to "give the company's commander opportunity to exercise his men in marching." It would also provide the men "some recreation and rest from the fatigue work of the garrison."

The quiet continued through the summer despite a few reports of Navajos trespassing with their sheep. When Hooton investigated one of these reports, he discovered that there was no cause for concern: "[T]he party making the complaint had no claim there. He was not one of the prominent settlers" and "responsible men in the vicinity" did not want the Navajos interfered with "as they were on very friendly terms."

Access to clean water was one of the most pressing concerns for one camp, which was located near impure water. After using this water, the troops came down with what was diagnosed as typhoid fever. Once they moved to higher ground near better water the situation improved.

Water was an ongoing concern in this semiarid region and caused additional conflict between the Indians and the settlers. As Swaine reported, the settlers dismissed Indian claims to water because the settlers thought that "they [the settlers] would use it more productively." But the Indians needed water, too. The debate over water rights would continue long after Fort Lewis was closed.[19]

To prevent troubles, troops remained in the field and scouts investigated rumors well into December. One incident reported by Capt. William Conrad centered on the ever-present whiskey and a hut on the land that had been returned to the reservation. Much to the dismay of settlers, such land disputes required a trip to Santa Fe to present the case to the land authorities there.

Disputes over claims to this land worried Swaine, who hoped they would be resolved by spring and the lands restored to the tribe. If not, he feared that it would "probably become necessary to establish another summer camp there." By year's end, the Ignacio Ute agent told the post's commanding officer that Red Jacket "promised good behavior" and that the agent did not "believe reports to the contrary are true."

A week into 1887 found Red Jacket's and Mariana's bands facing off against the settlers in McElmo Canyon. The settlers charged that the Utes had wandered off the reservation. But once again, an investigation revealed that the Utes were not to blame; Swaine reported that the cowboys and the cattlemen had appropriated the only water on that portion of the reservation at Navajo Springs, several miles inside the reservation. Swaine complained that the cowboys had also intimidated settlers, "and though they hesitate to speak against the cowboys, they repeatedly refer to the fact that the Indians are deprived of their lands at Navajo Springs, leaving it to be inferred that they are the original cause of their troubles." Swaine recommended that the agent demand the land back and remove his Indians. These recommendations were followed.

As the conflict continued, Swaine recommended that a subagency be established at Navajo Springs because this site was too far from Ignacio to be managed effectively from there. But he hesitated to order soldiers to the site, fearing that there would be "a great risk of suffering on their part." Deep snow would assuredly cut them off from their base of supplies. A scout was sent instead and reported some depredations on settlers' property, but the crisis passed once the onset of winter calmed matters.

Utilizing the railroad out of Durango, one troop of cavalry went to Amargo, New Mexico, in February 1888 to prevent "trouble between Jicarilla Apache and Mexican" stockmen. They stayed until April, when a property owner demanded the troops be withdrawn from his land. Soldiers returned to Amargo in July to remove settlers from the Jicarilla reservation. That same month troops moved into the Blue Mountains "to compel bands of roaming Southern Utes and so-called Pahutes to return to their reservations." These troops remained in the field until August.

The unsettled situation in the region calmed down as the end of the decade neared, but a few isolated reports of trouble continued to crop up. Following the pattern established by its older neighbors, the new hamlet of Cortez asked for troops in July 1888. A letter supporting the request claimed that "[the Indians] will take Cortez by night and destroy the inhabitants therein." Considering the small size of the settlement, that would not have been impossible. Cortez was located near the vortex of the earlier troubles at Mitchell Springs and adopted that region's heritage of worry and distrust.

In response, Sixth Infantry captain Stephen Baker was sent to investigate the situation at Cortez. He did not seem to be too worried because he decided to visit the cliff houses and adjacent ruins in Mancos Canyon along the way. Once in Cortez, he found the people "generally did not fear Utes or any other tribe." The few Utes around "do beg annoyingly" and some people "seemed to think that stray Indians in demanding food were impudent." The claims made in the letter to the post, requesting troops, "did not seem to be believed by anybody."

Yet, the letter apparently voiced the fears of some residents in Cortez and nearby McElmo Canyon. They still wanted a troop presence and complained to the Department of Missouri. Fort Lewis was notified that "troops should have been sent" in response to the initial request. Again Baker traveled to Cortez to assess the situation.

This time he found a general uneasiness because of "Ute insolence." Reports surfaced of Utes' ordering "women and in some cases men" to cook food for them. Baker visited the Big Bend and Disappointment Valley country and learned that Indians had killed some calves and colts. The settlers were concerned primarily about allowing the Indians to roam away from the reservation. In the "now comparatively settled country," people "declare such a state of affairs can't last long without collision." Baker agreed that the Utes should be removed if they "insist on the right to hunt outside the reservation." The danger, however, did not seem great enough to send troops into the vicinity. But the stubborn residents of Cortez disagreed and ultimately were successful. In September, the Sixth Cavalry established a field camp nearby and patrols were sent out to calm uneasy settlers.

But the officers who investigated the Cortez complaints repeatedly stated that they had been exaggerated. Finally, the troops were ordered back to the post on October 12. One officer offered his opinion on the matter: "There is a great desire to have a military post established in that section as an aid to colonization and for the money it would bring into the county rather than from any real necessity of protection." Those same desires had spurred demands for posts and troops throughout the West for years, as seen in places such as Durango, Denver, Dodge City, and Cheyenne.

Fanning the fires of an Indian scare developed into an extracurricular sport among westerners wishing to expand their army business in slow times or sometimes even in good economic times. William Byers, in his *Rocky Mountain News*, expressed this sentiment more explicitly than most: "Our people have a right to some of the patronage of the government."

In spite of efforts to the contrary, the situation had calmed down to the point that Capt. Adam Kramer was able to lead a practice march of the rest of the troops of the Sixth Cavalry, following the Department of Missouri's recommendations. The practice march served two purposes: first, it was a good training exercise for the troops, and second, it advertised to the public that the army was in their neighborhood. Kramer devoted various days to practicing tactics, setting up camp, defending against convoy attacks, preparing a field hospital, skirmishing, and day and night signaling. Kramer reported that discipline was well preserved, with the exception of a few cases of drunkenness: "Much [less] than would have been expected in view of the fact the troops were paid off immediately before leaving and that there were not only many liquor saloons in the route, but the command was even followed by whiskey peddlers, however the precautions adopted to restrict sales were successful." Even less trouble appeared when troops from Fort Lewis served as an escort for the Indian commissioners going to southern Utah.

With the region becoming settled, demands for troops were spurred more by the desire for the money Uncle Sam brought in than by any real fear of Indian hostilities. As such, Fort Lewis's days were numbered.

The year 1890 found the troops occupying themselves by escorting the paymaster, with the commanding officer charged with carefully checking his detachment "to see that each man's belt is filled with proper ammunition." The officers, with plenty of time on their hands, studied tactics and had time to ponder questions about at-ease marches. Evidence of the post's diminishing significance, the real problem of the year was the conflict over timing of the annual practice march and the paymaster's appearance. It was requested that he defer his now monthly appearance for a week because "to pay on the march would insure an avalanche of whiskey dealers to follow and annoy our camps, causing trouble, affecting discipline."

The last full year of the post's occupancy found the usual rumors, occasional patrols, and Utes and Navajos off their reservations. Once again, a report of Indians roaming off the reservation in the Blue Mountains came to the attention of the post's commanding officer, now Capt. Tullius Cicero Tupper, also a Civil War and Indian war veteran cited for gallantry and meritorious service in both. In response to this report, he sent out a patrol of one officer and six men, ordering them to go as far as practicable "this season of the year [November]" and find out what was happening. But the concerns appeared to be far from serious. Tupper stated that the principal complaint against the Indians hunting beyond the reservation limits "is the fact they scare the cattle."

The Utes also complained. An April 1891 report correctly pointed out that Whites often crossed the Ute reservation with herds of stock, which "results in losses and annoyance to the Indians." Additionally, the Utes expressed their concerns about the Denver & Rio Grande Railroad's proposed line between Durango and Albuquerque, which would cross their land. The Indian police actually ordered surveyors off as trespassers. Captain Sumner Lincoln noted that the Southern Utes had not given them permission to be there, and the line was not built.

As the fort's days dwindled in 1891, nearby residents worried that the Utes could cause problems.[20] Yet, once again, the real concern related more to the peril of losing the financial windfall that Fort Lewis represented than to actual hostilities. Thus the days of a military presence in southwestern Colorado ended.

The soldiers of Fort Lewis had fought no battles or even serious skirmishes. Amazingly, it appears that not one man had been killed in combat. The post had never been attacked or even seriously threatened. Troops had scouted, pursued, and marched long distances and even had been in the field for months at a time. They had set up temporary camps in isolated corners of the region and maintained a military presence for the settlers as well as the

Utes, Navajos, Piutes, and Apaches. Perhaps most importantly, Fort Lewis's troops had upheld the rights of all people, even the Indians, despite those who wanted to move the tribes somewhere else and open their reservations—"gardens of Eden," abounding with natural resources—to ambitious Whites for settlement.

The troops had separated the Navajos and Utes and tried to keep them and the farmers and ranchers away from each other's land and animals. Much of the rural land that had been open in 1880 was settled by 1890. During this decade, La Plata County had increased in population fivefold and had had neighboring Montezuma County carved out of it. A new railroad, the Rio Grande Southern, now went where only horses and wagons traveled before, from Durango westward, circling around the San Juans. Tourists were arriving to view the scenery, visit the homes of the ancient "Aztecs," vacation in the mountains, and dip in the hot springs for health and relaxation. Some tourists even wished to see the Indian-fighting army they had heard and read so much about.

The reassuring presence of Uncle Sam's military had helped to open up this land. Although not exactly a frontier when the army arrived, this region could not be called settled until the late 1880s. Farming, ranching, coal and precious metal mining, tourism, agriculture, railroads, urbanization, and lumbering had all become part of southwestern Colorado's growing economy. Fort Lewis, as a protector and a consumer, played a significant role in the development of this area.

The post and its garrison had served a somewhat passive role in the settlement of the West. As Colonel Swaine wrote to one of his field officers in June 1885, "Your firmness and display of troops will achieve the result that the spark of war may not have an opportunity to kindle the hearts of these young bucks." He added, "[Your] display of force will also give confidence to citizens." Fort Lewis was not the only fort to serve history in this manner. As historian Robert Utley indicated, western forts often gave settlers "reassurance if not always protection."[21]

In addition to its reassuring presence, Fort Lewis provided economic stability to the region. Locals did not take this advantage for granted and probably exaggerated their fears at times just to keep those government dollars coming. Again, this dependence on the fort by locals was typical, as evidenced by Gen. Phil Sheridan's comments about a Texas fort: "exaggerated reports, gotten up, in some instances, by frontier people to get a market for their produce, and in other instances, by army contractors to make money."[22]

Fort Lewis was a part of that long string of posts scattered throughout the prairies, deserts, and mountains that protected, opened, and even promoted the West. Its lifespan was short and it never ranked as one of the major posts, but in many ways Fort Lewis's story is more typical of a western fort than those of its better-known contemporaries. Most have read about Fort Laramie, Fort Apache, or Fort Abraham Lincoln, but Fort Lewis was almost unknown beyond the borders of southwestern Colorado. No officer or enlisted man gained fame here. No legends remain to be handed down through the generations. Yet, as the troops marched out for the last time, they must have had a certain satisfaction in a job well done.

SIX

The Army Loved
to Dance

We'll break windows, we'll break doors
The watch knock down by threes and fours;
Then let the doctors work their cures,
And tinker up our bruises.

"Garry Owen"

Life at Fort Lewis in the 1880s offers a microcosm of late nineteenth-century America. The post was similar in many ways to rural, small-town America, with the possible exception of having a larger variety of immigrants and far fewer women and families than the average farming town in Illinois or Nebraska. It had religious services, a school, a library, recreation, housing problems, entertainment, a store, gardens, and even complaints about the weather. The post had its upper and middle classes (officers) and its lower middle class (noncommissioned officers and enlisted men).

Without question, Fort Lewis initially mirrored other out-of-the-way western military posts in the nineteenth century. The fort's accessibility was increased with the improvement of the twelve-mile-long road leading into

Durango. When the railroad reached the community in July 1881, the fort could no longer be considered remote.

During his nearly two years there from 1881 to 1883, post surgeon Bernard Byrne left an excellent firsthand account of life at the post, in which he described the fort's seasonal routine:

> Winter at Fort Lewis was a dreary time. Shut in from the outer world by heavy snows and bitter winds, we had to depend upon ourselves for amusements and recreation. Our social life was spent almost entirely on dinners, card parties, musicals and so on, and the rivalry was acute. In fact, as months passed, we became too critical. We saw each other too intimately; factions were formed, unkind remarks repeated; we approached the time when cool bows replaced the former cordial greeting. As in a large family, no peculiarity escaped censure. The military parades and concerts given once a week would often soften this hostile spirit.
>
> Then summer would break upon us and all was changed. We forgot our grievances in the magic of perfect weather. . . . Outdoor sports and activities were kept up all day.
>
> We had picnics into the mountains under ideal conditions, horseback rides through gorgeous scenery that made one glad to be alive.[1]

Indeed, the post's location along the La Plata River looking north to the La Plata Mountains provided a spectacular setting.

Surviving those cold, snowy months required planning. On January 13, 1888, the *Durango Herald* noted that the people at Fort Lewis "make the best use of winter months" by organizing social clubs and "make it a point to give entertainments and dances every week or two." Durangoans often joined in the fun, and the newspaper noted that "those who have the pleasure of attending, report the Fort people very sociable."

As Byrne described in his journal, winter came early and did not quickly let up its grip. The long valley coming out of La Plata Canyon caused snow to funnel in from the mountains to the site of the post. The abundant snow interfered with troops at Fort Lewis and in the field. Because it frequently blocked roads in every direction, soldiers often asked for early discharges to be sure that they would not be stuck at the fort past their time of service. The possibility of serving extra time was a concern for Spencer Reeves, who asked to be "discharged before the expiration of his term of service" to avoid the "snow blockades likely to occur on the railroad." Robert Schuhast requested the same thing in November 1886, forty-one days before the end of his term of service, because "of the deep snows prevailing about that time." Even as early as December 1880, before the men had faced a winter in the canyon, four men asked for and were granted discharges to avoid getting stuck.

The worst winter weather took place during the infamous winter of 1883–1884, earning the moniker "winter of the century." Snow up to twenty-five feet high blocked the Denver & Rio Grande Railroad. To avoid running out, Durango merchants borrowed 2,000 pounds of sugar from the post, which had sufficient stores to pamper the town's sweet tooth. Troops could not respond to a request to come to Mancos to help cattlemen harassed by Navajos. Snow five to eight feet deep stopped them. For both the post and Durango, the only way out was to travel south to Fort Wingate, a six-day journey. Not until April did the roads clear enough to make travel possible. After that terrible winter, many troopers requested early discharges in the fall to avoid getting stuck for another winter. The freezing weather also caused its share of problems.

The region's abundant snowfall caused problems every winter and forced the officers to carefully manage their troops. In November 1886, Lieutenant Colonel Swaine reported to his district commander that deep snow had made it difficult to supply troops in the field so he had reduced the force along the San Juan River. During the winter of 1890–1891, the post received nineteen feet of snow, which shut down mail delivery for twenty-eight days. And the possibility of snow closing the railroad was a particular concern for the post commander. As General Superintendent Robert E. Ricker explained to the quartermaster of the Department of Missouri, the railroad intended to keep the road open, "unusual storms and snow blockade excepted."

Yet, often this goal was unrealistic. In March 1891, a report observed that it would "be necessary to shovel tons of snow" to open the road. In February alone they had received sixteen feet of snow. Sometimes, however, the abundant snowfall could work to an individual's advantage. Two soldiers en route to Fort Lewis wired that they were snowbound at Fort Logan outside Denver and would be delayed for an unspecified time.

Keeping warm was another challenge. Determined to carefully manage fuel, coal, and wood consumption, the army from September 1 through April 30 parceled out allowances to the various buildings, including offices, homes, the hospital, and barracks, to avoid running out before the end of the season and to prevent sudden, heavy expenditures in response to the freezing weather and cold winds that whistled down the canyon from the La Plata Mountains.[2]

For some, the elevation took its toll, causing shortness of breath or more serious ailments. At least one officer worried about the elevation's effect on the sun's strength: "[T]he sun at this great altitude is powerful." Campaign hats were a necessity to counteract the bright sun and its glare and in 1885 the post ran short when these hats were left off the annual supply estimates.

To help pass the long winters at the post, the residents of Fort Lewis attended parties and dances and traveled to town, when possible. According to Byrne, the officers generally got along. As seen with the relationship between Crofton and Peshine, however, there were problems at this lonely post. Tensions among Fort Lewis's small corps of officers probably existed. After all, these officers were not serving a prime tour of duty and they may have worried that their careers were not on the right track. Personalities can play a decisive role in such situations.

Something as seemingly straightforward as the selection of quarters could generate problems for the entire post. For example, when 1st Lt. Thomas Townsend requested quarters, he was told he could select "any vacant quarters or quarters occupied by officers of a junior grade of rank," as was standard practice in the army. By electing to move into an already occupied bunk, he could cause a domino effort, displacing a number of men. Obviously, this situation had the potential for creating much turmoil and unhappiness at the post.

This issue became yet another problem in Peshine and Crofton's ongoing feud, when Crofton refused to have quarters vacated for Peshine. When an officer junior to Peshine received quarters superior to his, Lieutenant Peshine charged "prejudice, discomfort and injury of a senior" officer. He relied on "army custom from time immemorial," 1863 regulations, and a prior decision of the War Department to support his case.[3]

Peshine's complaint notwithstanding, the officers' quarters at Fort Lewis seem to have been adequate or better. The July 4, 1885, issue of *Idea* described them as excellent in an article about 1st Lt. Medad Martin taking his family to live at the post: "[T]he happy family will go to their splendid home" at the post.

As with Peshine and Crofton, the complaints about living quarters mostly stemmed from perceived slights rather than from the quality of the accommodations. Recent West Point graduate Amos Shattuck protested the transfer of his cook to the commanding officer, stating that "it is the custom of this post to employ enlisted men as servants and cooks." Shattuck believed himself to be "entitled the same privilege as other officers serving at the post" and carried his protest all the way to the department commander, who declined to intervene.

But sometimes officers needed to be reprimanded for behavior problems. Second Lieutenant Edward Ord got in trouble for being absent two days without leave. After an investigation, the department warned Ord that his "reputation for being tardy, careless and thoughtless" caused concern. "Further lapses in this direction will not be overlooked." Ord straightened up and served into the twentieth century. Occasionally officers were reprimanded for less serious matters, such as failure to exercise horses, nonattendance at a duty call, or oversleeping at reveille. One officer, who must have been a sound sleeper, claimed that he had slept through first call, the morning gun, and reveille; this excuse was deemed unsatisfactory by his commanding officer.

A more significant infraction by an officer took place in late 1886 involving 2nd Lt. John Shaw of the Sixth Infantry. A native New Yorker, Shaw had come up through the ranks, advancing from private to corporal, to sergeant, and then to first sergeant between June 1875 and June 1880. In June 1880 he was promoted to second lieutenant, and was one of the few men in the postwar army to pass between enlisted and officer ranks. Accused of "having drawn his pay four times for December 1886," he was arrested. In May 1887 the army "dropped" Shaw from the service.[4]

Sometimes officers were pulled into disagreements between companies. The officers of Companies A and D argued about Company D's forcible taking of a root cellar used by Company A. This "unjustly unmilitary and illegal" action was ultimately resolved and an extra "root house" was dug.

Isolated as the post was, that did not mean the officers failed to study and discuss the latest tactics, regulations, and related topics. In the winter of 1889–1890, they met twice a week. A junior officer might present a paper "upon a professional subject, either original or copied," before a meeting or in a study session. This was the officer's lyceum; regulations in the 1880s required all officers at all posts to participate. An army veterinarian also came to Fort Lewis to give instructions to officers and troops.

Fort Lewis's isolation caused numerous officer requests for leave. A wide range of reasons prompted these requests. Captain Gustavus Bascom asked permission to go home and take care of his sick wife in Ohio; Swaine went to New York and Ohio on an 1884 leave; Capt. Will Daugherty traveled to Michigan to complete his degree as a master mason; and Capt. Mott Hooton for his health asked "to go to his home to take a rest from official duties and recuperate." Both officers and enlisted men were granted furloughs or leaves, the length of which could be even three, four, or six months.

Concerned about officers' health, including their vision, the army in 1889 relieved all those forty-five years of age or older from compulsory target practice. For the officers remaining at the post, life went on with their varied obligations to meet before their tour of duty ended.

Hunting was one way for the officers to blow off steam and relieve the tedium of life at the post. In his memoir, Byrne described hunting as particularly popular with the officers. Not just a sport, hunting provided welcome fresh meat for the company mess. The frequently requested hunting passes were issued, along with pack mules and as many as a dozen enlisted men, for support for a week or longer, which indicates that these trips were not purely recreational. Some hunting trips seemed to be more for sport, as when Colonel Swaine took a week off in the fall of 1886 to hunt and fish.[5]

From the outset, a few women—laundresses or wives of officers or enlisted men—lived at Fort Lewis. Sometimes the soldiers' wives worked as laundresses, but generally laundresses were not military wives. As a scholar noted, "[N]o one ever referred to laundresses as ladies." Officers' wives were readily and enthusiastically accepted into Durango society, but laundresses and even the wives of enlisted men were shut out.

At the post, the different social classes mostly stayed to themselves, but isolation and necessity led to some interaction. In her study of army wives, Anne Butler found that the harshness, danger, and new experiences of life in the West challenged the more traditional eastern ideas of womanhood, civilization, and class, causing "the officers' wives to lower prejudices and expectations" and "help[ing to] form bridges between groups of women at western outposts." This breakdown of class, race, and social barriers led these women to gain new insights into and appreciation of other classes and the society as a whole.

The children at Fort Lewis must have found life exhilarating. Boys especially had a grand playground of a river, plateaus, woods, and nearby mountains. They could ride, hunt, fish, hike, play baseball, and do almost anything else that boys dreamed of doing in the grand adventure of living at a military post. Young girls, on the other hand, were more circumscribed in what they could do, because their mothers did not want them to become tomboys. The children also benefited from the educational opportunities at the fort, which were better than average.

Marrying an army man led to a life of frequent travel and participating in the male-dominated military life. It meant sharing the isolation and loneliness, physical hardships, and often poor quarters of remote western posts. It meant worrying about whether her husband would return when he left on a campaign. Contrary to their children's relatively carefree lives, army wives faced more than their fair share of worries as they tried to provide a stable home life and instill Victorian American values in a young generation not always so accepting of middle-class standards.[6]

The ready supply of alcohol and prostitutes also caused problems for these women. Unwilling to adjust their expectations on these issues, women at the post and in Durango condemned the "hog ranch" (a saloon located close to the post), red-light district, and prostitution. The Woman's Christian Temperance Union, which had a strong chapter in Durango, worked hard to ban the sale of alcohol at army posts, but it is not known how involved the army wives were in this cause. Without question, they were aware of and affected by the problems caused by "Demon Rum." And it was particularly bad around paydays, when drunks would pick fights, pass out, and cause general mayhem.[7]

The post trader's store was one source of alcohol and other, less troublesome problems. A vital institution at the isolated frontier post, this store sold items such as cigars, writing paper, playing cards, needles, tobacco, and liquor and also served as a community center. The officers at the post fixed up the backroom as a clubhouse, and Byrne, a frequent customer, recalled hearing the sounds of trading going on as civilians and soldiers came in to purchase items at the store.

The post trader's store was managed by John Price, who had been appointed by the post council in 1880 and who also served as postmaster. There initially was some controversy over this appointment, when the post trader at Pagosa Springs argued that he should have received the appointment. He had appealed his case to the Secretary of War, but lost.

Price's tenure was marked by a variety of complaints concerning overcharging for inferior products and not accepting checks. Most of the complaints, however, involved liquor. Originally the army allowed alcohol at military posts, but an executive order that was part of an 1885 reform move prohibited it. The War Department informed post commanders that the order "is imperative and admits to no exception." Yet, some exceptions evidently existed because the post surgeon declared that California sherry could be placed on the "list of light wines and may be sold as such."

Despite the ban, John Price continued to sell alcoholic products with the tacit acknowledgment of the post's officers. Two years after the executive order, the adjutant general in Washington warned the commanding officer that "greater vigilance in the future is expected from those in authority at Fort Lewis, and that Mr. Price the Post Trader must be given to understand that the slightest departure from this order hereafter will result in forfeiture of his appointment."

Alcohol was plentiful and it was impossible to keep it away from the post. When Pvt. Patrick McSweeny showed up at the post drunk, rumors claimed he had purchased a pint of whiskey from the trader. An investigation revealed that he had returned drunk from Durango and "at the time had two quart bottles of whisky, offering that to everyone he came into contact with." Price escaped trouble that time, but later was charged with selling "ardent spirits" to hospital attendants "without written request from the post surgeon" and selling enough wine to a musician to make "him stupidly drunk."[8]

The saloon, called the "hog ranch" by locals, that was located within "two miles of the post flag staff" was yet another source of the devil's brew and prostitution. The land on which the saloon had been built had belonged to a homesteader, who had already taken up this land before the establishment of the military reservation. He proved up on the land and in 1883 sold it to an entrepreneur who promptly opened a saloon.

The new owner, Ed Rebstock, gave Swaine a great deal of trouble. In August 1885 Swaine complained to the adjutant general in Washington that the saloon's proximity "is not only a great annoyance at all times," but the owner expressed the intent to undermine "the interest of discipline in my command." Rebstock's methods were distracting at the very least; he would trail after the troops in the field, bringing along a wagonful of tempting liquor. The officer in charge protested to the civil authorities, arousing the ire of Rebstock, who, according to reports, "threatens now to draw soldiers to his place by means of *dance girls as well as whisky*." Rebstock also owned a saloon in Durango, where he advertised "the finest whisky in the San Juans sold over the bar at two drinks for a quarter."

So long as the post trader was not allowed to sell whiskey to soldiers, it was "impossible to devise means to prevent the men visiting low drinking places." Swaine contended that "good discipline could be maintained when the privilege was exercised under supervision," such as with a post store. Thus, Swaine recommended that "under the trying circumstances," the post trader be allowed to sell liquor "to thwart the evil designs of outside parties."

But it seemed that nothing could stop the nocturnal visits of wayward soldiers to the hog ranch around payday. An entrepreneurial trooper made it easier for these men when he made available "a kind of livery stable for his comrades" to use for their excursions, "going to the 'shacks,' which is extremely detrimental to the discipline of the post." He even had the audacity to stable his horses at the fort! Once the post commander found out about this, the private was "not to be allowed to keep any animals whatever which bused transportation within the limits of the reservation."

So-called hog ranches dotted the western landscape, serving a variety of customers. They offered gambling, prostitution, and whiskey, quite often of a questionable nature. More than one soldier found himself court-martialed after being found at the ranch and charged with "absence without authority" or "absent without permission," and more were hauled in for being drunk during or following a visit.

For soldiers willing to travel a little farther, Durango offered better liquor, entertainment, and women. The popularity of Durango's attractions is evidenced by the growth of Durango's red-light district in the 1880s. The quality of liquor, entertainment, and the "fair but frail" definitely rated better in the city. In comparison, hog ranches generally were the bottom-dwellers of the red-light world.[9]

Although officially prohibited from selling alcohol, Price had only restricted, but not eliminated, sales. The issue of Price's selling liquor came to a head when Capt. Javan Irwin filed a complaint in 1887 about the trader selling intoxicating liquors to the soldiers and others. Irwin's complaint, combined with pressure from Washington, forced Price to remove liquor from his store in July 1887. Swaine, supported by the post council, then recommended that Price be deposed as post trader and that a post canteen be established. The canteen opened in November 1888.

Canteens were clubs for enlisted men and became popular in the 1880s. Based on the British army model, canteens were supposed to keep the men away from gambling, drinking, and whoring at the hog ranches and in nearby towns. The canteen offered beer and light wines, as well as wholesome amusements. Officers hoped that the canteens not only would solve some disciplinary problems but also would improve morale and put an end to the traders' price gouging.[10]

Captain Adam Kramer wholeheartedly supported the canteen's establishment, stating that the trader had the soldiers entirely at his mercy with his monopoly and high prices for inferior products and "limited quantity and variety of goods." After the canteen opened, Kramer was able to boast for the first time in his more than twenty-five years of service that no man in his company had been "confined since 'pay-day' and none of the company now is in the guard house." Believing the canteen at least partially responsible for this result, Kramer bluntly and firmly stated in his long report of August 1888 that the canteen "will be better for discipline and comfort of the men than any post trader, while proximity of Durango (twelve miles) affords facility for trading not common to the canteen." In his report, the captain voiced his support for the sale of new sweet cider, which he felt "more conducive to temperance and good order if properly controlled as it is than the sale of either beer or alleged light wine elsewhere."[11]

Major Tullius Tupper, who replaced Swaine, also enthusiastically supported the canteen in his report to the adjutant general in Washington: "I have observed very little drunkenness and believe that as a rule the men are inclined to behave themselves better than under the old Post Trader system. The greatest danger to the canteen system will probably be found in the desire for excessive profits for benefit for company funds." At Fort Lewis, these profits were divided between the companies and the hospital. Tupper did handle one controversy regarding the proposed establishment of an officers' club at the canteen. The one that Byrne had mentioned was apparently gone and the post's officers now wanted one to be added to the canteen. Tupper felt it impracticable to attach three rooms solely for the officers' use and recommended that if they wanted a club, it "should be fitted up at their expense."[12]

The canteen had a lunch counter featuring pies, cakes, ham and eggs, iced milk, tea, and coffee. Games like dominoes and checkers were available, and cigars, tobaccos, iced lemonade, stationary, and "a long list of other articles needful for soldiers" were sold as near to cost as practicable with the "object constantly in view being to sell cheaply." A tenpin alley was "reconstructed" from an earlier one and opened free to those wanting to play. As the companies already had enough billiard tables, the canteen did not have any.

A "beer department," separate from the canteen, sold the "best obtainable quality" by "drink, draught, and bottled," not the "inferior article of Denver or Durango beer." Alcoholic offerings were strictly controlled as the canteen would not sell "other compounds under the guise of being nonalcoholic." In reality, national consumption of beer in the United States jumped during the 1880s (to an estimated 13.5 gallons per capita by 1890!) as nickel beer surpassed hard liquor as the drink of choice for many.[13]

Interestingly, Price continued as trader during this period, because the Secretary of War was content to allow the store and canteen to exist simultaneously so long as the canteen did not "infringe" upon the trader. Despite, or perhaps because of, his willingness to flout the prohibition, Price had more than a few supporters, even among the officers. Some officers had written a letter supporting Price, who reopened his store in July 1888 after a brief closure. The sign in his window read "Enlisted Men's Saloon" and "new stock is fresh and cool." One private, who seems to have been actively writing only during 1888, wrote a letter supporting the reopening: "If men must drink, it is much better to furnish liquor" at the post than "necessitate visiting the Hog Ranch."

The competition between the new canteen and Price's store produced more controversy. Price protested that his "right for exclusive sale of goods" was infringed on, "causing a falling off of receipts." Meanwhile, the Secretary of War decided that canteens should replace trading establishments and on January 31, 1889, revoked Price's appointment, giving him ninety days to conclude his business. But Price managed to keep his appointment and store, even securing official approval to continue as post trader "until the post shall be abandoned."[14]

The situation at Fort Lewis reflected what was happening throughout the army. Post traders had protested the establishment of canteens. In 1888 and 1889, the government vacillated between forbidding the sale of alcoholic beverages and directing that canteens not be conducted to infringe on the traders' rights. Many officers supported the establishment of canteens, citing, as Kramer had, that canteens reduced drunkenness and improved discipline. Ultimately, in early 1889, near the end of Fort Lewis's existence, the War Department decided in favor of the canteens. Obviously, there existed two sides to the discussion about Price and his tradership. Price served a need but he occasionally stretched the bounds, which was typical in nineteenth-century America.

In addition to the trader's store and the canteen, the troopers had other recreational outlets. An amusement room included billiard tables. And, in the absence of a formal physical training program, sports proved beneficial to the physical well-being of the men. Boxing, foot racing, wrestling, an early form of football, and baseball, which was the most popular team sport, were most popular at the posts. Blacks and Whites mingled freely in these activities, color forgotten if a man could hit, field, run, and help the post's nine to victory. More genteel individuals could try "Presbyterian billiards" (croquet) or even cricket.

Perhaps the most popular "sport" was gambling, which rivaled drinking as the scourge of western forts. Officers' attempts to eliminate gambling were unsuccessful; it was easy enough for the players to relocate to a site away from prying officers. The post trader's store often served as a favorite retreat, which perhaps is another reason why some officers opposed that institution. But gambling could be found everywhere.

To counter the negative influences of alcohol, gambling, and prostitution, Fort Lewis, like other western posts, had a library, school, and chapel. The reading room and library were open twelve hours a day and contained books, journals, and newspapers (Colorado and national). The money allotted per year per company amounted to $22. At its peak population in 1884, Fort Lewis had eight companies, giving it a library budget of $176.

The selection of reading materials available to the men was outstanding and even aroused concern at least once because it seemed more than the post could afford. Post commander Maj. Robert Hall in April 1884 ordered $112.53 of daily newspapers, including papers from Chicago, Denver, Kansas City, New York, Omaha, San Antonio, San Francisco, St. Paul, and Washington, D.C. The magazines covered an equally wide spectrum, from *Harpers* and *Frank Leslie's Illustrated* to *Puck*, *Forest and Stream*, and the *Grand Army Gazette*. Interestingly, when the *Army and Navy Journal* refused to supply its paper at a requested rate, the quartermaster general in Washington struck it from the list of newspapers available.

Supplementing the library was the school, which offered classes for children and adults living at the post. Many recruits had little or no education, relying on the army for an education of sorts. Frequently, it was the post chaplains who organized the schools at western posts with many of these chaplains devoting much of their time to educational activities. It is not clear if this situation was the case at Fort Lewis, but many of Fort Lewis's chaplains operated the post library in addition to their other duties.

Finding good teachers was a challenge. Teachers were typically drawn from the ranks of enlisted men, for whom teaching was extra duty. Occasionally, if discipline was bad, a noncommissioned officer would temporarily take over, but he had to receive departmental approval to do so. The adult school met during off-duty hours and taught the three R's to immigrants and illiterates. The quality of teaching was uneven and the schedule could be unpredictable. At least one term was canceled because the required books had not yet been sent. Generally funds for books came from post and regimental funds because the War Department provided no direct financial support for the purchase of schoolbooks. Inadequate facilities and textbook shortages also caused problems.[15]

The children's classes were held separately according to a special regulation of the army. The children had their own teacher, who occasionally examined volunteers for the adult school to see if they were "well acquainted with the branches taught." Finding qualified teachers must have been a considerable problem at many western posts. Tupper once requested that a trooper whose company was leaving Fort Lewis be transferred instead to a company remaining at Fort Lewis because "his services are invaluable as a school teacher and can be replaced with the greatest difficulty" and "not at all with the material here." Finding qualified teachers definitely presented a problem at Fort Lewis. To gain some extra pay, Jacob Moore, the post schoolteacher in 1890, also served as the census enumerator.

At one point, the officers became concerned that their children went to school with those of the enlisted men. Captain Powell and others requested a separate school for their children, but the post adjutant refused based on financial grounds. He told the officers that they "may make arrangement" for the private instruction of their children, "provided such instruction does not interfere with the requirement of the regular school."

Religion was a part of military life at the post, but it is unlikely that chaplains served the garrison continuously throughout the decade. Occasionally the soldiers attended services conducted by a minister or priest from Durango. Services were held in the school building or other rooms, and temperance meetings utilized the post hall because the fort did not have a chapel for most of its life. Without a designated chapel, the chaplains faced a disadvantage in gathering a flock on Sundays.

The other obstacle chaplains faced was the enlisted men's lack of interest in formal religion. Many officers seemed indifferent to a ministry at the posts as well. No requests came from Fort Lewis for a post chaplain. The temperance movement perhaps created a conflict between the chaplains, who saw drunkenness as a formidable problem, and the soldiers.

Even if Fort Lewis had requested a chaplain, it might not have been possible to provide one. There were not enough chaplains to serve all the military posts, and Fort Lewis must have been low on the priority list. The dearth of chaplains might have been the result of Protestant churches' lack of interest in the military services for evangelistic and military activity, even as they expanded their missionary campaigns after the Civil War. And not all chaplains measured up to being the sole person responsible for providing adequate sermons, personal counseling, and religious training. Also, Durango was close enough to easily satisfy ministerial functions such as marriages and baptisms.

In 1889, however, the post did have a chaplain, but one who did not present a favorable impression. Going against the typical anti-liquor position, he planned to sell liquor at a fair held to raise funds to fix up the post chapel until he was stopped by several officers. At the fair, only beer and light wine, as "refreshment only," were ultimately allowed. When this chaplain, identified only as the Rev. W.J. Larkin, retired for medical reasons, he left behind debts with Durango businessmen and the post canteen plus an overdrawn checking account. Even as the post closed, measures were being taken to secure the money from his pension. Larkin "hopes to be able to accommodate" his creditors, an officer wrote.[16]

The library, school, and chapel services remained available to the men at the post throughout the 1880s and obviously were used and supported to the point that they remained open. They were civilizing influences both for the garrison and for nearby civilians who took advantage of the opportunities. Whatever else may be said about these three institutions, "the participants had certainly become better soldiers, and in the final analysis, that is what the army demanded most."[17]

In 1885 a bowling alley ("ten-pin alley") and shooting gallery were built to entertain the troops. This construction project nearly ran out of money and was saved by a contribution from the post fund. It is not known how much the bowling alley and shooting gallery were used, but reports indicate that the bowling alley was not well maintained. "Badly placed" in the midst of the storehouses, the bowling alley was reported as "somewhat unsafe as regards to fire" in 1889.

Fort Lewis also provided a good core of musical entertainment. The post had a band and a singing troop, the "Ft. Lewis Original Minstrels," who performed at the post and nearby towns. Dances, lectures, picnics, and horse races also gained their devotees. Sergeant George Courtright fondly described the activities available: "There was a large recreation hall at the northeast end of the fort. In this was a good stage with curtain, backdrop, and well-painted scenery. Many amateur plays were given there. There was no lack of amusement." The recreation hall described by Courtright was typical for western posts. There might not have been a chapel, but Fort Lewis had a place to dance. As the saying went, the "army loved to dance."

Other social activities at the post and in nearby Durango occupied the men. Union veterans of the Civil War could attend meetings at a Grand Army of the Republic post in Durango. Some groups were more philanthropically minded, such as the group of officers who in December 1883 contributed money to help complete the pedestal for the Statue of Liberty.

Holidays such as Christmas, Thanksgiving, the Fourth of July, and Decoration Day (particularly for Civil War veterans) were observed. The participation of the Fort Lewis drummers, fifers, trumpeters, and band proved popular at these observances in nearby communities where Union veterans resided in substantial numbers. The garrison paid tribute to deceased individuals, such as Presidents James Garfield and Chester Arthur and Gens. George Crook and Phil Sheridan, with special ceremonies.

The quiet activity of gardening both passed the time and benefited the garrison as a whole. Beans, carrots, onions, squash, rutabaga, pumpkins, corn, okra, eggplant, celery, and horseradish root were grown. Wisely, some company gardeners started seeds in hotbeds before planting. Aided by mules that pulled plows, cultivators, planters, and other farm instruments, the men worked to cultivate their gardens in less than ideal conditions. Some seeds proved nearly worthless, late and early frosts created havoc, and insects ate more than their fair share. Even the post's resident hogs and cattle enjoyed a nibble now and then. The elevation, arid climate, and short growing season also made gardening a daunting challenge. The men used their engineering skills to irrigate company plots, which were located near the post.

But the gardens were worth the trouble; they added seasonal variety to meals, made scurvy less of a problem, and provided a healthier diet. The harvest from Fort Lewis's gardens was supplemented by farms in the surrounding agricultural communities. And the men turned the quiet pastime of gardening into a sport. Surgeon Byrne recalled the friendly rivalry among the soldiers over which garden produced the finest crops; the winning company received a dance.

Indeed, disputes broke out over these gardens, which must have been the source of company pride and represented an investment of time and money. One such dispute resulted from a troop being transferred before it could harvest its vegetables. The F Troop of the Sixth Cavalry was transferred to Fort Wingate; the troopers asked M Troop from Fort Leavenworth, the troop that replaced them at Fort Lewis, for reimbursement for the cost of their seeds because they had not received what they considered a just return. But the members of M Troop also had a grievance because they had received nothing for the garden they left behind, which they described as "more than double the value of what they received here."

Captain William Carter of M Troop investigated as "carefully and thoroughly as possible" to decide the value of the garden products received by his troop. The 1,600 heads of very poor cabbage, according to Captain Carter, were "thrown out to the hogs." His men also harvested a "few potatoes so small as to be of no market value," forcing the company to purchase about $100 worth of potatoes from a local ranchman. "In plain words, the garden here was a failure and F Troop ought not to expect M Troop to pay under this circumstance since the vegetables were hardly worth digging and hauling." Carter believed that the harvest was not worth much; even seven dollars would be "a high valuation" for the things received, but "I presume it will be necessary to pay for them."

Not content, F Troop's commander hinted that the garden's poor yield was the result of M Troop's neglect and that his company considered the garden worth $90.62. Not until the following March, a full six months later, was the matter settled without "further" adjustment. Such episodes proved common among forts in the West as companies transferred quite frequently. Companies seeking reimbursement for left-behind crops consumed much time as they filed numerous reports and appeals.[18]

Citizens of neighboring towns interacted with Fort Lewis in a variety of ways as the post continued to make a significant impact on the nonmilitary life of southwestern Colorado. Some families lived on or near the post and their children probably attended the post school; some used the hospital as Byrne described and others occasionally rode in to purchase goods from the trader.

Infrequently, a "destitute citizen" needing some help would straggle in. Congress never gave the military official authority to treat civilian ailments and accident victims, but civilians could generally count on ranking officers to approve treatment and many routinely expected it. One report, however, reveals that Captain Kramer ordered a civilian seeking assistance off the post immediately. It is not known why.

Sometimes the interaction between civilians and the military post was the result of misdeeds. In June 1887, two wayward civilians were arrested for stealing government supplies and turned over to Durango authorities. Because state authorities did not have jurisdiction over military reservation matters, the police were unable to take further action. Because the goods had been recovered, the post commander decided to simply order them off the reservation; no doubt they never came back.[19]

The fort's predominant masculine world—with its gambling, drinking, and prostitution—resembled that of a mining town rather than a farming community. For the men stationed there, Fort Lewis probably offered a more relaxed life and enjoyable environment than the typical western frontier garrison, despite its small size and relative isolation. Fort Lewis should have been a pleasant tour of duty for the soldier from the deserts and dangers of New Mexico, Arizona, and Texas or from the hot, windy high plains of Nebraska, Kansas, and Wyoming.

GOD OF BATTLES

In Shakespeare's *Henry V*, King Henry, just before the battle of Agincourt rages, "O God of battles! Steel my soldiers' hearts." The victory went to the English that day, and although the officers and troopers at Fort Lewis never engaged in such an epic event, they were part of a defensive line in the post–Civil War West. As such, they provided a valuable service and eventually joined their comrades in the legendary saga of the settlement of the American West.

The officers were professionals, but most of their men were new recruits who served only one tour of enlistment before moving on. No fame and glory rode with them out of Fort Lewis and they did not engage in any storied campaigns. The daily routine of duty at this isolated post in southwestern Colorado was broken only by patrols and camping in

135

the field. Yet, their experience was typical for the army in the 1870s and 1880s.

Most of them left no photographic record of their lives at Fort Lewis, but a few images—mostly those of officers—have been saved.

Ninth Cavalry on patrol. Courtesy, Wells Fargo Bank, Pagosa Springs

Company A, Twenty-Second Infantry, at Fort Lewis, ca. 1885. Courtesy, Colorado Historical Society

Troopers practicing field medicine while on maneuvers. Courtesy, Center of Southwest Studies

Wedding photograph of Sgt. Conrad Oldershausen and Elizabeth Graham. She was a post cook and he was stationed at Fort Lewis when they met. Courtesy, Donna Lauer

Utes occasionally visited Fort Lewis. The post briefly served as their agency headquarters. Courtesy, Duane A. Smith

Troopers line up in front of their barracks in the mid-1880s. Courtesy, Montana Historical Society

Twenty-Second Infantry soldiers and one civilian strike up a jaunty pose. Courtesy, Montana Historical Society

Band concerts furnished important entertainment at Fort Lewis. No photographs exist of a band at the post, but these relaxed members of the Sixth Cavalry Band played there. Courtesy, Arizona Historical Society/Tucson

The Ninth Cavalry Band, shown here in the Santa Fe Plaza, was a popular attraction wherever it performed. Courtesy, Museum of New Mexico

After serving as commanding officer at Pagosa Springs, Maj. Francis Dodge, Ninth Cavalry, received the Medal of Honor for gallantry in action during the Meeker troubles. Courtesy, U.S. Army Military History Institute

Fort Lewis at Pagosa Springs did not impress Maj. Alfred Hough. Courtesy, U.S. Army Military History Institute

Lt. Col. Robert Crofton was the first post commander of Fort Lewis on the La Plata River. Courtesy, U.S. Army Military History Institute

Young Lt. John Peshine raised questions about Crofton's priorities. Courtesy, U.S. Army Military History Institute

Capt. Mott Hooton supported Navajo rights against settlers' complaints. Courtesy, U.S. Army Military History Institute

Capt. Adam Kramer believed that the post school needed more than one teacher. Courtesy, U.S. Army Military History Institute

Capt. Tullius Cicero Tupper (top row, fifth from left) chased down rumors in 1890, before moving on to the troubles at the Pine Ridge reservation. In the front row, second from the right, sit Capt. William Carter and next to him, Capt. Adam Kramer. Courtesy, U.S. Army Military History Institute

"Many men in my command are about barefooted and need clothing generally," reported Capt. Henry Carroll about his Ninth Cavalry troopers. Courtesy, U.S. Army Military History Institute

A much younger post adjutant, Maj. Robert Hall, found the heavy snowfall in 1884 to be a grave problem. He also later served as post commander. Courtesy, U.S. Army Military History Institute

Not all Fort Lewis life focused on military matters. Col. Peter Swaine, Capt. William Conway, Capt. Charles Miner, and their families went on a fishing trip. *Courtesy, Montana Historical Society*

Officers of the Twenty-Second Infantry at camp on the Pine River between fishing jaunts. *Courtesy, Montana Historical Society*

Both William and Fanny Corbusier left accounts of their lives at Fort Lewis. Here they are with their family while stationed at Fort Grant, Arizona, in January 1888. Courtesy, Arizona Historical Society/Tucson

SEVEN

Uncle Sam's Bonanza

We'll beat the bailiffs out of fun,
We'll make the mayors and sheriffs run;
We are the boys no man dares dun,
If he regards a whole skin.

"Garry Owen"

Despite the words of this verse of "Garry Owen," Fort Lewis and Durango got along very well, though now and then a spat. In a real sense, they needed each other. So did Fort Lewis and La Plata County. The impact of the Fort Lewis garrison was evident in census returns. The Colorado 1885 census showed that the county population had quadrupled over what it had been five years earlier. The 4,495 citizens of La Plata County in 1885 had increased marginally to only 5,509 in 1890, partly because of the military situation at Fort Lewis. The year 1885 was a peak period of garrison strength, boosting the 1885 population. By the 1890 census, the post, on the verge of abandonment, did not contribute significantly to La Plata's population. Rather, Durango and its subsequent railroad were responsible for the boom in La Plata's population.

The construction of Fort Lewis on the La Plata River and the settlement of neighboring Durango on the Animas River started within a month of each other, in August and September 1880. On November 15, 1879, the *La Plata Miner* had forecast that a new town would be established in the Animas Valley within a year. The prediction came true when Denver & Rio Grande officials, stymied by Animas City's refusal to meet the railroad's terms, decided to start a rival community that would become the railroad hub of southwestern Colorado.

The resulting town became known as Durango. The town's first survey stake was driven on September 13, 1880. To its upstart rival, Animas City lost most of its businesses and a third of its population, languishing as the iron horse chugged by on its way to Silverton and the San Juan mines. Animas City's day as the preeminent city in southwestern Colorado vanished in a twinkling.

Backed by the railroad, Durango attracted more than 2,000 enthusiastic people, who crowded into the new "metropolis" by Christmas, doubling La Plata County's population from the previous summer. Most of the new residents were Protestant and of northern European stock and many had lived in Colorado before arriving on the banks of the Animas. Merchants, doctors, lawyers, laborers, housewives, ministers, saloon keepers, and the like—they represented a typical cross section of a western town.

Durango evolved into a unique mining, smelting, and agricultural community with railroad connections. The railroad boomed urbanization here as it did throughout post–Civil War America. Gaining the desired tracks ensured a community's future. Those that failed to attract the railroad found themselves in deep trouble, if not terminal decline.

Nothing exemplified the symbol and substance of modern industrial America better than the railroad. Americans had fallen in love with the iron horse and its potential to improve their lives. The Denver & Rio Grande, Colorado's "baby railroad," took its narrow-gauge tracks (three feet as opposed to the standard gauge of four feet, eight and a half inches) to every mining region it could, overcoming seemingly insurmountable obstacles along the way. Locals welcomed its coming with open arms; the day of the "jubilee" had dawned.

The army had discovered the railroad's usefulness during the Civil War, the first American conflict in which it played a major role. Now, in the West, railroads transported troopers and supplies with an ease, speed, and thrift (a quality Congress particularly adored) unmatched in frontier history. It also cut the range of the Indian tribes into smaller segments, thus making the military's job with regard to the Indians simpler, if still difficult.

To sustain its growth, Durango had the railroad, coal mining, farming and ranching, tourism, smelting, lumbering, and abundant land to homestead. Best of all, in the 1880s, it had Fort Lewis. The presence of the garrison afforded safety and peace of mind. The fort provided an economic bonanza that was the envy of other less fortunate Colorado towns. For a decade, the post was the strongest economic pillar underlying Durango, the "new wonder of the southwest." And Durango's newspapers eagerly promoted their young community, "the magic city," from the beginning.

Despite their lingering local misgivings about Washington, the pioneers took advantage of Uncle Sam's economic support as they established new settlements in the West. The settlers benefited from the federal government's virtually giving away land and natural resources, establishing territorial governments, granting statehood, underwriting railroads, defending settlements, or establishing Indian reservations. Durango, too, prospered from a host of these governmental efforts, the most obvious of which was Fort Lewis.

Economic growth was limited only by the imaginations of residents who had something to sell or some service to provide. For Durangoans and residents of the surrounding area, Fort Lewis represented a financial windfall of marvelous possibility. Early settlers, who were often strapped for cash, could not have asked for a better resource and it was right at their back door. Fort Lewis became one of the largest purchasing and employment agencies in southwestern Colorado, a fact that locals did not overlook.

The Denver & Rio Grande had looked favorably on La Plata County because of its abundant coal resources. Coal mining began with the establishment of Durango and Fort Lewis and the post was an excellent customer. Locally mined coal was hauled in wagons (until the Rio Grande Southern Railroad was built) to the fort and was used to heat barracks, quarters, and offices for most of the decade.

Coal was also found within the boundaries of the military reservation, and the military planned on eventually developing this reserve to ease transportation costs. The army wasn't the only one with this plan. At least one overeager Durangoan, Andy Shore, tried to mine it without permission in 1884, but the army quickly put a halt to his claim jumping.

The military reservation also contained many trees, which could be cut for fuel. The military awarded contracts that specified exactly where and how much an individual or company could harvest. During the early construction of 1880–1881, military and civilian workers were employed in lumbering. Even in later years, the army continued to let contracts for lumber needed in further building projects. As part of his responsibilities, the fort's commanding officer worked to limit illegal cutting on the military reservation. Once, the commander had to deal with concerns about whether a sawmill on Lightner Creek was built on military reservation land. He also had to make sure that the post had an adequate supply of lumber, even if the prices seemed high. When the post commander purchased wood at nine dollars a cord in 1880, double the going rate of four to five dollars, it angered more than one taxpayer.

A steady stream of troopers, visitors, and wagons covered the twelve miles between town and post. For a short time, a stage carried mail and passengers between the two, but typically a buggy or buckboard limited to two passengers and a small amount of freight covered the route five times a week. Some enterprising civilians earned additional income by transporting recruits and dismounted soldiers from town to post at a rate of $1.50 per person when no other transportation was available.

Freighters eagerly bid on government contracts to haul supplies from Durango to the post. This could represent quite a windfall. The *Herald,* for example, noted on June 17, 1882, that three carloads of supplies had arrived and would soon be loaded on government wagons. Early in the decade, they had received payment of one dollar per hundred pounds, but by 1889 the rate dropped to twenty cents. The contract remained a good one, however, with dependable pay and steady work over the short haul to the fort.[1]

Only part of the road between Durango and Fort Lewis was public. The rest belonged to the Durango, Parrot City, and Fort Lewis Toll Road Company, which was operated by famous toll road and railroad builder Otto Mears. Thus, when Fort Lewis sent a semiweekly wagon to Durango for market supplies for officers and companies, the quartermaster paid the toll for the former and the companies paid their own, which to many seemed unfair. As one officer said, "[I]f right in one case, it is right in the other." Post commanders questioned whether the toll company had the legal right to collect tolls at all since some six or seven miles of the road possibly traversed the reservation. The toll road company, in turn, complained about late payments and the army's avoiding the toll gate, as 1st Lt. Benjamin Cheever did in October 1888. Using a detour on a practice march to Pagosa Springs, he avoided the charge of one dollar per horse, a quarter for a two-mule team, and a nickel for each pack animal, plus assorted charges for four- and six-mule teams. The amount that Cheever should have paid totaled $105.85.

A crisis struck in April 1883 when the toll road was closed to public transportation "on account of arrears running back to June 1, 1882." At least one officer promptly suggested that the road "lying on the military reservation be closed until the matter is settled." The matter eventually was resolved after reaching the Treasury Department. A May report to Washington pointed out that the toll road had existed before the government established the reservation and thus it was necessary that a "reasonable toll be fixed and paid to the company."

Even after the military agreed to pay the necessary tolls, the toll company worried about competitors building roads and requested at least once, in 1884, that Fort Lewis deny a request by La Plata County commissioners, who wanted to build a free road through Ridge's Basin. Supported by a petition from the citizens of La Plata County, the commissioners needed Washington's approval because a portion of the road cut through the reservation.

Captain Javan Irwin responded and pointed out that the government could not take sides, then went on to elaborate on some of the problems the post was facing. The toll road in the wet season proved "almost impassible for heavy teams" but "to my knowledge the county route runs through soil even more spongy." He questioned whether the proposed road would be "better or even as good as the toll road" during those wet seasons of the year. A free road, however, even if it was a mile or two longer, would be an advantage to the government during the dry months.

The Secretary of War ended the discussion in July 1885, when he rejected opening a public road through the reservation. No one is sure how profitable the toll road was, although Mears noted that he eventually sold out because it "did not pay well." Both soldiers and civilians regularly avoided tolls by taking a horseback trail "over the hill." Particularly after the problems of the homesteader and the hog ranch, the army definitely did not appreciate interloping by civilians.[2]

Other local business benefited from the fort's proximity. The telegraph line that ran between the post and town returned a profit for the local operator; the federal government paid the Durango operator twenty dollars each month to handle the post's business. The railroad earned revenue, transporting troopers, baggage, and carloads of supplies. To facilitate the logistical aspects of such a large project, the army hired a quartermaster agent in Durango at $100 a month through 1886, which was excellent compensation at the time. The freight master at the Durango depot received $50 to $60 per month. For at least some of these years an "old veteran" held this position.

Hotels and restaurants provided services for troopers and officers staying overnight in town. Banks prospered somewhat through individual deposits, although the Department of Missouri disapproved of company funds being deposited locally, even if the First National in Durango had a national bank charter. This was no surprise, considering the shaky reputation of some private and state banks in this era.[3]

Local newspapers also profited from the post's existence. The *Durango Herald* acquired a subscriber through the institution of the post library and gained news items with which to beguile their readers. Caroline Romney, for example, entertained her readers with a long account of the Fort Lewis ball in February 1881. She proudly listed all who attended and concluded, "All in all the party was a most brilliant success, of which the entire garrison may be proud." San Juan Hardware, "having heard the post needed garden tools and utensils," sent their price list and hopefully made a new customer.

Durango and La Plata County also obtained a few settlers from Fort Lewis. John R. Leonard, a onetime government agent, and his family settled in Durango, opening a cracker factory and investing in mines in Silverton. Other discharged soldiers may have joined them, but how many is unknown.

Durangoans also appreciated the positive publicity the community received from being near Fort Lewis. For the timid souls worrying about the West's rough connotations and the nearby presence of Utes, Fort Lewis might have encouraged them to visit, invest in local businesses, or even settle in the area. Fortunately, the garrison did not create any bad publicity as did some other western posts, which became notorious for their race riots, fights, and drunken brawls. Local contractors made considerable money throughout the decade as Fort Lewis built new additions and required ongoing repairs. The army gladly accepted a local firm's bid of $10,044 to construct the fort's hospital, as it was more than $1,000 under the estimate. When post construction originally began, 50,000 regular bricks and 40,000 adobe bricks were purchased on the open market, a boon for local firms.

As previously mentioned, farmers and ranchers also benefited from the market Fort Lewis provided. The demand for hay to feed the fort's animals at $60 a ton meant a steady income for the local supplier. The fort also offered farmers an opportunity to bid on the garrison's milk contract, with "exclusive privilege of the same until revoked." Vegetables, too, were needed to supplement the companies' gardens. Beef, purchased throughout the decade at six to eight cents per pound, helped immeasurably to make local ranching profitable, as did the fact that the government reimbursed anyone who lost cattle to "depredations," as they loved to call anything that disappeared around Indians.

Occasionally, local folk overpriced themselves, particularly in the early years. In September 1880, the post quartermaster requested permission to go to the open market, even as far away as Fort Leavenworth, Kansas, if he could not buy potatoes and onions at less than the local rate of three cents a pound. Finding goods at reasonable prices was made possible by the Denver & Rio Grande, which prevented the locals from having a monopoly. The railroad posed both a blessing and a threat to Durango's citizens and nearby farmers in their dealings with the fort. It lowered the cost of living and made transportation easier, but it also allowed the importation of cheaper supplies. Local businessmen and farmers often faced stiff competition to win military supply contracts.

In an emergency, however, the local suppliers had the advantage. At least one unnamed contractor from faraway Yankton, South Dakota, failed to fulfill his obligation to supply oats to the fort and this "caused much trouble and anxiety." Perhaps he underbid his competitors, then was faced with the reality of shipping the oats to southwestern Colorado.

Even those who won bids sometimes faced difficulties. A Durango merchant demanded that the post adjutant pay a bill for a pair of skates, after "three or four" bills produced no result. Another businessman had several unpaid bills and wanted the company commander to get the "monies due." One civilian, William Wannamaker from Cortez, simply wanted reimbursement for wood consumed by the cavalry camping on his land.[4]

The fort offered excellent wages for people with a variety of skills, from herders to blacksmiths and painters to construction superintendents. Bricklayers received a daily wage of $4; blacksmiths, $2–$5; and carpenters, $2–$2.80. Superintendents could earn $100 per month; engineers, $75; wagon masters, $60; teamsters, $30; and packers, $20. Corresponding wages in town were lower: a daily wage for bricklayers was $1.75–$2.50; for blacksmiths, $2.00–$4.00; and for carpenters, $2.00–$2.25.

As expected, monthly post returns indicated the number of civilians employed at the fort was highest during construction, quadrupling the typical number. March 1881, for instance, listed forty-one civilians, including twenty-seven carpenters, two bricklayers, and twelve teamsters. More typical were the returns for December 1886 and April 1888, listing ten and nine workers, respectively. Fort Lewis was an important employer, but not the largest in the Four Corners. The mining districts were too well established and Durango quickly grew too large to give the post a major employment role. Army dollars were still important, however, and the military dollar multiplied as it passed from hand to hand, helping farmers, laborers, merchants, and ranchers.

Sometimes a civilian found himself removed from the post. In 1888, the post adjutant, 1st Lt. Zerah Torrey, informed a civilian photographer he could not continue his photographic gallery at the fort and told him "you will be removed." What caused this remonstrance remains unstated. The next year, however, Durango photographer Jacob Boston was allowed to set up for a three-day stay at the "old photograph gallery which has been moved."[5]

The wages earned by civilians working at the post probably tempted more than one soldier to desert or request discharge. Lawrence Welsh requested a discharge "to better his condition in the world." He wanted to use the capital he had saved to start a boot and shoe business in Durango, which, he suggested, "would benefit the country more than his services in the army." The army approved the request.

The post occasionally offered assistance to local law enforcement. In 1883, troops were asked to help guard a "colored man" accused of murdering Bruce Hunt, a popular bank official. Yet, before they arrived, vigilantes lynched the miscreant for being involved with a gang of bank robbers who had killed Bruce Hunt.[6]

The fort's contracts, jobs, and economic benefits quickly drew Durangoans' attention, but so did general goings-on at Fort Lewis. The military presence was felt in Durango in an assortment of ways, and locals appeared at the post for events ranging from dances to baseball games. The garrison played a role in its neighbor town's life and the resulting social interaction was amazing. This was particularly true between officers and Durango's middle and upper classes. Estelle Camp, wife of Durango's preeminent banker, explained that Durango had only two classes: the "cultured, well educated, traveled class," including the "army people [officers and families] of Fort Lewis," and the "wild and wooly followers" of mining, lumbering, and cattle ranching. Young Durangoan Nettie Jackson did not remember such distinctions but she clearly remembered General Sherman's visit. Her father had served three years under Sherman during the Civil War and was part of the Committee of Welcome that met Sherman's train to "extend courtesies." Jackson remembered, "[My father] insisted I be at the station with him at ten o'clock that morning so he could introduce me to the General. To my surprise and embarrassment the old General put his arm round me and stooped and kissed me. But my pride in the matter was quite extracted when later I learned that kissing *all* the girls was quite an indoor sport with General Sherman." She also recalled the accident that marred his inspection: "The cannon used to fire the official salute" exploded, costing the gunner one of his arms.

Nettie's reminiscences included descriptions of other, more typical social events involving the "young officers of the post [who] were much in evidence in the social affairs of Durango." Social engagements at the post brought out Durango's society. Caroline Romney, in her *Record*, enjoyed describing such affairs for her readers. On February 19, 1881, she related one trip to the fort for a "complimentary ball" in great detail. Romney and the other partygoers traveled on a dark night in an "omnibus wagon," rolling "up hill and down dale, along fine mesas, along narrow ledges, down steep pitches. Our hair stood on end, a good part of the way. We lost our rear passenger out in the snow on two occasions when our vehicle gave a tremendous lurch." The troopers had gone to great lengths to ready the garrison for this dance, removing bunks from a barrack to clear a space for dancing and decorating the dancing area and the dining room with "festoons of evergreens" and a large number of pictures and flags. Caroline Romney's description of the supper, with the variety of foods available, brings to mind the appearance of Charles Dickens's Spirit of Christmas Present in *A Christmas Carol*. Caroline noted that "all in all the party was a most brilliant success, of which the entire garrison may be proud."

A party at the Grand Central Hotel on Washington's birthday followed, hosted by "five attractive [officer] bachelors." The "Grand Promenade" opened festivities at nine, and "Home, Sweet Home" closed them at one. Caroline concluded, "There were many elegant dancers on the floor, pre-eminent among whom were the gentlemen and ladies of the military."

A dinner and dance at the fort the next year found ambulances sent into town for the guests. At the celebration, party guests learned the "German," a new dance. They returned to town the next morning, after having breakfast and watching the guard mount, "with loud praise for the very cordial treatment they received" and the "most delightful time imaginable."

Fort Lewis's officers frequently attended social events and balls in Durango, such as the one given by the Hook and Ladder Company in May 1882. Occasionally, the military band came with them. The *Herald*'s report of a Thanksgiving ball in 1881 praised the Fifteenth Regimental Band for being "superb" and listed the names of all twenty-one members. Single young men in uniform, such as the three "handsome" lieutenants who came into town for the stockmen's ball in April 1885, managed to turn quite a few young ladies' heads and were popular dancing partners. Events such as these led to a few marriages, including that of Lt. William Davis and Laura Will. She was quickly introduced to army life when her husband was transferred to New Mexico. Sometimes Durango entertained fort marriages, such as

Bernard Byrne's in January 1881 and Sergeant Courtright's in September 1883.

Perhaps the most popular attraction at these social events was music, and the musicians from Fort Lewis were extremely popular. Indeed, military bands gave the army an excellent public relations tool. Bands also entertained the post and nearby communities and provided ceremonial pomp to public celebrations.

The splendid twenty-piece Fifteenth Infantry Band, including a drum major, highlighted a May 1881 parade and an 1882 firemen's parade. Reports indicate that the Fort Lewis Band played at the stock grower's ball and a grand ball celebrating Washington's birthday a couple of years later. The *Idea*, on November 1, 1884, advised its readers that the Wednesday afternoon band concerts at the fort "are of very high order." The band also played for a Thanksgiving ball at Animas City and a number of the soldiers attended, along with members of Animas City's high society. Part of the band also played for the Durango production of Gilbert and Sullivan's popular musical *The Mikado*. The Fifteenth Infantry Regimental Band had quite an experience when traveling to Silverton in 1882 for the Fourth of July festivities and to celebrate the Denver & Rio Grande's arrival in that community. Leaving the Durango depot, the "magnificent band" struck up "The Girl I Left Behind Me" and "discoursed the most inspiring strains of music frequently during the trip." Six coaches full of a "jolly looking crowd" traveled north on the new line to the end of the tracks three miles from Silverton. After traveling by carriage the final three miles, they led the parade and their "soul inspiring music" was the highlight of the day. The Fort Lewis Band very much impressed the *San Juan Herald* on July 6, 1882. Its members camped on Silverton's Snowden Street, erected ten tents, and "gave that portion of our city quite a warlike appearance." As at Durango, Silverton's reporter proclaimed that the band's parade repertoire electrified folk along the sidewalks by "discoursing the most inspiring strains of martial music." The band ended the highly successful day at the grand ball, furnishing the "music perfect" for the dance, with a bass viol and first and second violins. It provided a "rare treat" for "our mountain town."[7]

The *Herald* crowed, "One of the best bands in the country," about the Twenty-Second Infantry's band. After another concert by this band, the newspaper enthusiastically reported that "such grand and exquisite music is rarely ever heard as that which greeted the ears of our people today." The post's "excellent band of twenty-four musicians," the *Idea* thought, helped break the "monotony and dull routine of soldier life." In April 1888, when the army transferred the band to Fort Lyon, Colorado, Durangoans had "their last opportunity to hear them" when they played the intriguingly titled "Hum Drum." Unfortunately, no paper bothered to publish a review. At least one person asked, "Why don't some local tooters organize a brass band now that the Twenty-Second Infantry band has departed?"

The newspapers highly praised these affairs. The *Herald* could not restrain itself on one occasion and said that southwestern Colorado seldom heard such "magnificent music." Such phrases proved a familiar opening for music performances, which bewitched Durangoans. The Fort Lewis Minstrels, along with a brass band and orchestra, played two nights in Durango in 1885 and gave "a grand and superb" performance. They returned in February 1888, and the *Herald*'s review praised the "first class entertainment. We believe we voice the sentiment of all present when we say that the Ft. Lewis boys gave a fine exhibition for amateurs."

In addition to musical offerings, the post invited Durangoans to attend plays and concerts there. Sometimes even the troopers put on productions. The post's recreation hall contained a "good stage with well painted scenery." The *Idea*, on May 30, 1885, highly praised that hall as "splendid" and "supplied with stage and scenery at the post." In the same issue, the paper stated that the Chicago Comedy Company, which had garnered accolades for performances staged in Durango, planned to go to Fort Lewis for "one week in response to an invitation. Besides the army there, there are a great many citizens who are theatre goers." The only potential problem was lodging, as the post adjutant wrote one company, "[Y]ou may experience some difficulty making arrangement [for] your company for the reason no hotel accommodations are at this post." The troupe probably stayed in Durango.[8]

Baseball fever infected Americans after the Civil War, which had spread the game both north and south. It gave the troops a break in the monotony of garrison duty, provided an exciting pastime for players and spectators, and offered an opportunity to bet. In 1881, the post on the La Plata had existed for less than a year before enlisted men of the Thirteenth Infantry organized a baseball club with two teams. These athletic events stirred up a friendly rivalry between town and garrison and became a social event for all involved. A Durango team journeyed out to the fort and lost 20–19, after which both teams and their guests "enjoyed a splendid supper prepared for the occasion by the Crofton Club." Part of the day included horse races and a "spirited and highly entertaining stag dance after supper." Returning home, the Durango boys gave "loud praise for the hospitable treatment they received at the hands of the soldiers." Charles Lawrence, one of the Crofton Club's "first nine" players, happened to be in solitary confinement the day of the game. Wanting to play, he pleaded for his release, promising "to give no cause for complaint in the future." The post records remain silent on whether or not authorities granted the petition.

The two teams split two games played in September. Durango's mayor, John Taylor, gave a speech, a reported "masterpiece of eloquence," following the game, in which Fort Lewis "honorably defeated" their rivals. The "boys took their defeat very good naturedly" and "were treated well" by the soldiers. Home-field advantage paid off for the Durango team a couple of weeks later when Fort Lewis's team came to town for a game. Afterward, the Durango team took the "Fort Lewis boys to the Pacific Slope Restaurant" for dinner.

The next May, Fort Lewis won the game, despite the captain of its team suffering a badly cut nose and lip and having three of his teeth loosened. At this time, players generally did not use gloves, so fielding ground balls on the rough, uneven diamonds took skill and courage. The *Idea* spoke for generations of discouraged fans when it commented after a July 1885 defeat, "Our boys should practice a little more before they try to compete with those who possess the advantage of almost daily practice." Silverton, on the other hand, cheered on its nine to a 31–18 trouncing of Fort Lewis in an 1886 game on the Fourth of July.[9] Durangoans did not despair every time. When the Fort Lewis "muffers" challenged the Durango "base ballists," they organized and prepared for the game. Townsfolk nearly deserted Durango, noted the *Herald* on June 21, 1887, owing to the fact that everybody "who could get conveyances" journeyed to Fort Lewis to witness the baseball game. The local nine returned happily to Durango, "speaking highly of the hospitable" treatment by the garrison. They indeed appeared very "hospitable," as Durango won 27–17. Whether it was baseball, shooting matches, or even horse races, locals could find a sport to follow. Gun clubs held shooting matches, usually with the host sponsoring a dinner after the bout. Durango arms enthusiasts faced the post's best regimental marksmen, who competed at national shooting competitions, making for some stiff competition. The army's greater interest in marksmanship was facilitated by these local competitions, which gave their marksmen practice and the excitement of a match.[10]

Durango offered Civil War veterans at the garrison an opportunity to socialize with their comrades with the activities of the Sedgwick Post No. 12 of the Grand Army of the Republic (GAR). After a slow start in the early postwar years of the 1860s and 1870s, the GAR had increased membership by the time Fort Lewis was founded. It had been a political force early on but then lost its drive as the country tired of the "bloody shirt" slogans of the Grant era and moved away from the emotionalism of the war. Early in its career, the GAR had been closely tied to the Republican Party, with soldiers being advised to "vote as you shot." Republicans loved to tar Democrats as the party of secession while praising the heroic "boys in blue." But by the time of Fort Lewis's establishment, the GAR no longer had an overt political purpose and instead focused its resources on pensions, war memorials, and aid for indigent veterans. Veterans serving at Fort Lewis, such as James Felt, John Moan, and Charles Gould, joined and participated in Durango's chapter while stationed at Fort Lewis. In all, the Sedgwick Post had nearly two dozen Fort Lewis men on the rolls during the 1880s, some of whom may have served under "Uncle" John Sedgwick, one of the most popular Union generals.[11] When Denver hosted the national encampment of the GAR in 1883, Coloradans beamed with pride. Even Colorado governor James Grant, an ex-Confederate, told the veterans that the principles of the Union "were not only triumphantly vindicated by the sword in 1865, but today enshrined in the hearts of people from Maine to Georgia." Some unreconstructed southerners might not have agreed. To him and the other proud 1883 hosts, the "blessings of a free, a prosperous and a united country" towered as triumphantly as Pike's Peak. Reflecting its heritage, Durango's GAR post always took a prominent role on Memorial Day and often marched together in parades. As the years went by, the "boys" marched a little more slowly and their numbers started to dwindle, but their pride did not diminish.

Decoration Day in Durango, originally set aside nationally to honor Union soldiers, often featured the fort's band, soldiers, and officers. Other nearby communities also tried to get some military representation. By the end of the decade, the day had come to honor all "the beloved dead," not just Union soldiers. As the editor of Silverton's *San Juan Democrat* wrote in the May 24, 1884, issue, the years since the war came to a close "have served to obliterate all sectional feeling, so don't let us forget that day." No doubt some unreconstructed rebels and patriotic Yankees with long memories did not agree and held strong feelings about their former enemies being so honored.

Durango offered temptations, so the troops came into town to enjoy the red-light district, creating occasional disturbances. Silvertonians chuckled over a fight between the harlots' "professional champions" and some officers. Apparently the officers "insulted" the girls and in the ensuing fight the "soldiers beat a hasty retreat," with one lieutenant "escaping with a piece of an ear missing." Both Durango and Silverton liked to take swipes at each other's supposed lawlessness, in addition to coming up with other ways to besmirch their rival's image, which was probably the case here. The *Idea*, at the same time as the brothel incident, reported some leading Silvertonians skipping town because of the possibility of a grand jury investigation. Although Durango's police records do not identify the occupations of those arrested, the most common charges and fines involved drunkenness and fighting. In addition, at least one soldier found himself arrested for fast driving. Despite the protests of chaplains, doctors, and other morally concerned citizens, military authorities tolerated prostitutes, whiskey sellers, and gamblers as part of life. With a large population of young, single men, prostitution flourished. Furthermore, as in Durango, sometimes temptations beckoned beyond government land and there was little the army could do to curb the lure of the glittering attractions.

Sin fascinated Durangoans, as it did others, and thus the "hog ranch" captured attention. A series of courts-martial in the summer of 1888 intended "to stamp out the bad habit indulged" in by "quite a number of otherwise good soldiers." Their crime was "paying nocturnal visits to the hog ranch." Such episodes titillated some, appalled others, and shocked proper Victorian Durangoans.

Presiding officer Capt. Stephen Baker "pretty severely dealt" with the soldiers who, since payday, had indulged. He minced no words: "This is a vile den kept by one Rebstock, and is about two miles from the post." The soldiers had to travel only a few more miles to visit Durango's red-light district.

Enlisted men, particularly around payday, enjoyed the variety of pleasures available in Durango, and often paid the consequences of their actions. In May 1889, eight to ten of them (the *Herald* did not seem to know the exact number) were arrested for being absent without leave while enjoying the pleasures of Durango. Loaded into a four-mule team wagon, they received a cavalry escort back to the post. Another enlisted man, having changed into civilian attire and believing himself safe, flagged the train down at Animas City. He had the misfortune of meeting a lieutenant aboard who promptly arrested him.

Countering these untoward activities was religion. When no chaplain was available, which was quite often, local ministers and priests stepped in to fill the void. Durango also provided the nearest point to attend services if none was available at the post. Father Fitzsimmons traveled to Fort Lewis in July 1888 and preached a "powerful and eloquent sermon." He traveled with an Episcopal priest who, according to the *Idea*, gave an "impressive and eloquent" sermon on the spiritual and military duty of the Christian soldier.

Like those "magnificent" bands, "eloquent" sermons appear to have been habit. The garrison reciprocated, when possible, once giving entertainment to aid Durango's Methodist church.

The relationship between Fort Lewis and Durango appears to have been positive throughout the decade. When a large segment of the town burned on July 1, 1889, including the red-light district, where the fire started, the commanding officer sent troops into town to prevent looting and offered any other help that was needed. The papers covered events at the post extensively. Readers learned about troop movements, construction projects, courts-martial, and a host of items. They were intrigued that the post served briefly as the Southern Ute Agency headquarters for the latter part of the decade, placing two perceived protagonists together. Indeed, the newspapers' coverage seemed endless. In October 1885, a series of fires struck the post, with arson the suspected cause. The *Idea* covered the story and advised its readers to "be very careful about approaching the post after dark," since Fort Lewis had taken extra precautions to prevent further trouble. The number of guards was increased from nineteen to twenty-six at eight guard posts, many of whom were uneasy at their posts, and the fort advised that "no man, citizen, or soldier would be allowed out of quarters after taps."

The only post correspondent to Durango newspapers appeared briefly in 1888, signing himself as "private." He regaled readers with popular tidbits about life at the post, such as details about the "enlisted men's saloon," telling them that its "new stock is fresh and cool." In his reports, "private" took readers into the guardhouses and to a "very restricted dance" for officers only. Commenting on the women at the post and in Durango, he wrote that the officers proclaimed, "They have struck a post inhabited by some of the most beautiful and accomplished girls in the State, and this is saying a great deal, as Colorado is famed for its beautiful maidens."[12]

Also of interest to Durangoans was the post's involvement with the mysterious ruins found throughout the region. Although Fort Lewis had no historic relics to send to the National Military Museum in Washington, as Congress had requested, the post sat near these amazing ancient ruins. The secretary of the Smithsonian Institution asked about the "advisability of an exploration of the Aztec [*sic*] ruins" in the vicinity of the fort. Virginia McClurg, one of the women who eventually helped create Mesa Verde National Park, secured a cavalry escort to accompany her to see some of the ruins in Mancos Canyon. Officers visited some ruins as well, including Byrne, who spent most of his visit worrying about the rattlesnakes he might encounter amid the rubble. Fort Lewis, despite complaints from Mancos, Farmington, Durango, and Cortez folks during the troubles with the Navajos, Utes, and Piutes, appears to have had a good relationship with the communities and residents throughout the Four Corners region. They all benefited from the post's presence, and, in turn, the enlisted men benefited from Durango's proximity to the post. In a modest sense, the garrison emerged as one of the region's tourist attractions.

Unlike some of its contemporaries, Durango did not go bust when Fort Lewis closed. Army financing had helped establish the town and aided in business expansion. By the late 1880s, Durango had forged a solid economic base. After a brief struggle it became the La Plata County seat and established railroad connections to the San Juan mines and the outside world. Other towns did not, as Michael Tate explains in his *Frontier Army*: "Their town would not rise phoenix like out of the ashes of military abandonment."[13]

By the end of the decade, the Secretary of War and Congress realized that many of the western posts no longer served a worthwhile military purpose. Prodded by cost-conscious eastern voters who did not want to finance a huge standing army, Washington continued to cut the military and made a list of military forts that could be closed. Fort Lewis was on that list.

EIGHT

THE LAST TO LEAVE

The hour was sad I left the maid,
A ling'ring farewell taking
Her signs and tears my steps delay'd
I thought her heart was breaking.

"THE GIRL I LEFT BEHIND ME"

In the early 1890s, plenty of signs appeared that Fort Lewis's days were numbered. Voters in the East grew increasingly skeptical of the so-called Indian
troubles in the West and frustrated with the ongoing financial drain. The
army, pushed by Secretary of War Redfield Proctor, evaluated all posts to
determine which could be sacrificed to save more important installations.
The consolidation of western posts made more sense now that troops could
be moved efficiently by rail. The establishment of Fort Logan near Denver
provided such a post for Colorado.

Major Indian war campaigns decreased steadily throughout the 1880s,
culminating in a final struggle with the Sioux in 1890–1891. Southwestern
Coloradans really had not encountered anything more than minor troubles
regarding their Ute and Navajo neighbors. Western settlers felt more secure

now and less dependent on the military posts for protection. The day of the small western post was nearing its end.[1]

Life continued at Fort Lewis, even as the post faced closure. Perhaps there were a few more requests for transfers or dismissals, but for the most part it was business as usual. A report from Major Tupper indicates that some soldiers were still cultivating gardens at Fort Lewis in 1890. In his report, Tupper lists the variety of farm tools (including three plows; two each of seeders, cultivators, and harrows; and ten hoes) and the approximate cost. And farm animals continued to reside at the post. The hospital maintained one cow, and the four companies now stationed at the post had a total of eighty-four pigs. The cavalry troops had their horses, and mules served all the companies.

Assistant Surgeon William H. Corbusier was transferred with his family to Fort Lewis from Fort Hays, Kansas, arriving in Durango on November 15, 1889, and at the post the next day. They arrived but their luggage did not. The surgeon's remembrances of the post give a snapshot of life in Fort Lewis's waning years. Once, he and his son Hal were caught in a heavy snowstorm while he was in the mountains treating a patient, and it took them all night to travel back to the post. "Just in time," Corbusier recalled, "to keep a rescuing party of cavalry from going after us as Little Mother [had told Major Tullius Tupper that] I would be back in time for sick call and I had never failed." His wife, Fanny Corbusier, also recorded some information about her family's brief stay at Fort Lewis. The "air was dry and crisp" and the elevation affected her and her husband: "our hearts beating faster on exerting ourselves." They selected frame quarters at the "west end of the officers' line." She liked their quarters, "which were very comfortable ones" and warmed with coal from a nearby mine. She continued, "The lower floor was up at least six feet so the rooms were not damp. We borrowed bedding and took our meals at mess for two weeks, at the end of which our baggage arrived and we started housekeeping."

Their mother remembered what fun her sons had with the goats they drove when not in school. Fanny was not impressed with her sons' teacher at the post school: "The soldier teacher usually had a drink with the Chaplain [William Larkin] on his way to school every morning and had a bottle in his desk in the schoolroom until the boys found it and threw it out." Her husband also remembered the teacher as "a drunken Roman Catholic priest." According to Fanny, the chaplain was not in service long after this incident and the teacher finally retired in February 1891. Meanwhile, her son Harold "had German under Private Bromstead of the Sixth Cavalry,

Phil, violin lessons from Private Stewart, and Latin and Literature from me."

The other Corbusier son, Frank, found himself in a little trouble with the chaplain, who had asked the boy to help him with a turkey shoot. In return, the chaplain promised to give Frank a turn. Fanny recalled: "He didn't know Frank very well, or he would not have given him the first shot. Frank put a bullet through the turkey's head, ran to the box, grabbed the turkey, and came home as fast as his legs could carry him, not heeding the chaplain's call that it was a mistake."

An influenza epidemic hit the post in January 1890 and Corbusier notes, "I treated about 120 cases." Unfortunately, he had approved a month's leave for his assistant and had no help during the crisis. William Corbusier "couldn't rest, as he had so many cases to treat and no one to assist him." The constant work and strain undermined his health and he wrote, "I could no longer go on." He was in bed for a month "before we could take him to a lower altitude," wrote Fanny. Major Tupper telegraphed for another surgeon. After a great deal of difficulty whereby "twenty feet of snow on the railroad" piled up "and no trains could get through," another surgeon finally arrived at Fort Lewis to relieve Corbusier from duty.[2]

With the help of Lt. William Carter, the Corbusiers' neighbor who had been very kind during William's illness, Fanny got everything ready to ship. "We had removed things to vacant quarters next to ours and worked so quietly that Father couldn't hear a sound." On April 9, the Corbusiers left Fort Lewis. "As we descended the mountains he felt better, and we had him carried in a chair up to the second story of the Hotel Strater." The Corbusiers left the next morning, going through cuts in snowdrifts "probably twenty feet" where the "blockade had been."[3]

The post once again lacked a doctor. The army offered a contract position in an attempt to entice local doctors. Although what they offered did not tempt any physician to sign on permanently, seasoned Durango doctor William Winter, who had served as acting surgeon in 1884, agreed to serve on a temporary basis until a doctor arrived from Fort Leavenworth. He received $60 for his services at the post that winter.[4]

The army continued to enforce its claim to the military reservation and kept a close watch for illegal activity. A military report found no evidence of illegal cutting of hay or wood, or unauthorized homesteading, on the military reservation. It was discovered, however, that "cattle graze on the reservation distant from the post." Investigating this matter occupied the officers as they sought to determine the owner of the "unknown" bovine and "drive them off." Near the fort, civilian employees legally kept cows, as did "one soldier for sale of milk to the garrison."

Most of the activity on the reservation, however, was the result of building by the Rio Grande Southern Railroad. The railroad, on its way from Durango around the western San Juan Mountains, received permission from the Secretary of War in July 1890 to "operate and maintain a railroad, telegraph and telephone line" across the reservation. Secretary of War Redfield Proctor limited the company's right-of-way to 100 feet and warned the railroad not to cut timber "for any purpose." The Rio Grande Southern also was required to restore any roads damaged during the construction process to the condition "when entered upon" and "immediately make good to any damage it may do to United States property." The commanding officer worried that the survey ran through the "best pine timber on the reservation," possibly stripping the fort of much-needed timber. Construction started with a few problems. The Southern broke the post telegraph line, which the railroad promptly repaired, and promised in the event of another future breakage to "see it repaired at once." Fort Lewis watched as the remnants of its isolation disappeared. Passing through Wildcat Canyon, the rails came within a couple of miles northeast of the post. Fort Lewis even received its own station—a simple shelter and a platform—although it came far too late to be of much use.

Troops moved in and out in a steady stream, once leading to five changes in the post quartermaster in eight months, causing "some demoralization," observed Tupper. In 1891 Tupper himself would be replaced by Capt. Sumner Lincoln.[5] Despite the turmoil, the same issues at the fort persisted. Complaints once again made their way to the postmaster general in Washington about the Durango postmaster's refusal to deliver mail to a carrier on Sundays. The complaints got results. The post office told the Durango postmaster that it did "not see any hardship in separating mail" to Fort Lewis and "handing it over" to couriers. He could make the delivery "without necessitating opening your office to the general public." And despite the fort's imminent closure, the companies stationed at the fort needed recruits to fill their ranks. Snow persisted in causing problems, impeding troop movement for months at a time.

In April 1891, reports described a particularly terrible winter that had stopped all troop movement since the previous December. Nineteen accumulated feet of snow resulted in twenty-eight days without mail and erased the possibility of getting "any place in any kind of conveyance." Even in early April, it was "impracticable to move a wagon properly loaded two miles from this post." Post commander Lincoln sent this information to Washington with a clear agenda in mind, as he noted that the "last remarks are made with the view of inviting attention to the value of Ft. Lewis as a point from which to conduct Indian operations," an idea that Washington was already considering.

But in the meantime, the smaller garrison at Fort Lewis had to contend with the effects of the winter snow. Before the season ended, two cavalry barracks were "down crushed by snow" and "tons" of snow had been shoveled. "A great deal of work," Lincoln remarked. With fewer men at the post, not all the buildings could be protected, even though the men worked hard.

Unlike the post's early years, no military maneuvers chasing hostile Utes or Navajos occupied the troops in 1890 or 1891. Tupper did, however, recommend a September 1890 practice march, choosing the autumn season out of practicality. Parties of Navajos and Utes had "been in the habit of roaming about this country during the fall months engaged in hunting and selling blankets." Troops in the field would have a "salutary influence," yet Tupper also knew their travel abroad might worry civilians, who might assume that the troops were responding to problems with the Utes or Navajos.

Among those still stationed at the post was Heath Eldridge's father, Bogardus, a first lieutenant in the Tenth Infantry. He was part of a new breed of army officer with no Civil War experience, having joined the military in 1876. Years later, Heath wrote his recollections of the post's final year and his experiences as a young boy there. Although the signs of the fort's impending closure did not intrude much on his childhood, his reminiscences present a clear picture of a fort in decline and are the only view of Fort Lewis from one of the post's children.

What Heath remembered most about that year was the "beautiful snow," which provided great adventure for a little boy. It started snowing at the end of October and seemed to continue almost every day until March. "After each snow fall it was the custom to break out the roads by riding six mules single file, then a snow plow was used, pulled by six mules to clear the roads." The snow was such a "menace" that soldiers were called out at night to clear the roofs before buildings collapsed. In this small garrison, there were "not enough men to go around to shovel and one night two unoccupied barracks collapsed under the snow's weight," which greatly impressed Heath. Heath marveled at the fact that a soldier jumped off the roof of his two-story home into a pile of snow "without injury." He probably wanted to try it himself, something his worried mother certainly would not have condoned. The garrison made the best of the winter situation, finding some sport amidst all the snow. A Norwegian post carpenter knew how to make skis and skiing was one of the few endeavors that the men could easily do. Heath remembered, "I had a pair and I used them to go across the parade ground to the post school." One of his friends had a burro that could be coerced into towing a sled, which provided hours of fun.

At the post school, the boys cut tunnels in the snow that had been pushed off the roof, and in them found a "fine place" to play. A soldier served as their teacher, and they studied from the "famous McGuffey Readers."

The Eldridges had a striker, or family servant, whom Heath's father paid. He milked the family cow, brought in coal, took out ashes, and did other jobs, and he ate meals with the family. The enlisted men, probably out of envy, referred to a striker as a "dog robber" or a "hand shaker," because it was said that he robbed a family's dog of food and shook hands for favors. These terms had long been used by the army. The Eldridge family also had a "good cook," and they ate "hearty breakfasts." Heath recalled, "We also had eggs from our chickens and generally ate two for breakfast."

Heath liked Capt. Sumner Lincoln, whose hobby was photography and who "often took photographs of us." Born in Massachusetts, Lincoln had an interesting career. Enlisting as a private in 1861, he was "honorably mustered" out as a lieutenant colonel of the Sixth Vermont in 1865. A year later, he rejoined the army as a second lieutenant and reached the rank of brigadier general before retiring. Clearly, Lincoln had a profound influence on young Heath, who must have felt honored by the captain's attentions. Yet, Heath's mother, afraid of guns, disapproved when Lincoln gave her two boys their own toy guns. Heath wrote, "The Colonel [his Civil war rank] was like an uncle to us." Heath had a tough run of luck with his pets while at Fort Lewis. "We had our pets, but due to the large number of skunks, the domestic cat did not thrive. Our first dog was a water Spaniel called 'Curley.' Just as we got used to him, he disappeared. Our questions to our parents received no satisfactory answer. Possibly he had hydrophobia. Skunks were supposed to spread it." Heath's next pet was a rabbit that "went to rabbit heaven," followed by another spaniel, who managed to survive.

In his journal, Heath wrote that he remembered hearing coyotes howl in the hills at night and once lived through an "Indian scare." The troops were off on a practice march when "a rumor went around that Indians were going to attack." The Gatling gun was made ready before the rumor was proven to be false. Not surprisingly, "the returning troops received a royal welcome" from the nervous stay-at-homers. "The band played 'When Johnnie Comes Marching Home' to greet them."

Always worried about potential trouble from the Utes, his mother would keep her children in the house when Utes roamed about the post, although Heath remembered, "We would look at the Indians with curious eyes through the window." Attitudes toward the Utes had changed and they often freely wandered around the grounds, selling "pine nuts, bead work, and moccasins."

One highlight Heath remembered well was the appearance of a Scottish Highlanders Piper band that furnished music for an officers' picnic and out-door dance. Heath wrote, "It was the first time I had seen the highlanders in kilts. The chaplain of the Post was quite active and I think he had a hand in obtaining the band." Musical entertainment such as this was becoming rarer, a dramatic change from a past when Fort Lewis had been famous for its music.[6]

Even as young Heath recorded his vivid impressions of the post, Fort Lewis was slowly closing down. In May 1890, the post commander had been informed that, because of the "contemplated abandonment of Fort Lewis," the department wanted a careful estimate of stores on hand and needs for the next quarter. The quartermaster wished "to avoid accumulation" of articles at the post and requested a "special requisition of only such articles [that were] absolutely necessary." Some goods stored at the post had already been disposed of by sale.

By December 1890, the planning for the reinterment of burials, including some family members of soldiers, from Fort Lewis to Fort McPherson National Cemetery in Maxwell, Nebraska, was complete. In November and December 1891, two Durango contractors performed one of the last acts at the post, removing the bodies, placing them "in substantial pine boxes," and shipping them out by rail. They disinterred twenty-nine soldiers and dependents out of the "about forty persons in all" in the cemetery. The untouched burials were those of civilians who had lived nearby and been buried in the military cemetery.

As the post's senior officer, Capt. Sumner Lincoln sent a long report in July 1891 detailing the actions that had been taken to abandon Fort Lewis. All stores not required by the garrison through October 1 had been moved to Fort Logan. Two wagons and the "twelve youngest, most active mules" went to Fort Sill, along with twelve "excellent pack mules and complete packing outfits." Nearly all surplus clothing had been sent to other posts, and "all serviceable ordnance and ordnance stores [were] shipped to the Rock Island [Illinois] arsenal." The Department of the Platte, which after a reorganization was now responsible for Fort Lewis, received "all serviceable signal equipment" and stores.

The redistribution of stores took care of most of the post's concerns. Nevertheless, Lincoln still worried: "This post is well-equipped in every respect and the amount of property and buildings to be disposed of are so considerable that it is desirable that the boards and inspections considered necessary be ordered as soon as practicable."[7]

But the garrison did not have everything it needed. In July, 112 cans of corned beef arrived to supplement the "travel ration" for the troops leaving the post. The fort also lacked the materials needed for shipping the government's property, such as boxes and crates, nails, screws, and so forth. Thus, a special requisition went out for these materials. General Order No. 50 in July ordered that steps be taken toward "looking to the abandonment of Fort Lewis," so that the troops could be "withdrawn on or before October 1." In that same order, the Secretary of War authorized the abandonment of several other posts. In addition to Fort Lewis, General Order No. 50 closed Fort Shaw, Montana, and Fort Abraham Lincoln, North Dakota, from which Custer's Seventh Cavalry had ridden fifteen years before on the fateful 1876 campaign that ended at the Little Big Horn.

Each post commander was ordered to forward a withdrawal schedule "showing a detailed description of, and condition of, public buildings" remaining on his post and reservation. The commanders were also to include the value of each building and whether the buildings could be used to "advantage at other military posts or stations." The frugal army never missed an opportunity to reuse buildings, a sound policy considering their budget woes.

All public property was to be disposed of by shipment or by sales or auctions. Then a nominated custodian, a "reliable person," would take charge of the buildings remaining at the post. The buildings would be taken care of in this manner until "the Interior Department is ready to receive them."

The activity surrounding the post's closing increased the number of reports and requests going back and forth, as the special correspondence about the closure was added to the typical regulation reports. One report included a bit of correspondence involving "wire woven bunk bottoms," of which those in poor condition were sent to the St. Louis depot for restoring. Those not thought "worth the cost of transportation should be submitted for action" by inspectors, who could authorize their disposal. The army had warned Lincoln about not shipping "worthless camp and garrison equipment."

In August, public sales became popular with civilians in the area. Heath Eldridge's father served as assistant acting quartermaster during the hectic period. He requested the authority to employ an auctioneer for a period not to exceed five days, "at a rate not to exceed $10 per day." Among the items sold were mules, a spring wagon, desks, and other goods unusable by the military. Lieutenant Eldridge reported that a total of seventeen desks remained at the post, but only seven remained in a condition good enough to "warrant the expense of shipment." The final sale of surplus military items occurred on September 14, allowing the post to be abandoned four days later.

Captain Lincoln's final report on the condition of Fort Lewis described what was left of the post. The rifle range was not in a good state, and the barracks and quarters languished "in very poor conditions." The stone guardhouse, however, was in "excellent condition," and the brick hospital was in "good condition." The post garden was also "in very good condition" and would serve as a "valuable auxiliary for the soldiers' ration" as they prepared to leave. In closing, Lincoln offered his praise of the library, the contents of which had been shipped to the Omaha depot. He considered the collection that Fort Lewis had acquired to have been an "excellent one regarding quality, condition, and number." That once-heated debate between the canteen and the post trader had receded, with the canteen victorious. Lincoln concluded that the post canteen had proven "an entire success," and the management of it had been "entirely satisfactory." Considering the lack of recruiting success over the past decade, his final observation "that there is very little desirable material for recruits found in the vicinity" is completely understandable. Few enlistments had occurred at the time of the abandonment, continuing a decade-long pattern.[8]

The post quartermaster and assistant worked overtime to get everything ready to ship or sell. Their completion of the ever bothersome reports justified what was, or what was not, done. Now that it was time to vacate the post, the now completed Rio Grande Southern, with its side track to the Fort Lewis station, came in very handy. The travel arrangements for Company E of the Tenth Infantry show the logistics involved. Two officers and thirty-seven enlisted men, plus one officer's wife, a servant, and one soldier's wife with two children, needed to travel along with 20,000 pounds of property and baggage. Lincoln explicitly ordered the Denver & Rio Grande agent at Durango to arrange for a special train to Antonito, otherwise the former occupants of the fort "would have to wait there all night." He also reminded the railroad agent that the baggage cars were to go to Santa Fe "without charge." La Plata and Montezuma County residents watched these goings-on with concern. They realized the economic impact of the fort's closure and would miss the often-rousing social outlet the fort had provided. They protested in the form of letters and meetings, expressing their fears of an Indian uprising to members of Congress. But they were more scared of losing the jobs and contracts provided by the post, which had never defended civilians from anything more than rumors or minor trouble.

Fort Lewis's closing was inevitable and had been held off as long as possible. In 1889, the state's two senators, Henry Teller and Edward Wolcott, as well as House representative Hosea Townsend had protested the Secretary of War's proposal to abandon Fort Lewis. To them, "with the Southern Utes and the Jicarilla Apaches located so near that post as they are, the post has served as [sic] excellent purpose of keeping the Indians quiet." The lawmakers added, "We are of opinion that the abandonment of the post at this time would place the people of that vicinity in a very dangerous position." Colorado's congressional delegation wanted the post to remain "at least until the removal of the Indians," a hope shared by many other Coloradans.

They had swung enough political clout to have the abandonment deferred for a time. Secretary of War Redfield Proctor politely replied that the army had "no intention of entirely withdrawing the troops," so long "as there may be any necessity for their presence." But he added, "The inadequacy of the water supply, along with other military reasons has suggested to the department the desirability of gradually withdrawing the troops from Fort Lewis, with a view to its ultimate abandonment, or by reducing its garrison to a strength sufficient to protect the settlements." The water issue referred to by Proctor had resulted from farmers taking too much water for irrigation above the post, leaving Fort Lewis with an insufficient supply. Proctor's actions were based on an earlier report that recommended abandonment with "no hesitation." The report also commented, "the elevation is so great and its isolation so gloomy that the garrison—officers and men—are affected unfavorably in health and spirits."[9]

But Durangoans were loathe to let the post go without a fight. In a May 18, 1891, article, the editor of the *Durango Weekly Tribune* urged his readers to fight the closure, even as he conceded that "probably the post will be abandoned" now that only forty-seven men remained there. In his opinion the facts did not "warrant the abandonment," and they should "make a move" to have a few companies garrisoned at the post. The editor argued that having troops around "would be better" for a country "not yet far removed from the frontier." After years of promoting itself as settled, civilized, and far removed from the frontier, Durango seemed willing to change its tune, albeit only for a moment. Whenever post closures were announced, protests such as this one were typical and often were spurred by economic concerns. Noting the emotional reaction of local leaders to shutting down a nearby military installation, Gen. William T. Sherman observed: "Every such city from Maine to Texas has a local pride in its fort and garrison. Any attempt to withdraw the garrison or remove the flag is met by local opposition, often impossible to overcome."[10]

But Fort Lewis's supporters could do nothing now that Washington and the War Department had made their decision. At least it was an exciting time for Heath Eldridge and his family, who were the last to leave. When the post's pumping engineer forgot to fill the reservoir prior to stopping the pumps, the reservoir ran dry and the family "was forced to get drinking water from the irrigation ditch in front of their house." His mother wisely insisted it be boiled.

Heath and his family drove an army ambulance to Durango, where they stayed the night. The next day they boarded the Rio Grande Southern. The last of the post's troops moved to Durango at the same time. The telegraph operator tapped out the last military message on his key on September 18, then the line went silent, as the army's stay at Fort Lewis came to an end.[11]

All was not completely quiet at the post, however. Joe Coppinger had secured a contact to haul supplies and materials to the post four years before and now continued his work at the abandoned post. He freighted away tons of ammunition, rifles, artillery, and munitions. Coppinger also hauled five tons of drugs and medicines to Durango, where druggist and hotelier Henry Strater purchased them for $350. Soon Coppinger finished his work, leaving only the custodian there to watch over buildings and property. But even as Fort Lewis was closing, plans were being made for its future. Under the authority of a July 31, 1882, Act of Congress, unoccupied military barracks would "provide [an] additional Industrial training school for Indian Youth." General Order No. 189, from the Adjutant General's office in Washington and dated November 12, 1891, stated that "the unoccupied military post of Fort Lewis, Colorado, and its buildings and appurtenances, are to be hereby set aside for Indian school purposes." What remained of the post, mostly run-down buildings, became the official property of the Department of Interior in February 1895, giving it complete control over the buildings and land.

The former post became one of two Indian schools in Colorado, although many were located throughout the West. The other was the Teller Institute, near Grand Junction. Fort Lewis seemed an ideal location, as it was adjacent to several tribes. During its operation, Fort Lewis had always contained an educational component, which now became its primary function.

In 1892 the first of the young students arrived. Durangoans, although unhappy about losing the military, had not completely lost access to Uncle Sam's deep pockets. The fort remained an Indian boarding school until 1910 when the buildings and land were sold to the State of Colorado with the stipulation that Indian students be offered free admission to any public school located at Fort Lewis. The state opened first a rural high school and then a junior college at Fort Lewis. The junior college campus was moved to Durango in 1956 and became a four-year college in 1962. Throughout these changes, the Fort Lewis name and the pledge to educate Native American students were retained, as Native American students still can study tuition-free at Fort Lewis so long as they meet admission standards.[12]

The post's military legacy faded from memory as a new century and new interests arrived. The automobile, movies, ragtime music, aeroplanes, and the electrifying Theodore Roosevelt in the White House transformed the West of a bygone century into romantic legend. Durango's interest turned elsewhere as the Spanish American War, the new American empire, and the onrushing world crisis that led to World War I seized headlines. In the midst of the new, global events, the old post seemed a quaint relic of a vanished era.

The Indian-fighting army receded into history as well. The last hope of the tribes, trapped on reservations, became the ghost dance, a futile attempt to bring back the old times. The last conflict had ended with the tragic fight at Wounded Knee in South Dakota on December 29, 1890, with some of Fort Lewis's own present at the battle. Two hundred seventy years of America's other civil war ended on that cold, bleak, snowy December day in South Dakota. And with it came the end of the era of the western military post.

Ahead for the United States was the 1898 Spanish American War, which gave America an empire and a starring role on the world's stage. This "splendid little war," as Secretary of State John Hay called it in writing his friend Theodore Roosevelt, led to the Filipino Insurrection, which cost more lives and lasted longer than the war in Spain. One of the earliest casualties was Heath's dad, Capt. Bogardus Eldridge, who was killed on October 2, 1899, in fighting near Bacoor, Luzon.

Strike the Tent

The flags are furled, the bugles silent, and no one marches on the drill field. The regimental bands have not sounded for over a century, nor has the cavalry ridden out to answer pleas for help or to patrol the Four Corners region. Guards no longer walk where buildings once stood, reports have been filed away and gathering dust for decades, and inspections fade into the events of long ago. The men, women, and children who once called Fort Lewis home have gone, too.

Fort Lewis, trapped between the Civil War generation "touched by war" and the dawn of the twentieth century, seems like a quaintly obscure artifact of yesteryear. Overshadowed by military events elsewhere in the country and other more significant forts, Fort Lewis quietly faded from memory, becoming a closed book of a military yesterday.

What then of Fort Lewis? Has it any significance? Or is it simply part of a legendary, even romantic, past that entices and intrigues those who encounter it but yields little to the epic saga of the settlement of the American West?

From the military point of view, Fort Lewis was a success. As Col. Peter Swaine expressed in June 1885, the troops in the field protected the interests of both settlers and Indians and carried out their duties with respect for both sides. Indeed, much of their time was spent investigating rumors, and care had to be taken to avoid responding inappropriately to unfounded reports. A display of force would "give confidence to citizens," and Swaine added that the "spark of war may not have an opportunity to kindle the hearts of these young bucks." Investigation of rumors took up a great part of the army's time. Another order stated, "You discriminate with care between representations of dangers which are real" and those "non substantial [*sic*] and improbable." Conceptually, cautiously checking on rumors would not only investigate the truth of the matter at hand, but it was critical that the army investigate rumors without fueling them by continuously patrolling the area. Residents worried that the continued "exaggerated conviction of danger" might discourage "many who contemplate settlement" and impede "growth and prosperity." Who would want to settle an area that required the army to keep the peace?

The army realized the multiplicity of roles it played, as noted in a September 1888 report from a practice march into the Cortez area, commanded by Capt. Adam Kramer. The army's presence at Fort Lewis bolstered the economy by providing government contracts and jobs. It also quieted apprehensions and might have dissuaded some from causing mischief. Finally, and perhaps most importantly, the army helped promote settlement and shape development. Kramer's report concluded by describing the "immense possibilities for farming and settling in the Montezuma Valley," stating that this "hitherto barren waste is now promising great fertility by the introduction of irrigation." Encouraging words for prospective settlers.[1]

Fort Lewis brought smiles to the faces of farmers, freighters, coal miners, carpenters, businesswomen and -men, denizens of the red-light district, ranchers, and blacksmiths; almost everyone who had a product or service to sell benefited. They all saw Uncle Sam as a rich uncle who would help them make their dreams come true in this new land. Fort Lewis's mission was the same as that of other frontier forts: to prevent trouble, to defend settlements and settlers, to protect Indian lands, to act as a police force, and to help open the West to settlers. Without question, it fulfilled its duties in southwestern Colorado. Nothing particularly heroic transpired here; the troopers were simply performing their duties. Garrison life—rigidly organized, uniformly routine, boring, and often uneventful—slugged onward day after day. Through reveille, taps, drills, inspections, various calls, practice, guard duty, mess calls for uninspiring meals, reports, and fatigue details, life relentlessly continued on in the common features of a military day. The undermanned companies patrolled, marched, and settled into field camps in the late spring, summer, and early fall, then hunkered down the rest of the year in the lonely isolation of Fort Lewis.

For the most part, the garrison had the support of locals and did not face public mistrust and criticism. Westerners in particular were often skeptical of too much federal control, landownership, and defending tribal rights.[2]

For the garrisoned soldiers, it probably was simply another assignment, albeit one located in relatively pleasant surroundings compared with other western posts. These volunteers suffered the most from lack of military action as they found little military glory at the fort. One soldier described his experience as "glittering misery." Their reactions were typical, from resigned acceptance and boredom to dissatisfaction, drinking, and desertion.

The soldiers at Fort Lewis represented a cross section of Americans. Some were recently arrived immigrants who hoped to use army life to become "Americanized," while other recruits enlisted to get to the promised land of the West. More than a few joined to escape troublesome pasts. For the young blacks in the Ninth Cavalry, enlistment in the army was seen as an opportunity for a better life not available in civilian life. Their restlessness, which sometimes evolved into carelessness and often cockiness, mirrored the America of their day. Petty criminals and undesirables were found among them, plus a smattering of saints.[3]

Many found themselves accused of "conduct to prejudice of good order and military discipline," a catchall charge. The soldiers, particularly around payday, got into trouble at the post, at the hog ranch, and in town, although they rarely faced charges of any serious weight.

A select few tried to educate themselves by attending the post school. Officers and their families were often the only ones present at the post's irregular church services.

They complained about the food, enjoyed band concerts, worried about the arrival of the paymaster, worked unenthusiastically at fatigue duty, cheered the post baseball team, and went off the post occasionally to "let off steam." They enjoyed holidays and did not generally seem to mind being on campaign or in field camps along the San Juan River.

Although the Sixth Infantry and Cavalry were stationed longer at Fort Lewis, the Ninth Cavalry stood out in locals' minds. While they garrisoned there, the Ninth represented the largest percentage of Blacks ever in La Plata County and southwestern Colorado.

Did they face the discrimination so typical for this age? They might have, but it has not been documented. Certainly the Ninth Cavalry did in Texas, Nebraska, Wyoming, and elsewhere. But the White and Black troops seemed to have gotten along in southwestern Colorado as there appear to have been no racial incidents in Durango. It would be inconceivable that the local press would not have picked up such a story, as they always did on the state and national beats. Unlike some communities that had racial problems when Black troops were stationed nearby, Durango did not. Hays, Kansas, for instance, saw three lynched after a killing, and San Angelo, Texas, experienced a race riot. Fortunately, Durango avoided such tragedies.

Some of the officers who served at Fort Lewis eventually became generals, such as Henry Carroll, Robert Hall, William Carter, and Sumner Lincoln. Medal of Honor recipients Carter and Francis Dodge both served at the post but earned their medals elsewhere. In fact, no enlisted man won the Medal of Honor while stationed at Fort Lewis, because the garrison never faced combat.[4]

For many the romantic image of the western army of the post–Civil War decades has replaced the reality of the military's role in western settlement. Fiction and Hollywood seized this image of the late nineteenth century as the facts of the events slipped into the sunset. John Ford and John Wayne movie images of this army did much to reinforce the public's delusive beliefs about the military's role in western settlement. But Fort Lewis's saga portrays a more accurate and typical story of the times. In 1921, Gen. Charles King described his experiences while campaigning against the Indians. He called it a "thankless task" and noted that it was a "perilous service" that demanded leadership, soldiership, morale, and discipline. To him the troopers "cleared the way across the continent for the emigrant and settlers, who summer and winter stood guard over the wide frontier, [and] whose lives were spent in almost utter isolation."[5] In other words, it was not a life of heroic rescues and glories.

What remains of Fort Lewis today? The site became an agricultural station when the junior college was moved to Durango in 1956. Only two buildings that date back to the post's working days are still standing. Both are visible at the northern end of the old parade ground. Except for these two old-timers, none of the buildings survived the partial dismantling of the site after the move to Durango. The old military reservation (now an agricultural station) has been reduced to 6,200 acres and a New Deal library now sits in the middle of the parade ground. Newer homes sit on the west side of the parade ground where the officers' quarters were once located. Framing the east side are new buildings where barracks once stood.

Along with the two post buildings, the rifle range and a couple of dumping grounds are remnants of the soldiers who lived and worked here. Occasionally the site hosts groups, who usually meet in the library. Most who travel in this area do not know or appreciate the history of Fort Lewis. That will change when a historic marker is placed at the site along the highway; a historic walking tour also is planned.

The Utes and Navajos still live where they did when the last reveille echoed through Fort Lewis. Their lifestyles have changed over the years, and now their high school graduates attend Fort Lewis College. The college, too, has changed. After moving to a mesa above Durango in 1956, it eventually became a four-year school in 1962, a very different Fort Lewis from the one the troops knew. The troops would not recognize Durango either.

Ranchers, farmers, and coal miners, along with suburbanites who have left the city for rural life, live near the old fort. Water remains a critical issue, and the La Plata River is usually little more than a stream. Up the river from Fort Lewis, only a pale shadow remains of the coal camp of Hesperus, while miners dig out coal right next to what remains of the old post's reservation. Mining in the neighboring La Plata Mountains has long since ceased. Big Bend, where troopers once camped, lies under McPhee Reservoir, and the ruins at Mesa Verde are now protected as a national park.

The Rio Grande Southern Railroad has been gone for fifty years. County roads follow its route, houses squat on its right-of-way, and in some places the old track site can still be seen. The Denver & Rio Grande is gone, too, along with its tracks south and east beyond Durango. But its descendant, the Durango & Silverton, still runs over the tracks where the Fort Lewis baseball team and its supporters once traveled between the two towns.

Durango and Cortez have grown while Silverton has shrunk, its mining past more of a memory than a reality. Big Bend migrated to Dolores and Ignacio has become the Southern Ute government seat instead of the reservation headquarters. Most of these communities don't take much note of their onetime military neighbor and protector. They are more interested in their former mining camp neighbors, which as ghost towns have become tourist meccas.

As the post's flag was lowered for the final time and taps echoed, few people understood or appreciated Fort Lewis's many contributions to the

Four Corners region, and this is still true today. The post did more than just send its troopers riding after hostile Indians or save settlements from a fiery demise. Its varied contributions reveal the true legacy of the western army.

For the Navajo, Ute, and Piute, Fort Lewis helped to decisively shut the door on their old ways of life. For the onrushing settlers, the garrison offered peace to seek their dreams but could not guarantee their success. For the men who served there, it was simply a segment of their careers. Their memories of the place assuredly did not include brave deeds and thrilling exploits.

Now the post is but a pale ghost of bygone times. Where they danced. Where they lived. Where they worked. Where they dreamed. Where they drilled. Almost all is gone—gone like the world in which they served. Physically, little remains to tell visitors that once this place stood on the "picket line of civilization" and that once Fort Lewis thrived and assisted in settling and developing this region.

The people who once lived and worked at Fort Lewis were there to protect a generation of Americans and their settlements in a beautiful land of mountains, plateaus, deserts, and river valleys. The soldiers, their wives, and their children came and left. We can know them only through the written record they left behind.

Their generation was nearly gone as they last left the abandoned post, which no longer served a useful purpose in a land far removed from the frontier of yesteryear. It had become, as a dying Robert E. Lee said, time to "strike the tent."[6]

> So now farewell to war and strife
> Hard tack no more can find me
> I'm going home to a quiet life
> With the Girl I left behind me.[7]

NOTES

PROLOGUE

1. *Dodge City Times*, September 21, 1878.
2. *Dodge City Times*, September 14–October 5, 1878; Merrill J. Mattes (ed.), *Indians, Infants and Infantry* (Denver: Old West Publishing, 1960), 51, 61; *The War of the Rebellion* (Washington, DC: Government Printing Office, 1886), series 1, 48:1245–1247; series 2, 15:537, 539.
3. Robert G. Athearn, *William Tecumseh Sherman and the Settlement of the West* (Norman: University of Oklahoma Press, 1956), 137–143; Robert G. Athearn, "The Montana Volunteers of 1867," *Pacific Historical Review* (May 1950): 131–132.
4. *Dodge City Times*, October 5, 1978; William Lewis file, Post Record, Center of Southwest Studies, Fort Lewis College.
5. This creek has been variously identified as Starving, Famished, or Punished Woman's Creek. According to the Cheyennes, they named the stream "Punished

189

Woman's" long before the Whites arrived. Here a Cheyenne woman committed adultery and was given up to a band of Dog Soldiers. Afterward, the tribe would wait until they arrived at this stream to chastise any woman guilty of infidelity. Stan Hoig, *Fort Reno and the Indian Territory Frontier* (Fayetteville: University of Arkansas Press, 2000), 244.

6. Sources for section on Lewis and the 1878 campaign: *New York Times*, September 20, 21, 28, 1878; October 5, 1878; *Rocky Mountain News*, September 19–30, 1878; *Harper's Weekly*, October 19, 1878; *Biographical Register of the Officers and Graduates of the U.S. Military Academy* (Boston: Houghton, Mifflin and Company, 1891), 382–384; Hoig, *Fort Reno*, 70–71; Paul Hutton, *Phil Sheridan* (Lincoln: University of Nebraska Press, 1985), 334–335; Francis Headman, *Historical Register and Dictionary* (Washington, DC: Government Post Office, 1903), 631; *Tenth Annual Reunion of the Association of the Graduates of the United States Military Academy* (New York: D. Van Nostrand, 1879), 38–40; Mari Sandoz, *Cheyenne Autumn* (New York: McGraw-Hill, 1953), 55, 70, 76, 78; George B. Grinnell, *The Fighting Cheyennes* (Norman: University of Oklahoma, 1958 [reprint]), 404–408; Robert Carriker, *Fort Supply* (Norman: University of Oklahoma Press, 1970), 90–108, 127–128; William Lewis file, Post Records, Center of Southwest Studies, Fort Lewis College. The battle site is known as the "Squaw's Den Battleground" and was the site of the last Indian battle in Kansas.

7. William Lewis file, Post Records, Center of Southwest Studies, Fort Lewis College.

8. Ibid.

9. Ibid.

10. Bernard James Byrne, *A Frontier Army Surgeon: Life in Colorado in the Eighties* (New York: Exposition Press, 1935), 11. Byrne claimed that Lewis was a descendant of Meriwether Lewis. Bvt. Col. E. Bergmann, March 15, 1867, report that included earlier report, Post Records 1, Center of Southwest Studies, Fort Lewis College (these were photocopied from the National Archives and hereafter are cited as "Post Records" with box number, which refers to the collection in the Center of Southwest Studies).

11. Orders, October 18, 1878, Post Records 1; W. Osburne letter, August 15, 1888, Post Records 4; *Colorado Transcript*, November 29, 1876; *La Plata Miner*, quoted in Mary Ayres, "History of Fort Lewis," *Colorado Magazine* (May 1931): 85.

12. Robert Utley, *Cavalier in Buckskin* (Norman: University of Oklahoma Press, 1988), 42–43; Robert Athearn, *William Tecumseh Sherman*, 345–349.

CHAPTER ONE

1. Sources for the section on the founding of Fort Lewis: Lt. C.A.H. McCauley report, January 27, 1879, Post Records 1. For the naming of the post and site location, see Commanding Officer, District of New Mexico Orders, October 18, 26, 30, 1878; Capt. W. Hartz report, December 4, 1878, all found in Post Records 1. General Orders

#2, Gen. John Pope, February 17, 1879, Post Records 1, created the military reservation. A brief sketch of Fort Lewis's history may be found in Robert W. Frazer, *Forts of the West* (Norman: University of Oklahoma Press, 1965), 38–39.

2. Lt. C. McCauley Report, January 27, 1879, Post Records 1.

3. November 1878, Post Returns, National Archive Microfilm #624, Center of Southwest Studies, Fort Lewis College; Reports to District Commander, November 8, December 4, 7, 12, 1878, Post Records 1.

4. Report to District Commander, December 30, 1878, Post Records 4.

5. Reports to District Commander, December 7, 12, 30, 1878, January 1, June 16, 1879, Post Records 1; January 1, April 16, 1879, Post Records 4.

6. Dodge to Postmaster General, March 4, 1879, Post Records 4.

7. Report to District Commander, May 11, 1880, Post Records 4.

8. Dodge to Postmaster General, March 4, 1879, Post Records 4; Special Order No. 12, 1879, Post Records 2; Report to the District Commander, July 18, 20, 1879, Post Records 1; April 6, May 11, 1880, Post Records 4; Special Order No. 59, August 29, 1879, Post Records 1.

9. Don Rickey, *Forty Miles a Day on Beans and Hay* (Norman: University of Oklahoma Press, 1963), 93–98, 110; General Order #1, December 6, 1878, Post Records 1; Circular, January 3, 1879, Post Records 2; Board of Survey Reports, January 20, February 25, March 11, April 20, 1879, July 21 (quotation), August 21, 1880, Post Records 1; Council of Administration Report, April 9, June 30, 1879, Post Records 3; Reports, February 5, July 15, 1880, Post Records 1; Dodge to Adjutant General Washington, May 31, 1879, Post Records 4.

10. August 23, 1880, Post Records 1.

11. Charles L. Kenner, *Buffalo Soldiers and Officers of the Ninth Cavalry, 1867–1898* (Norman: University of Oklahoma Press, 1999), 23–25; Reports to District Commander, June 23, July 2, 11, October 20, November 9, 1879, February 9, 10 (quotation), 12, March 4, 6, August 9, 27, 1880, Post Records 2; Special Order #56, August 22, 1879, Post Records 1; Jack Foner, *The United States Army Between the Two Wars* (New York: Humanities Press, 1970), 3–5.

12. Edward M. Coffman, *The Old Army* (New York: Oxford University Press, 1986), 371–373; Thomas R. Buecker, *Fort Robinson and the American West, 1874–1899* (Norman: University of Oklahoma Press, 2003), 64–65.

13. Reports of Post Commander, July 11, 28, October 1879, Post Records 1.

14. Reports to District Commander, April 10, July 11, 31, October 18, 1879, Post Records 1; Report to District Commander, January 2, 1880, Post Records 4; *La Plata Miner* (Silverton), July 5, 1879. For a comment by a Ninth Cavalry chaplain on attitudes toward Mexicans, see Frank N. Schubert, *Voices of the Buffalo Soldier* (Albuquerque: University of New Mexico Press, 2003), 214. For further comments on Blacks and Hispanics in this area, see Duane A. Smith, *Rocky Mountain Boom Town* (Boulder: University Press of Colorado, 1992), and William Leckie, *The Buffalo Soldiers* (Norman: University of Oklahoma Press, 1967). Neither minority group had many settlers in southwestern Colorado until after the turn of the century.

15. *La Plata Miner,* May 3, July 5, 1879; *Rocky Mountain News,* April 25, 1879; Reports to District Commander, October 19, November 12, 13, 16, December 12, 14, 16, 1878, January 2, 11, March 8, April 14, 1879, Post Records 1; Special Order #7, January 22, 1879, Post Records 3; Special Order #12, February 1, 1879, Post Records 1; March 13, 21, April 6, July 20, 1880, Post Records 4.

16. The 1880 Census, Archuleta County, Colorado, Microfilm copy, Center of Southwest Studies.

17. See Richard Ellis, *John Pope* (Albuquerque: University of New Mexico Press, 1970), Hutton, *Sheridan,* and Athearn, *Sherman.* For Sherman's visit, see *La Plata Miner,* May 17, 31, 1879. For General Pope, see Reports to District Commander, August 19, 28, 1880, Post Records 1.

18. Robert G. Athearn, *William Tecumseh Sherman and the Settlement of the West* (Norman: University of Oklahoma Press, 1956), 245–247; Roy Morris Jr., *Sheridan: The Life and Wars of General Phil Sheridan* (New York: Crown Publishers, 1992), 375–376; *The White Tecumseh: A Biography of General William T. Sherman* (New York: John Wiley & Sons, 1997), 331–333; Paul Hutton, *Phil Sheridan and His Army* (Lincoln: University of Nebraska Press, 1985), 180–182; Sheridan in his *Memoirs* wrote that the "inordinate hatred of the Indian" on the frontier more than once "failed to distinguish friend from foe," thus exacerbating the army's difficulties. Philip Sheridan, *Personal Memoirs* (New York: Charles L. Webster, 1891), 87–88.

19. Alfred Hough to Mary, October 16(?), 1879, Hough Papers, University of Colorado Archives; Robert Utley, *Frontier Regulars* (New York: Macmillan Publishing, 1973), 338.

CHAPTER TWO

1. Don Rickey Jr., *Forty Miles a Day on Beans and Hay* (Norman: University of Oklahoma Press, 1963), has the verses to the song. For an overview of the Utes, Meeker, the San Juans, and the "war," see Marshal Sprague, *Massacre* (Boston: Little, Brown and Company, 1957), and Carl Ubbelohde, Maxine Benson, and Duane A. Smith, *A Colorado History,* 8th ed. (Boulder: Pruett, 2001).

2. Allen Nossaman, *Many More Mountains* (Denver: Sundance Books, 1993), 264–265.

3. Ibid.; Mary Ayres, "History of Fort Lewis," *Colorado Magazine* (May 1931): 85; Utley, *Frontier Regulars,* 338–339; Records, October 11, 1879, Post Records 1; October 10, 11, 1879, Post Records 4; *La Plata Miner,* December 30, 1882.

4. Hough's story is found in the Alfred Lacey Hough Papers, University of Colorado Archives, and Robert G. Athearn, "Major Hough's March into Southern Ute Country, 1879," *Colorado Magazine* (May 1948): 97–107. Hough had the habit of running his sentences together, separated only by commas. Except in rare cases in which meaning was not easily understandable without minor changes, they have been left in their original form.

5. Hough to Mary, October 17, 26, 1879, Hough Papers; Hough, "Autobiography," which was written in May 1880, some seven months after the incidents he describes.

6. Hatch was a brevet major general. Brevet ranks had been given out for "gallantry and meritorious" service during the Civil War and usually referred to a specific battle. Hatch earned this honorary rank from his heroic service in the battle of Nashville, Tennessee, in December 1864. In peacetime, officers reverted to their regular rank. Many of the officers who served at Fort Lewis held a brevet commission. See Francis B. Headman, *Historical Register and Dictionary of the United States Army* (Washington, DC: Government Printing Office, 1903), 1:510; William H. Leckie, *The Buffalo Soldiers* (Norman: University of Oklahoma Press, 1963), 7–8.

7. Hough to Mary, October 17, 23, 1879, Hough Papers. Andy Chitwood, "Animas City," in *Pioneers of the San Juan Country* (Colorado Springs: Out West Printing, 1946), 100–102, furnishes a map on which, in around 1940, Chitwood drew the places where troops camped on both sides of the Animas.

8. George Courtright, "Memoirs," 1–2, Center of Southwest Studies.

9. Hough to Mary, October 26, November 1, 13, 1879, Hough Papers; *La Plata Miner*, November 22, 1879; George Courtright, "Memoirs," 1–2, Center of Southwest Studies.

10. Hough, "Autobiography."

11. *La Plata Miner*, November 29, December 20, 1879, January 3, 1880.

12. Courtright, "Memoirs," 2.

13. Hough to Buell, December 13, 1879; Hough to Mary, November 23, 26, December 16, 21, 25, 1879; Hough, "Autobiography"; Athearn, "Major Hough," 109; Courtright, "Memoirs," 2.

14. *La Plata Miner*, May 8, 1880; Col. George Buell Report, May 14, 1880; Sherman to Sheridan, April 23, 1880, Fort Lewis Records, Fort Lewis, Colorado.

CHAPTER THREE

1. Col. George Buell Report, May 14, 1880; Sherman to Sheridan, April 23, 1880, Fort Lewis Records, Fort Lewis College.

2. Headquarters of the Army to Adjutant General's Office, Post Records.

3. Buell Report; Secretary of War to Department of Missouri, June 1880; Undated memo, December 1880; Headquarters of the Army to Adjutant General's Office, September 20, 1880; Inspector General Report, September 1, 1881; War Department Memo, April 6, 1928 (all found in Fort Lewis Records, Fort Lewis College).

4. Post Records, National Archives Microfilm #624, Center of Southwest Studies, Fort Lewis College; New Mexico District to Crofton, July 9, 1880; Reports to New Mexico District, September 17, 29, December 18, 1880; January 20, 1881, Post Records 1; Department of Missouri to Crofton, September 23, 1880; Report to General Sheridan, September 24, 1880, Post Records 2. Otto Mears was given credit for suggestion of the La Plata site. See Helen Searcy, "The Military," in *Pioneers of the San Juan Country*

(Colorado Springs: Out West Printing, 1942), 1:67; "Message from the President of the United States," 47th Congress, 1st Session, Exec. Doc. 146, 3.

5. For the construction of Fort Lewis, see Reports, August 31, September 4, December, 4, 31, 1880, April 26, 1881, Post Records 1. Reports, October 6, November 10, 20, 1880, March 15, April 1, May 31, June 30, 1881, Post Records 2. New Mexico District to Crofton, July 11, 30, 1880, Post Records 1. District Commander to J. Peshine, April 26, 1881, Post Records 2.

6. For the Crofton mess, see Post Returns, March, July, and August 1881, Microfilm #624; Reports to Commander, New Mexico District, January 20, 29, 30, February 7, April 23, 1881; Peshine to Department of Missouri, December 24, 1880, Post Records 1; December 26, 27, 1880, January 29, 30, July 13, August 10, 20, 21, 1881, Post Records 2.

7. Byrne, *Frontier Army Surgeon*, 66; *Durango Record*, February 19, 1881; *Durango Herald*, October 20, 1881. For the December report, see 1st Lt. H. Cavenaugh, December 18, 1880, Post Records 1.

8. Adjutant General Washington to Crofton, January 21, February 2, 1881; *Rocky Mountain News*, January 29, 1881, August 2, 1884; Reports to New Mexico District, July 16, September 25, 1880, Post Records 1. Reports to New Mexico District, November 27, December 4, 19, 1882, January 28, 31, March 4, April 20, May 8, 1883, Post Records 2. Pagosa Springs Post File, Center of Southwest Studies.

9. Leo Oliva, *Fort Hays, Front Army Post* (Topeka: Kansas State Historical Society, 1986), 61; Report to Department of Missouri, March 12, 1884, Post Records 4; John Pope, Robert Lincoln, and William Sherman Reports are found in "Message from the President of the United States," 47th Congress, 1st Session, Exec. Doc. 146, 1–3; Report, April 6, 1881, Post Records 1; Inspection Reports, May 20, August 15, 1881, Post Records 2; Michael Tate, *Frontier Army* (Norman: University of Oklahoma Press, 1999), 117–118; Paul Hutton, *Phil Sheridan and His Army* (Lincoln: University of Nebraska Press, 1985), 29. Inspector General Report, September 1, 1881, Fort Lewis Records.

10. For Sherman's visit, see *Durango Herald*, September 22, 1883, Courtright letter, August 23, 1939, Fort Lewis Records, Center of Southwest Studies.

11. Swaine to Adjutant General of the Army, December 18, 1885, Post Records 4.

12. Second Lieutenant George Williamson, Report, April 26, 1890, Post Records 3.

13. Reports, May 31, 1883, June 30, 1887, Post Records 1; Reports, February 26, December 18, 1883, Post Records 2; Reports, April 1, 1884, May 25, September 5, November 13, 21, 1888, April 6, November 1, 1889, April 26, 1890, April 16, 1891, Post Records 3; Swaine to Adjutant General, December 19, 1885, Post Records 4; *Idea*, October 17, 1885.

14. *Idea*, September 27, 1884. For newspaper views, see *Colorado Jack Rabbit* (Silver Plume), September 13, 1885; *Silverton Democrat-Herald*, September 19, 1885; *La Plata Miner*, May 24, 1884; *Durango Herald*, May 21, 1887; *Denver Tribune-Republican*, August 30, 1885; *Durango Record*, September 17, 1881. For the reservation, see report dated February 8, 1882, Post Records 1; Report, March 2, 1881, Post Records 2. It is

unclear if the Twenty-Second Infantry regimental band, or even part of it, was stationed at Fort Lewis.

15. Capt. Adam Kramer to Assistant Adjutant General of the Department of Missouri, August 28, 1888, Post Records 3.

16. Reports, January 24, February 4, June 28, December 18, 1882, May 12, 1885, Post Records 2; Reports, February 4, 1886, September 17, 19, 1887, Post Records 3; Reports, February 6, 1888, Post Records 4.

17. Byrne, *Frontier Army Surgeon*, 27.

18. Reports, May 31, June 30, 1881, July 29, August 31, 1884, October 29, 1885, Post Records 2; Reports, October 5, 1887, October 31, 1889, January 1, 1890, Post Records 3; Reports, November 17, 19, 1886, March 15, 1888, March 3, April 5, December 1, 7, 1889, Post Records 4.

19. Coffman, *The Old Army*, 384–389. Fort Robinson, Nebraska, was another healthy post: Buecker, *Fort Robinson*, 68–69.

20. Byrne, *Frontier Army Surgeon*, 39, 97.

21. Ibid.; T. Cunningham to Surgeon General, December 16, 1884, Fort Lewis Records; Reports, September 24, 1880, December 25, 1883, July 14, August 9, 1886, October 16, 1889, Post Records 1; Reports, November 3, 1880, January 1, November 22, 1882, March 15, 1883, April 24, 1885, Post Records 2; Reports, June 10, 21, July 28, 1886, April 30, September 17, 19, 1887, October 31, December 5, 1888, Post Records 3.

22. For the ordnances, see Reports, April 18, 30, 1889, January 2, 1891, Post Records 1; Reports, April 17, 1887, September 22, 1888, April 10, November 27, 1890, Post Records 3. For heliograph, see Reports, February 16, 1889, Post Records 1; Reports, May 27, July 30, December 22, 1881, June 30, December 11, 28, 1885, Post Records 2; Reports, December 18, 1886, January 8, May 20, August 17, 1887, October 16, 28, 1888, March 23, February 23, April 9, August 22, December 10, 1889, Post Records 3; Reports, November 7, December 18, 1890, Post Records 4; Rebecca Robbins, "Some Reflections on the Heliograph," unidentified article, author's collection. Field research confirmed that it was possible to send heliograph signals over this route.

23. These reports are found throughout the records. See, for instance, August 22, 1880, January 3, 1881, Post Records 1; February 4, 1881, January 13, 1883, March 6, September 17, 22, 1884, January 24, February 7, 1885, April 7, 1886, Post Records 2; January 10, June 3, December 10, 1887, July 18, 1888, March 13, 23, 1890, Post Records 3; May 26, 1885, August 31, 1886, September 30, October 23, 1888, Post Records 4.

24. Paul Hutton, *Phil Sheridan and His Army* (Lincoln: University of Nebraska Press, 1985), 331; Roy Morris Jr., *Sheridan* (New York: Crown Publishers, 1992), 368–370.

CHAPTER FOUR

1. This was probably the Twenty-Second Infantry band, which was stationed at the fort around this time. At various times the Sixth Cavalry and Fifteenth Infantry

bands, or parts thereof, were also at the post. The Durango newspaper usually referred to them simply as the Fort Lewis band.

2. The section on the soldiers at the post comes from the following sources: La Plata County, Colorado Census, 1885, microfilm copy, Center of Southwest Studies; S. Whitman, *The Troopers* (New York: Hastings House, 1962), 72, chapter 5; Edward M. Coffman, *The Old Army* (New York: Oxford, 1986), 222–223. Future general John Pershing never served at Fort Lewis, despite rumors to the contrary. See Frank Vandiver, *Black Jack*, vol. 1 (College Station: Texas A&M University Press, 1977).

3. For the Seventh Cavalry, see Douglas D. Scott et al., *Archaeological Perspectives on the Battle of the Little Bighorn* (Norman: University of Oklahoma Press, 1989), 248–250.

4. For the Ninth Cavalry, see William Dobek and Thomas Phillips, *The Black Regulars, 1866–1898* (Norman: University of Oklahoma Press, 2001), xi, xvii, 246; Frank N. Schubert, *Voices of the Buffalo Soldier* (Albuquerque: University of New Mexico Press, 2003), 47–48, 252; Charles L. Kenner, *Buffalo Soldiers and Officers of the Ninth Cavalry, 1867–1898* (Norman: University of Oklahoma Press, 1999), chapter 1; Reports, May 6, June 2, 20, August 6, 17, 20, 1881; Pope to Crofton, August 17, 1881; Reports, January 19, May 26, June 5, July 2, August 2, October 2, 1883. See also William Leckie, *The Buffalo Soldiers* (Norman: University of Oklahoma Press, 1967), chapters 1, 9. "Brunettes" was a common term of the period used in reference to the Black troopers.

5. See Record of Enlistment, Post Records for 1883 and 1887.

6. Reports, October 19, 1880, September 25, 1881, June 19, August 7, 21, 1884, Post Records 2; May 31, 1887, December 28, 1888, June 2, October 11, 1890, May 21, 1891, Post Records 3; December 1, 1886, Post Records 4; Jack Foner, *The United States Soldier Between the Two Wars* (New York: Humanities Press, 1970), 20; Michael Tate, *Frontier Army* (Norman: University of Oklahoma Press, 1999), 161–168.

7. April 23, 1890, Post Records 3.

8. Reports, August 14, September, 1880, January 2, 1888, Post Records 1; February 24, October 21, 1881, January 23, April 12, September 4, 1884, March 16, April 16, August 22, 1885, Post Records 2; December 16, 1888, January 18, 21, July 5, August 4, 1889, April 23, May 4, July 26, October 17, 19, December 18, 1890, Post Records 3; May 23, 1884, January 26, November 2, 1885, Post Records 4.

9. The desertion reports, telegrams, and court-martial review in the Fort Lewis records are numerous. For examples cited, see Reports, May 21, 1889, Post Records 1; October 16, 17, 1880, January 13, October 20, 1884, April 20, 1885, April 26, 1886, Post Records 2; March 6, 1886, June 18, December 12, 1887, May 21, 22, July 31, December 17, 1889, June 6, 1890, Post Records 3; July 25, 1884, May 27, 1889, Post Records 4; *La Plata Miner*, September 12, 1885; *Silverton Democrat*, May 24, 1884, July 10, 1886; Leo Oliva, *Fort Hays*, 45, 47, 49, 51; Howard and Crook quoted in Foner, *The United States Soldier*, 98–99, also see 6, 7, 10; Coffman, *The Old Army*, 375–376.

10. Foner, *The United States Soldier*, 19; Reports, August 18, 1880, Post Records 1; Reports, April 10, 1888, January 18, April 2, October 28, 1889, January 14, February 7, 1890, Post Records 3; April 15, 1888, Post Records 4.

11. Anne G. Butler, *Army Wives on the American Frontier* (Boulder: Johnson Books, 1996), xii, 129, 136, 138, 144–145, 147; Patricia Y. Stallard, *Glittering Misery* (Fort Collins: Old Army Press, 1978), 12–13, 128–129, chapter 2; Reports, September 17, 1880; extra-duty reports, November 1889, April 1890, Post Records 1; March 21, April 9, 1883, April 12, 1884, Post Records 2; April 3, 1886, August 11, 1889, June 21, 1890, Post Records 3.

12. Coffman, *The Old Army*, 278–280; Reports, January 6, March 8, 1881, August 16, 1883, January 11, 1884, May 24, June 2, 4, 9, 1885, Post Records 2; May 15, 1886, August 5, 1889; Post Records 3.

13. There are numerous reports and correspondence dealing with these topics. See, for example, Reports, September 13, 1881, February 14, 1882, January 4, 17, 1883, October 18, 1885, Post Records 2; February 2, June 24, 1886, February 24, 1887, Post Records 3; March 14, 1884, May 29, 1885, March 30, December 14, 1886, Post Records 4.

14. Reports, March 7, 1881, Post Records 1; August 11, 1881, August 15, 1883, April 21, September 14, 1884, Post Records 2; February 6, April 16, June 10, 28, 1886, March 30, October 1, 1888, February 13, 1889, July 26, 1890, Post Records 3; December 1, 1886, Post Records 4; Butler, *Army Wives*, 141.

15. Reports, April 16, 1881, Post Records 1; October 10, 13, 14, December 23, 1880, May 24, 1881, January 20, August 23, 1883, February 7, 1884, December 18, 1885, Post Records 2; April 9, 1887, Post Records 3.

16. Foner, *The United States Soldier*, 24. Reports dealing with courts-martial, drunkenness, and prisoners are found for every month in the post records. Particular cases referred to are as follows: Reports, December 19, 1880, Post Records 1; October 18, 30, 1880, January 14, November 17, 1883, September 23, 1884, Post Records 2; February 15, 1887, April 8, 1890, Post Records 3. Don Rickey, *Forty Miles a Day on Beans and Hay* (Norman: University of Oklahoma Press, 1963), 156–159.

17. Records, April 17, 1890, January 5, 1891, Post Records 3.

18. Michael L. Tate, *The Frontier Army* (Norman: University of Oklahoma Press, 1999), 64–67; *La Plata Miner*, September 12, 1885; *Silverton Democrat*, May 24, 1885; Reports, June 1, 1881, December 17, 1883, Post Records 2; April 1, 1891, Post Records 3; November 8, 1886, Post Records 4. For the post office dispute, see the numerous reports, dispatches, and so forth from June to August 1891, Post Records 3.

19. June 2, 22, July 2, 3, 6, August 13, 1891, Post Records 3.

20. August 12, 1883, Post Records 1; August 29, 1883, May 1, 1885, Post Records 2; January 15, April 6, October 25, 28, 1888, April 29, May 4, 1889, Post Records 3; April 23, 1886, April 27, 1889, Post Records 4. Comments on paymasters appear throughout the records. See, for example, November 10, 1883, Post Records 2; November 7, 12, 1888, Post Records 3; Courtright, "Memoirs," 3.

21. Reports, September 25, October 1, December 25, 1880, January 14, 1889, Post Records 1; November 16, 1880, April 1, June 21, 1881, September 13, 1883, June 14, 1885, Post Records 2; November 1, 1887, August 7, 1889, Post Records 3; December 24, March 28, 1889, Post Records 4; Courtright, "Memoirs," 3, Center of Southwest Studies.

CHAPTER FIVE

1. Byrne, *A Frontier Army Surgeon*, 101; *Colorado State Business Directory*, 1880–1891; Reports, June 30, 1887, Post Records 1; February 6, 1888, Post Records 4. The *Silverton Democrat-Herald* on September 19, 1885, estimated 500 soldiers. Business directors often gave inflated population figures or published the optimistic numbers given by enthusiastic local boosters.

2. Monthly Post Returns, 1880s, National Archives Microfilm #624, Center of Southwest Studies, Fort Lewis College; Rickey, *Forty Miles a Day on Beans and Hay*, 75; Mark Danley, U.S. Cavalry Memorial Research Library, Letter, July 10, 2002; Foner, *The United States Army Between the Two Wars*, 2; John K. Mahon and Romana Danysh, *Infantry Part I: Regular Army* (Washington, DC: Center of Military History, 1984), 31–33.

3. Reports, October 19, 20, December 7, 1880, Post Records 2.

4. For the Farmington troubles, see Reports, January 18, 28, 29, February 2, 5, March 4, 9, 15, April 22, 25, 1881, Post Records 2.

5. *Durango Record*, April 16, 1881; *La Plata Miner*, April 16, 1881; Records, March 9, 10, 11, April 12, 13, 1881, Post Records 2.

6. Clayton Laurie and Ronald H. Cole, *The Role of Federal Military Forces in Domestic Disorders 1877–1945* (Washington, DC: Center of Military History, 1997), vii, 57–59, 75–76; Robert W. Coakley, *The Role of Federal Military Forces in Domestic Disorders, 1789–1878* (Washington, DC: Center of Military History, 1988), 3–4, 144–149, 171–172, 196–197, 348. See also Edward M. Coffman, *The Old Army* (New York: Oxford, 1986), and Michael L. Tate, *The Frontier Army in the Settlement of the West* (Norman: University of Oklahoma Press, 1999).

7. Reports, May 11, 26, 29, June 9, 1881, Post Records 2; H. Mitchell to Crofton, June 21, 1881, Post Records 2.

8. Augur quoted in Tate, *The Frontier Army*, 110; see also chapter 4. Reports, May 2, 6, 11, 13, 15, 23, 26, 27, 28, 29, June 9, 14, 19, 21, 23, 1881, Post Records 2; Henry Page to Crofton, May 6, 23, June 11, 1881; D. Williams to Crofton, May 2, 4, 1881; J. T. Williams to Crofton, May 9, 1881; J. Kirkwood to Secretary of War, June 2, 1881; H. Mitchell to Crofton, June 21, 1881, Post Records 2.

9. Byrne, *Frontier Surgeon*, 104–106.

10. *Durango Record*, August 13, 20, 1881; Reports, July 4, 6, 11, August 9, 16, 19, 30, 1881; Allen Nossaman, *Many More Mountains* (Denver: Sundance Books, 1998), 166. The Grand River is now the Colorado River.

11. H. Davis to Pope, August 15, 1881, Post Records 2; *Durango Record*, August 20, 1881.

12. Frank N. Schubert, *Voices of the Buffalo Soldier* (Albuquerque: University of New Mexico Press, 2003), 95–96; Reports, February 14, 24, June 12, July 4, 6, August 2, September 23, October 3, December 22, 1882, Post Records 2; *Rocky Mountain News*, July 7, 1882.

13. Reports, January 29, 31, February 12, March 8, 14, 27, April 7, May 11, July 16, 19, 31, August 5, 8, 31, September 7, 26, November 30, December 23, 28, 1883, Post Records 2; Wattles Records, Colorado State University.

14. A. Potter letter, January 18, 1884; John Bell telegram, July 24, 1884; Reports, July 1, August 17, 19, 1884, Post Records 1; Reports, March 9, 15, 17, 18, 24, 25, April 2, 21, 24, May 1, 8, 19, 28, June 17, 13, 26, July 2, 7, 9, 16, 20, 25, 26, 31, August 17, 18, 19, 20, 21, September 2, 4, 9, 13, 25, October 1, November 8, 1884, Post Records 2; Report, July 24, 1884, Post Records 3; Reports, March 7, 24, April 3, 7, 23, 25, 29, May 10, 18, 23, June 4, July 20, 23, 24, August 19, Post Records 4.

15. A. Potter letter, January 18, 1884; Reports, March 17, 24, 1884, Post Records 4; March 21, 25, 1884, Post Records 2.

16. March 17, 24, April 2, 3, 21, 1884, Post Records 2; April 3, 7, 23, May 23, 1884, Post Records 4.

17. July 20, 24, 1884, Post Records 4; July 16, 1884, Post Records 2.

18. For sources for the Dolores River trouble, see Report, September 14, 1885, Post Records 1; January 16, 29, March 8, 12, June 13, 19, 23, 25, 28, 30, July 1, 3, 6, 14, 15, 16, 28, August 6, 27, October 1, 3, 1885, Post Records 2; June 13, 16, 21, 22, 28, 29, 30, July 2, 3, 4, August 31, September 16, December 11, 1885, Post Records 4; *Georgetown Courier*, undated; quote in the *Idea*, July 4, 1885; *Idea*, June 27, July 4, 11, September 14, 1885; *Silverton Democrat*, July 4, 1885.

19. June 1, 5, July 10, August 7, 18, September 19, 1886, Post Records 3; June 14, 1886, Post Records 3; July 24, August 6, September 2, 15, 1886, Post Records 4.

20. For sources on Fort Lewis's last years, see Tate, *The Frontier Army*, 114–115; Reports, January 8, 10, 1887, Post Records 1; January 5, 17, February 16, March 8, April 25, July 8, 11, 14, August 6, 1887, July 21, August 1, 13, 31, September 7, 12, 17, 18, 19, October 4, 9, 10, November 22, 1888, August 17, 26, September 19, November 28, 1889, January 16, 27, February 7, October 28, December 8, 17, 1890, April 1, 2, 6, 1891, Post Records 3; July 11, August 3, 20, November 28, 1889, December 13, 15, 1890, Post Records 4.

21. Swaine to Major David Perez, June 22, 1885, Post Records 1; Utley, *Cavalier in Buckskin*, 43.

22. Sheridan quoted in Thomas T. Smith, *The U.S. Army and the Texas Frontier Economy* (College Station: Texas A&M University Press, 1999), 177.

CHAPTER SIX

1. Byrne, *Frontier Surgeon*, 101–102.

2. Reports, February 12, 1881, September 5, 9, 1884, Post Records 2; March 19, 1890, February 26, March 9, 1891, Post Records 3; February 21, March 13, 25, April 3, 5, 1884, November 5, 1886, Post Records 4.

3. See Chapter 4 for more information on Crofton's troubles. July 21, 1890, Post Records 3; June 4, 1885, Post Records 4.

4. For information on Shaw, see February 16, 1887, Post Records 1; Herman, Historical Register, 2:8780; December 27, 1887, July 17, 1889, Post Records 4; January 3, 4, 1889, Post Records 1.

5. Reports, September 15, 1880, December 16, 1884, August 31, 1886, August 15, 1888, December 3, 1889, Post Records 1; Reports, October 9, December 26, 1880, April 30, August 10, 1881, July 31, December 18, 1884, October 29, 1885, November 5, 1886, Post Records 2; Reports, August 18, 1886, August 18, 1888, January 4, 16, October 25, December 12, 1889, July 21, 1890, Post Records 3; June 4, September 21, October 2, 1885, December 27, 1887, February 10, July 17, October 28, 1889, March 1, 1890, Post Records 4. For Shaw, see Report, February 16, 1887, Post Records 1, and Heitman, *Historical Register*, 2:878.

6. Anne G. Butler, *Army Wives on the American Frontier* (Boulder: Johnson Books, 1996), xii, 129, 136, 138, 144–145, 147; Patricia Y. Stallard, *Glittering Misery* (Fort Collins: Old Army Press, 1978), 12–13, chapter 2, 128–129.

7. Edward Coffman, *The Old Army* (New York: Oxford, 1986), 350, 359–360, 388; Robert M. Utley, *Frontier Regulars* (New York: Macmillan, 1973), 87.

8. Ayres, "History of Fort Lewis," 88; Byrne, *Frontier Surgeon*, 28; Reports, August 8, 1880, Post Records 1; January 12, 1881, August 15, 17, September 22, 1885, Post Records 2; September 27, 1886, March 25, 1887, Post Records 3; April 21, 1884, January 12, October 9, 1885, May 2, 1888, Post Records 4; Foner, *The United States Soldier*, 28, 80.

9. *Idea*, November 1, 1884, July 25, 1888; Rickey, *Forty Miles*, 169; Reports, July 18, 1883, Post Records 2; June 5, 1890, Post Records 3; August 11, September 9, 1885, Post Records 4; Tate, *Frontier Army*, 127; Utley, *Frontier Regulars*, 87.

10. Coffman, *The Old Army*, 360–361; Thomas R. Buecker, *Fort Robinson* (Norman: University of Oklahoma Press, 1999), 69–70.

11. Adam Kramer to Department of Missouri, December 17, 1888, Post Records 4.

12. *Idea*, July 26, 1888. The tradership and canteen reports, letters, and so forth appear throughout the decade. Specific ones referred to are Reports, February 5, 1889, Post Records 1; February 11, July 13, 1887, January 14, August 28, 1888, April 7, 1890, Post Records 3; June 18, November 3, 13, 19, 30, December 17, 1888, May 2, June 30, 1889, Post Records 4. Rickey, *Forty Miles*, 201–203; Foner, *The United States Soldier*, 92–93.

13. Coffman, *The Old Army*, 360; Post Canteen II, Post Records 4.

14. January 14, 23, 1888, Post Records 3, December 13, 1888, June 30, 1889, Post Records 4.

15. Earl F. Stover, *Up from Handymen: The United States Army Chaplaincy* (Washington, DC: Department of the Army, 1977), 47–57; Tate, *Frontier Army*, 201–206; Coffman, *The Old Army*, 323–325; December 3, 8, 1886, December 9, 1888, February 7, 1889, August 21, 1890, Post Records 4.

16. Stover, *Up from Handymen*, 15, 31, 45, 62–64, 88, 235; Tate, *Frontier Army*, 199–202; 1st Lt. George Walker report, August 29, 1889, Fort Lewis Records; John Lucas and Ronald Smith, *Saga of American Sport* (Philadelphia: Lea & Febiger, 1978), chapter 9; William Dobek and Thomas Phillips, *The Black Regulars* (Norman: University of Oklahoma Press, 2001), 123, 129, 148, 158, 161–163; Records, May 3, 1889, April 10, 1890, Post Records 1; January 11, April 16, June 7, July 31, 1881, July 21, 1883, April

12, 1884, January 29, 1885, Post Records 2; January 3, 1886, June 14, 1887, November 16, 1888, February 12, December 9, 14, 1889, February 11, 14, 16, 17, May 10, June 6, August 21, 1890, April 1, 1891, Post Records 3; October 2, November 11, 1889, February 10, 15, 1891, Post Records 4; Tate, *Frontier Army*, 203–206. Oliva, *Fort Hays*, 55, 58.

17. Tate, *Frontier Army*, 212; see also chapter 8.

18. Byrne, *Frontier Surgeon*, 101; Courtright, "Memoirs," 3–4; Butler, *Army Wives*, 83–84; Records, May 24, 1884, November 24, 1888, Post Records 3; June 17, 1888, October 14, 1889, March 13, 1890, Post Records 3; March 9, 30, April 1, 1889, January 7, November 1, December 18, 1890, Post Records 4; Rickey, *40 Miles*, 205–207; Darlis Miller, *Soldiers and Settlers* (Albuquerque: University of New Mexico Press, 1989), 43–45; 1st Lt. George Walker report, August 29, 1889, Fort Lewis Records.

19. Records, October 11, 1880, July 23, August 8, 1883, Post Records 2; June 27, 1888, February 20, 1889, Post Records 3; Tate, *Frontier Army*, chapter 5, 175.

CHAPTER SEVEN

1. Helen Searcy, "The Military," in *Pioneers of the San Juan* (Colorado Springs: Out West Printing, 1942), 1:68–69; *Herald*, May 18, 1889; Darlis Miller, *Soldiers and Settlers* (Albuquerque: University of New Mexico Press, 1989), xiv; Reports, February 1, 1884, May 27, 1889, Post Records 1; October 9, November 30, December 31, 1880, June 1, 1885, Post Records 2; April 6, 10, 12, 1883, March 13, July 16, September 12, 1884, Post Records 2; October 2, 22, December 26, 1889, August 1, 1891, Post Records 3; May 24, June 6, 1884, June 4, 1885, Post Records 4; Michael Tate, *The Frontier Army* (Norman: University of Oklahoma Press, 1999), 127–129.

2. For information on the toll road issue, see September 12, 1884, July 16, 1885, Post Records 2; April 10, 12, 1883, October 22, December 26, 1889, Post Records 3.

3. Reports, August 23, 1880, Post Records 1; November 3, 1881, Post Records 2; October 7, 1886, July 30, August 6, 1888, June 14, 1889, Post Records 3; November 19, 1888, Post Records 4; Telegrams, April 5, May 7, 1883, Fort Lewis Records.

4. For information on the post's impact on Durango, see *Idea*, November 8, 15, 1884; Reports, September 20, 25, 30, 1880, Post Records 1; January 4, 1881, August 20, 1883, November 13, 1888, Post Records 2; May 12, 1881, August 20, 1883, Post Records 2; April 16, June 10, 1886, June 26, 1887, November 28, 1888, August 22, 1889, January 22, April 3, 1890, Post Records 3; Miller, *Soldier and Settlers*, 354–355.

5. For information on wages in Durango, see *Colorado Bureau of Labor Statistics 8th Annual Report* (Denver: Smith-Brooks, 1902), 91–93, 380. For a comparison of the military impact on civilians, see Thomas T. Smith, *The U.S. and the Texas Frontier Economy* (College Station: Texas A&M University Press, 1999), 133, 176, 179, chapters 4, 5, 9; Reports, March 17, 1881, April 8, 1889, Post Records 1; July 23, December 10, 1883, December 23, 1884; January 20, 1885, Post Records 2; September 20, 1888, March 31, 1889, Post Records 4. See also Miller, *Soldiers and Settlers*, for further discussion of the army as an employer.

6. Tate, *The Frontier Army*, 64–67; *La Plata Miner*, September 12, 1885; *Silverton Democrat*, May 24, 1885; Reports, June 1, 1881, December 17, 1883, Post Records 2; April 1, 1891, Post Records 3; November 8, 1886, Post Records 4. For the post office dispute, see the numerous reports, dispatches, and so forth from June to August 1891, Post Records 3.

7. *San Juan Herald*, July 6, 1882.

8. *Durango Record*, February 19, March 19, September 17, 1881, January 20, 22, 24, 1882; Florence Netherton, "Durango's First Newspaper," *Pioneers of the San Juan Country* (Colorado Springs: Out West Printing, 1946), 2:28–30; Edward Coffman, *The Old Army* (New York: Oxford University Press, 1986), 358; *Durango Herald*, October 20, November 21, December 1, 1881, May 26, July 8, 1882, June 1, 1886, January 13, 1888; *Idea*, September 27, 1884, February 7, April 11, 1885, April 3, 5, 1888; Letter, May 4, 1889, Post Records 4; Byrne, *Frontier Surgeon*, 67; *Animas Forks Pioneer*, July 8, 1882; *La Plata Miner*, July 4, 1882; *San Juan* (Silverton), December 22, 1887; Unidentified letter, August 39, 1939, Fort Lewis Collection, Center of Southwest Studies; Allen Nossaman, *Many More Mountains* (Denver: Sundance Books, 1998), 3:184; George Courtright, "Memoirs," 4.

9. *Durango Record*, September 3, 24, 1881; *Durango Herald*, September 1, 1881, May 16, 1882; *Idea*, July 4, 1885, July 25, 1888; *Silverton Democrat*, July 10, 1886.

10. Coffman, *The Old Army*, 278–280, 355; Buecker, *Fort Robinson*, 70, 156; Ayres, "Fort Lewis," 87; *Durango Herald*, September 1, 1881, May 16, August 12, September 30, 1882, June 21, 1887; *Durango Record*, July 9, September 3, 24, 1881; *San Juan*, June 2, 1887; Reports, September 16, 1881, Post Records 2; *Idea*, July 4, 1885, July 25, 1888; Courtright, "Memoirs," 4; *Silverton Democrat*, July 10, 1886.

11. Sedgwick Post Records, Center of Southwest Studies, Fort Lewis College; Stuart McConnell, *Glorious Contentment: The Grand Army of the Republic, 1865–1900* (Chapel Hill: University of North Carolina Press, 1992), xii, 20–21, 25–27, 85, 115, 148, 167, 181, 207.

12. *Silverton Democrat-Herald*, May 30, 1885; *Durango Herald*, May 18, 1887, May 17, 1889; Records, March 25, October 3, 1889, Post Records 3; *Idea*, July 3, 26, August 1, 1888; Durango Police Record, 1880s, Center of Southwest Studies. For information on prostitution and other sins, see Coffman, *The Old Army*, 311–315; Frank N. Schubert, *Voices of the Buffalo Soldier* (Albuquerque: University of New Mexico Press, 2003), 111–113; and Buecker, *Fort Robinson*, 65–66, 71.

13. Tate, *The Frontier Army*, 135; see also chapter 5.

CHAPTER EIGHT

1. Edward Coffman, *The Old Army* (New York: Oxford, 1986), 402–404; Reports, March 9, April 6, July 11, 1891, Post Records 3; June 27, August 15, 1891, Post Records 4. Robert Frazer, *Forts of the West* (Norman: University of Oklahoma Press, 1965). Coincidently or not, within four years of the establishment of Fort Logan in Colorado, three posts had been abandoned—Crawford (1890), Lyon (1889), and Lewis.

2. Robert Wooster, ed., *Soldier, Surgeon, Scholar: The Memoirs of William Henry Corbusier, 1844–1930* (Norman: University of Oklahoma Press, 2003), 120–121. After Fort Lewis, Corbusier did not treat private patients.

3. Patricia V. Stallard, ed., *Franny Dunbar Corbusier: Recollections of Her Army Life, 1869–1908* (Norman: University of Oklahoma Press, 2003), 156–161; Wooster, ed., *Soldier,* 121. Both Corbusiers were confused about the direction the officers' quarters ran; the quarters ran north to south.

4. April 23, July 17, 22, 1890, Post Records 3; August 3, 1889, Post Records 4.

5. Reports, July 1, August 3, November 8, 1889, January 7, March 17, April 18, 19, 23, May 14, 22, July 22, 1890, Post Records 2. For the Rio Grande Southern, see W. George Cook et al., *The R.G.S. Story,* vol. 1 (Denver: Sundance Publications, 2001), and Mallory Hope Ferrill, *Silver San Juan: The Rio Grande Southern* (Boulder: Pruett Publishing, 1973).

6. W. Heath Eldridge, "An Army Boy in Colorado," *Colorado Magazine* (October 1955), 306–309.

7. *Durango Herald,* November 27, 1891; Reports, March 1, September 25, December 10, 1890, July 1, 1891, Post Records 3.

8. For information on the fort's closure, see Reports, May 2, July 21, 28, 1891, Post Records 1; July 10, 28, August 5, 1891, Post Records 3; March 4, May 20, June 13, July 2, August 15, 27, 1891, Post Records 4.

9. Teller, Wolcott, and Townsend to Redfield Proctor, October 17, 1889, Fort Lewis Report, September 7, 1889; Secretary of War to Teller et al., November 6, 1889, Fort Lewis Records.

10. Sherman, quoted in Thomas T. Smith, *The U.S. Army and the Texas Frontier* (College Station: Texas A&M University Press, 1999), 178.

11. Post Records, National Archives Microfilm #624, Center of Southwest Studies, Fort Lewis College; Eldridge, "An Army Boy," 309–310; Joe Coppinger interview, quoted in Fort Lewis College, February 15, 1937. Boxes of Post Records have several folders full of August and September 1891 material.

12. For information on Fort Lewis post military career, see Duane A. Smith, *Sacred Trust: The Birth and Development of Fort Lewis College,* rev. ed. (Boulder: University Press of Colorado, 2005). The State Land Board serves as caretaker for the remaining land. Colorado State University has a lease on the site for agricultural purposes and testing.

EPILOGUE

1. Michael Tate, *The Frontier Army* (Norman: University of Oklahoma Press, 1999), 304–306, 312; Reports, June 22, 1885, Post Records 1; August 15, September 14, 18, 1888, Post Records 4.

2. To place Fort Lewis in the larger scene, see Robert Utley, *Frontier Regulars* (New York: Macmillan, 1973); Michael Tate, *The Frontier Army* (Norman: University

of Oklahoma Press, 1999); Robert Utley, *Cavalier in Buckskin* (Norman: University of Oklahoma Press, 1988); William Dobek and Thomas Phillips, *The Black Regulars* (Norman: University of Oklahoma Press, 2001); Robert G. Athearn, *William Tecumseh Sherman* (Norman: University of Oklahoma Press, 1956).

3. William Leckie, *The Buffalo Soldiers* (Norman: University of Oklahoma Press, 1967), 258–259; Arlen Fowler, *The Black Infantry in the West* (Westport: Greenwood Publishing, 1971), 137–138; Leo Oliva, *Fort Hays* (Topeka: Kansas State Historical Society, 1986), 36; Bruce J. Dinges, "The San Angelo Riot of 1881," *Journal of the West* (Summer 2002): 35–44; Don Rickey, *Forty Miles a Day on Beans and Hay* (Norman: University of Oklahoma Press, 1963), 20, 28, 88–90, 350–353; Dobek and Phillips, *Black Regulars*, 90–92, 112, 249. See also Frank Schubert, *The Buffalo Soldiers* (Shippensburg, PA: White Mane Publishing, 1997), v–vi; Frank N. Schubert, *Voices of the Buffalo Soldier* (Albuquerque: University of New Mexico Press, 2003), 174, 177–179, 201–202, 244–246.

4. For the officers, check under individual names in Francis B. Headman, *Historical Register and Dictionary of the United States Army*, vol. 1 (Washington, DC: Government Printing Office, 1902). John Carroll, *The Medal of Honor* (Bryan, TX: privately published, 1979), lists the recipients for the Indian wars. Only 41 officers received the Medal of Honor, compared with 155 privates and 123 sergeants. The Eighth Cavalry received 90, by far the most.

5. King, quoted in Tate, *Frontier Army*, 304.

6. Douglas S. Freeman, *R. E. Lee* (New York: Charles Scribners', 1955), 4:492.

7. Silas D. Wesson, Diary, author's possession.

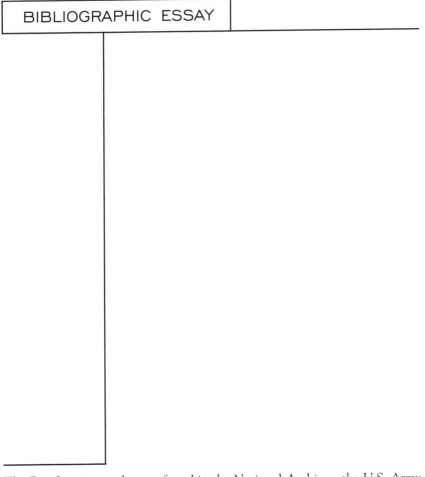

BIBLIOGRAPHIC ESSAY

The Fort Lewis records were found in the National Archives, the U.S. Army Military History Institute, and at the Center of Southwest Studies at Fort Lewis College. The center has copies of the material from the National Archives and also a collection of photographs, local and regional newspapers on microfilm, and other material related to Fort Lewis as a military post. For collections of other photographs, see the credits under individual photos.

A rather small number of books and articles mention Fort Lewis or the people stationed there. To find these materials, the reader is referred to the notes for each chapter. Researching Fort Lewis proved a fascinating project and the writer hopes it will inspire researchers to tackle other posts. As both Shakespeare and Sir Arthur Conan Doyle wrote, "The game's afoot."

INDEX